This facsimile

THE HISTORY O.

OF

WEST OR

KILPATRICK

first published in 1893

is re-published by
Clydebank District Libraries
& Museums Department

1995

ISBN 0 906938 11 2

Printed by
Cordfall Ltd
0141 332 4640

HISTORY OF THE PARISH

OF

WEST OR OLD

KILPATRICK

AND OF

THE CHURCH AND CERTAIN LANDS

IN THE PARISH OF EAST OR NEW KILPATRICK

BY

JOHN BRUCE, F.S.A. Scot.

LET KILPATRICK FLOURISH.

GLASGOW

JOHN SMITH & SON, Renfield Street

MDCCCXCIII

THIS VOLUME

IS RESPECTFULLY DEDICATED

TO

JOHN CAMPBELL WHITE,

FIRST LORD OVERTOUN,

FOREMOST IN EVERY GOOD WORK.

INTRODUCTORY NOTE.

I N presenting this volume dealing with the history of my native parish, I hope that in spite of its manifest shortcomings it will meet with a sympathetic reception from those connected with or interested in the district. Due acknowledgment will be given in the concluding chapter of the willing and valuable assistance rendered by many kind friends, accompanied by a list of the various authorities from which much of the information engrossed in the following pages has been derived.

J. B.

HELENSBURGH,
8th August, 1893.

TABLE OF CONTENTS.

ERRATA.

Page 2.—Duntocher and Clydebank charges are "*quoad sacra*" and not "*quoad omnia*," the former being disjoined in 1836 and the latter in 1875.

,, 17.—Line 16, for "John" read "Thomas Walker."

,, 59.—Line 7, for "his memory" read "to the Virgin Mary or our Lady."

,, 59.—Line 9, read "Isabella, Duchess of Albany."

,, 60.—Line 11, insert the word "do" after "tomb."

,, 128.—Line 2, for "1840" read "1843."

,, 203.—Arms of Fergusson Buchanan are wrong, for correct quarterings see Appendix, page 329.

,, 210.—Line 24, delete the words "of Moss and Auchentoshan."

VIEW FROM DALNOTTER HILL, A.D. 1812.

From a Water-Colour Painting by H. W. Williams.

WEST KILPATRICK.

CHAPTER I.

GENERAL DESCRIPTION.

THE important parish of West or Old Kilpatrick, which derives its name from Saint Patrick, the tutelary Saint of Ireland, is situated in the old province of the Levenax or Lennox, and stretches along the north bank of the River Clyde from Yoker Burn in the east to Gruggie's Burn in the west, a distance of some 7¾ miles, its utmost breadth from north to south being 5½ miles. In shape it is not unlike a triangle, with the base towards the river. It is bounded on the north and east by the parishes of Killearn, East or New Kilpatrick, and Renfrew, and on the west and north-west by that of Dumbarton. Originally East or New Kilpatrick—or, as it was anciently called, Drumry parish—was embraced within the boundaries, but on 16th February, 1649, "in respect of the largenes of the parish and for the better helping of the ministers' stipends," the Scottish Parliament agreed to the division as proposed by the Presbytery of Dumbarton.* In 1875, owing to the great increase of the population, Duntocher—which had been a *quoad sacra* charge from the year 1856—was constituted a parish *quoad omnia*, Clydebank being at same time similarly disjoined.

The parish contains several lochs and sheets of water, the largest of which are Loch Humphrey, in size 6 furlongs by 3 furlongs, and Cochno Loch, 4 furlongs by ¾ furlongs; the latter is said to have been the trout preserve for the Abbey of Paisley.

The scenery of the district—which is beautifully diversified—has long been admired, the view of the river and mountains westward from Dalnottar being considered one of the finest prospects on the Clyde. The scenery from that point has long been a favourite subject with artists, and, as early as the end of last century, Mr. Farringdon, Royal Academician, London, a man of eminence in his profession, was employed to take views on the rivers Forth and Clyde, and that from Dalnottar Hill was supposed by many to be the best in the collection.† This view, painted by Naysmith, was the subject of the drop scene of the old Theatre Royal, Queen Street, Glasgow, and it is said

---

* See Appendix A.
† Old Statistical Account, vol. v., Edinburgh, 1793.

£100 was offered and refused for it a few days before the theatre was burned down. At one time the road from Glasgow led right over Dalnottar Hill, thus affording to travellers every opportunity of enjoying the scenery. The following extracts from Stoddart's " Local Scenery and Manners in Scotland," * and Dibdin's " Tour in Scotland," † are of interest, as showing the favourable impressions the scenery from this point produced on cultured minds.

Stoddart writes—" Two or three miles further, you fall into the Dumbarton road, which here crosses the canal, and immediately begins to ascend Dalnottar Hill ; on reaching the top of which, near the house of — Davidson, Esq., a most beautiful view bursts upon you at once. On the left, in the vale below, flows the Clyde, with the canal carried close along its banks. On the opposite side of the river is Erskine, a well wooded seat of Lord Blantyre's, the green points of which, receding behind each other, form the head of the Firth of Clyde ; the river now swelling into an estuary, and appearing like a noble lake shut in by the bold and lofty Argyleshire mountains in the distance ; and immediately below you is the right bank of the Clyde, ornamented by a continued succession of pleasant

* London, 1801, page 200.
† London, 1801, pages 180 and 181,

points, from the small village of Kilpatrick, to the town
of Dumbarton, whose singular rock and castle already
strike you with admiration.   Upon the whole, the view
from Dalnottar hill is not only remarkable, as being
the first in this tour which presents an idea of the
grandeur of Highland scenery, but as combining, in an
eminent degree, many characteristics of the grand and
beautiful.

" The approach of evening induced me to take up our
night's lodging at a small public-house in Kilpatrick,
where, as we did not expect very luxurious fare or very
splendid accommodations, we were not disappointed."

While Dibdin writes—" We saw all at once the opening
view from Dalnottar Hill, with Dumbuck, Dumbarton
Rock, for the castle is at that place concealed, the
winding Clyde, and the extensive distance beyond Port-
Glasgow and Greenock, which formed altogether a most
beautiful and striking effect.   All other considerations
became suspended ; out came the pencil.   At this time
a light shower was passing off, which gave a pearly and
sober appearance to the view, massing objects together
and softening down all outlines."   (The drawing referred
to is in comparison with Williams,' which forms our
frontispiece, a very crude production, the locality being
barely recognisable.)   " Having achieved this feat, we
bade adieu to Dalnottar and its extensive ironworks,

and came to Kilpatrick, where, according to tradition, was born the tutelary saint of Ireland."

Miss Dorothy Wordsworth, who travelled through Clydesdale in 1803, writes in glowing terms of the Dalnottar view. The frontispiece is from an engraving of a water-colour painting by H. W. Williams, known as "Grecian" Williams, dated 1812. The detail is remarkably faithful, showing many points which are still recognisable.

The view from the Kilpatrick Hills, which, with Dumbuck, form the most southerly spur of the Grampians, is unsurpassed for variety of scenery, comprehending as it does the rugged grandeur of the Highland mountains and the softer beauty of the fertile fields and valleys of the Lowlands. The highest points in the district are as follows, and are taken from the Ordnance Survey Map :—

Fynloch and Duncomb, ...	1,313	feet.
The Slacks, S.E. from Loch Humphrey,	1,199	,,
Cochno Hill, ...	1,140	,,
Lang Craig, ...	1,140	,,
Loch Humphrey, ...	1,065	,,
West Muirhouse Farm,* . . .	800	,,
Hill of Dun, ...	681	,,
Greenland Farm, ...	600	,,
Dumbuck Hill, ...	547	,,
Craigunnock, ...	515	,,
Cochno Policies, ...	504	,,
Ardconnel or Sheep Hill, Auchentorlie, .	500	,,
Dumbowie Hill, ...	500	,,

* Highest inhabited house.

Edenbarnet Road, ...	461	feet.
Dumbar Hill, ...	428	,,
Blackmailing Farm, ...	300	,,
Carleith Farm, ...	207	,,
Duntocher R.C. Chapel, ...	200	,,
Drums, ...	200	,,
Dunerbuck Farm, ...	180	,,
Radnor Park, ...	150	,,
N. E. Boquhanran or Chapel Yard, .	100	,,
Gavinburn Farm, ...	80	,,

The land naturally is well drained, but from the proximity of the hills to the river none of the streams are of great volume ; the most important being Duntocher. Burn, which has its sources in Loch Humphrey and the adjoining slopes, and falls into the Clyde at Dalmuir.

The other streams are Yoker Burn ; Lusset Burn, Kilpatrick ; Auchentorlie Burn, Little Mill ; Milton Burn, and Gruggie's Burn, at the western boundary of the parish.

ROADS.—The parish is traversed from one end to the other by the highway leading from Glasgow to Dumbarton, and running parallel with the river. * About the year 1760 there were no passable roads for carriages owing to the want of bridges, for in floods the rivulets were unfordable. Ten years or so afterwards the Duke of Argyle, Lord Frederick Campbell, and Sir Archibald Edmonstone, one of the heritors of the parish, undertook

---

* Old Statistical Account. vol. v., page 229, Edinburgh, 1793.

to make part of the high road from Yoker to the town of Dumbarton, a stretch of about 8 miles, and to take the chance of the tolls for their indemnification, which at the time was considered a very uncertain security. The road was soon made in the completest manner, and in 1793, through the increase of the trade in the parish and the number of travellers, the turn-pike dues had repaid the money advanced. Towards the end of last century the road leading from Kilpatrick to Duntocher and East Kilpatrick, which was the old highway from Dumbarton to Stirling, was similarly improved, to the great benefit of the parish.

Another and very old road, passing through the Abbey lands, commences at Dalmuir, strikes northward from the Dumbarton highway to where N.W. Boquhanran Farm formerly stood, of which Mr. Walter M'Laren, now of Carleith, was the last tenant. The farm-house has had to make way for the villas erected there within the last few years. The road then runs thence eastward past N.E. Boquhanran or Chapel-yard, and on to Kilbowie, Drumry, Drumchapel, and Garscadden. At all points the parish is well intersected by roads kept in excellent repair, the metal required being mainly supplied from the whinstone quarry at Bowling.

In August, 1878, the Act to alter and amend the law in regard to the maintenance and management of roads and bridges in Scotland was passed, by which it was provided that 5 years afterwards, unless in the meantime the Act should be adopted, or tolls and statute labour be legally abolished in such county, the existing system should end.   Accordingly on the 1st of June, 1883, the tolls and gates throughout the parish were discontinued, and the roads are now maintained by an equal assessment on landlord and tenant—on the landlord solely when he occupies his own house.

On the Dumbarton road the toll-houses and gates were at Yoker Burn, Dalmuir, and Glenarbuck Burn, Bowling.   On the Duntocher road there was a check bar near the old Parochial Schoolhouse, Old Kilpatrick, and a toll-house at Law Muir and Canniesburn, New Kilpatrick.

CANAL.—The Forth and Clyde Canal, which has its western terminus at Bowling Bay, was, with great ceremony, declared open on 28th July, 1790.   The *Scots' Magazine* for August thus describes this interesting event :—

" Glasgow, 30th July.   The important event of opening the Forth and Clyde Canal or Navigation from sea to sea, took place on Wednesday, and was evidenced by the sailing of a' track barge belonging to the company of proprietors, from the basin of the canal near Glasgow, to the River Clyde, at Bowling Bay.   The committee of management, accompanied by the magistrates of Glasgow, were the first voyagers upon this new navigation.   On the arrival of the vessel at Bowling Bay, and after descending from the last lock in the Clyde, the ceremony of the junction of the Forth and Clyde was performed in presence of a great crowd of spectators, by Archibald Speirs, Esq., of Elderslie, chairman of the committee of management, who, with the assistance of the chief engineer, Robert Whitworth, launched a hogshead of water of the River Forth into the Clyde, as a symbol of joining the eastern and western seas together."

The first vessel to pass through was the sloop " Agnes," of 80 tons burthen, belonging to Port-Glasgow, and built at Leith for the herring fishery and coasting trade. This took place on 31st August, 1790; on 9th September, the sloop, " Mary M'Ewan," was the first to accomplish the passage eastward.

The opening of the Great Canal was attended with very advantageous consequences to the parish, and indeed to the county at large. It is said the use of the wheel-barrow was unknown in the west of Scotland until introduced in the construction of the Canal. Formerly the removal of earth and stones was accomplished by two men carrying a hand-barrow. At the 1st January, 1791, the Canal Company had expended in this undertaking above £330,000, the aqueduct over the Kelvin alone having cost £8,509. The extreme length of the navigation from Lock No. 1, on the River Forth at Grangemouth, to Lock 39, on the Clyde, is 35 miles.

Summit of the head level, ...	156	feet.
Medium width of the surface of the canal, .	56	,,
,, bottom ,, .	27	,,

Depth throughout, ...	8 feet.
Number of locks on the east, . . .	20
,, west, . . .	19
Length of the locks between the gates, .	74 feet.
Width between the walls, ...	20 ,,
Fall of each lock, ...	8 ,,

The sandstone used in building the sea-locks at Bowling Bay and many of the bridges upon the west end of the canal was taken from Auchentoshan estate.*

The canal, when first constructed, being deeper than the River Clyde the Liverpool traders, one particularly, called the "Ariel," a brig-rigged vessel, went to Port-Dundas and discharged her cargo there, not being able on account of her draft to reach the Broomielaw.

RAILWAYS.—The first railway in the parish was that from Balloch and Dumbarton, with its terminus at Frisky Hall, Little Mill, where the passengers were transferred to the river steamers.   It was completed in 1850.   The year 1858, however, was signalised by the completion of the line from Glasgow to Helensburgh, The line was opened for passenger and goods traffic on Monday, the 31st May of that year, under the most favourable auspices, the weather being very delightful. There was no formal demonstration at the opening; all the trains were largely patronised from both ends, as well

---

* Old Statistical Account, vol. v., page 229, Edinburgh, 1793.

as at the intermediate stations, upwards of 200 passengers having left Helensburgh for Glasgow by the morning train. The transference of Messrs. J. & G. Thomson's shipbuilding yard to the Barns estate led to further railway extension, and on 1st December, 1882, the Yoker and Clydebank Railway was opened for traffic. The Lanarkshire and Dumbarton Railway Company, having obtained Parliamentary powers in 1892, are now constructing a railway which will prove a serious competitor to the existing Line, but it is hoped that both Companies will find the traffic in passengers and goods sufficiently remunerative.

As already mentioned, the River Clyde forms the southern boundary of the parish. During last century the magistrates of Glasgow made great efforts to deepen the river, and found the principal obstacle was the ford at Dumbuck. Mr. John Golborne, Chester, the engineer employed to improve the navigation, having measured the depth of water there, found it to be 2 feet at low tide ; 14 feet opposite Dunglass Castle ; 2 feet at Kilpatrick sands, and recommended the construction of a quay at Dunglass, where vessels of large burthen could be moored at quarter flood. This was in 1769. In 1770 an Act of Parliament was obtained to contract the river by jetties, and deepen it by dredging " between the lower end of Dumbuck Ford and the bridge of

Glasgow, so as there shall be 7 feet of water in every part of the said river at neap tides." Improvements were immediately carried out, and Mr. Golborne reported on the 8th August, 1781, that at Dumbuck Ford, "we had the pleasure to find no less than 14 feet."

The following extract from Pennant's "Tour in Scotland," 1770,* is interesting, from the description it gives of the method of deepening the river at this time:—

"Take boat at (Glasgow) the quay, and after a passage of four miles down the River Clyde, reach the little flying house of Mr. Golborne, now fixed up on the northern bank, commanding a most elegant view of part of the county of Renfrew, the opposite shore. After breakfast, survey the machines for deepening the river, which were then at work. They are called ploughs; are large, hollow cases, the back is of cast iron, the two ends of wood, the other side open. These are drawn across the river by means of capstans, placed on long, wooden frames or flats, and opposite to each other, near the banks of the river. Are drawn over empty, returned with the iron side downwards, which scrapes the bottom and brings up at every return a half a ton of gravel, depositing it upon the bank; and thus 1,200 tons are cleared every day. Where the river is too wide, the shores are contracted by jetties."

Since then the river has been gradually deepened, but so recently as 1812 the "Comet," drawing only 4 feet, required to leave Glasgow and Greenock respectively at or near high water, to prevent it grounding in the river. The late Mr. Thomas Macgill, shipbuilder, who died in 1882, could remember seeing the "Comet" lie ebbed off

---

* Vol. i., p. 158.

Frisky Hall. On one occasion a disturbance having arisen among the passengers, a couple of the most obstreperous were quietly put over the side and allowed to wade ashore. Even in 1820 the sloop "John," of Bowling, drawing 5 feet, grounded on the Yoker sands, when going up the river.

In his book on the Clyde, Mr. James Deas, C.E., engineer to the Clyde Navigation, gives some curious information regarding the effect of the deepening, widening, and straightening of the river on the tides. In 1755 the Clyde at Glasgow was only 15 inches deep at low water, and 3 feet 8 inches at high water; thus giving a range of tide of only 2 feet 5 inches. It is now 15 feet deep at low water (writing in 1883), and 26 feet at high water; giving a tidal range of 11 feet. High water level has risen 9 inches since 1853, and low water level has fallen 23 inches within the same period, and 7 feet 10 inches since 1755. In 1800 the time of high water was three hours behind Port-Glasgow; now it is only one hour.

The deepening and straightening, as well as the embanking of the river has had a beneficial effect in preventing the overflow of the banks which used to take place after the prevalence of southerly winds, indeed so high were the tides that at times the Glasgow road between Yoker and Dalmuir was rendered impassable,

The launching of the "Comet" from the building yard of Messrs. John & Charles Wood, of Port-Glasgow, in June, 1812, was an event the successful results of which have tended in course of time to add materially to the commercial prosperity of the parish. Her dimensions were—40 feet keel, 10 feet 6 inches beam, and 25 tons burthen. In the *Greenock Advertiser* of 15th August, 1812, the following advertisement appears:—

STEAM PASSAGE BOAT,

THE COMET,

CAPTAIN WILLIAM MACKENZIE,

Between Glasgow, Greenock, and Helensburgh,

FOR PASSENGERS ONLY.

THE Subscriber having, at much expense, fitted up a handsome Vessel to ply upon the RIVER CLYDE, between GLASGOW and GRENOCK— to sail by the power of Wind, Air, and Steam—he intends that the Vessel shall leave the BROOMIELAW on TUESDAYS, THURSDAYS, and SATURDAYS, about Mid-day, or at such hour thereafter as may answer from the state of the Tide ; and to leave Greenock on MONDAYS, WEDNESDAYS, and FRIDAYS, in the Morning, to suit the Tide.

The elegance, comfort, safety, and speed of this Vessel, require only to be proved to meet the approbation of the Public ; and the Proprietor is determined to do everything in his power to merit public encouragement.

The Terms are, for the present, fixed at 4s. for the best Cabin, and 3s. the second ; but beyond these rates nothing is to be allowed to servants, or any other person employed about the Vessel.

The Subscriber continues his Establishment at HELENSBURGH BATHS, the same as for years past ; and a Vessel will be in readiness to convey Passengers in the COMET from Greenock to Helensburgh.

Passengers by the COMET will receive information of the Hours of Sailing, by applying at Mr HOUSTON'S OFFICE, Broomielaw ; or Mr THOMAS BLACKNEY'S, East Quay Head, Greenock.

HENRY BELL,

HELENSBURGH BATHS,
5*th August,* 1812.

The excitement along the banks of the Clyde when the "Comet" first voyaged down the river was very

great, all the country side crowding down to see the wonderful craft propelled by the "power of wind, air, and steam."

Prior to the introduction of steamers on the Clyde, the principal means of communication between Greenock and Glasgow, and the various places on the banks of the river, was by the fly-boats, which were constructed by William Nicol, of Greenock. They were about 28 feet keel, from 7½ to 8 feet beam, about 8 tons burthen, and wherry-rigged, and were, on the whole, well fitted up for passengers.

The boats generally started from Greenock with the first of the tide. If, however, wind and tide were adverse, which was frequently enough the case, no little labour was required with sails and oars to make any advance whatever, and both passengers and crew in such untoward circumstances were often right glad on getting as far up as Dunglass, to rest there for five or six hours till the next tide should favour their further progress, exchanging meanwhile, their irksome confinement for a ramble in the neighbouring woods, which in those days were extensive, and, in the season, afforded excellent nutting.

Sheriff Barclay, in his "Reminiscences of Glasgow,"* says with reference to this detention : " It was surmised that the 'flies' were intercepted there by a net or web in the shape of a tavern. The passengers had frequently to remain in their ark or get quarters in the 'public' until the morning's tide called them to resume their voyage. A story was told and vouched, that when a 'fly' had been thus arrested for the night, and the crew were called in the early and dusky morn to avail themselves of the favourable tide, the two boatmen, who had been meantime indulging in strong drink, set to work with their oars. With the dawn the passengers had a dreamy notion that they were making little or no progress, as the outline of the castellated rock still, phantom-like, appeared in the mist. Calling the attention of the rowers to their apprehensions, the fact was painfully realised by the following colloquy between the ancient mariners :—'Tonald, did you lift t'anchor?' and the

---

* Glasgow, 1880, p. 176.

discouraging reply, 'Na, Tougal, not me, but 'twas your tudy.'"

FERRIES.—Erskine Ferry, which still remains, was the principal passage across the Clyde. At one time the portage was at Ferrydyke, immediately under the terminal Roman fort at Chapelhill, from which the compound name, Ferrydyke, is derived, but a sandbank having formed in the river early last century, the ferry was removed up to its present position. There was a ferry at Dunglass later, and also at Bowling canal sea-lock. The former was withdrawn when the wharf at Frisky Hall was built, and the latter when the upper wharf, now dismantled, was erected for the benefit of the Glasgowegians who patronised the Sutherland Arms Hotel. At Dalmuir there was a ferry-boat, the last tacksman being the late John Walker, a worthy elder in the United Presbyterian Church, Old Kilpatrick.

CHAPTER II.

PREHISTORIC REMAINS.

THE recorded prehistoric remains are, all things considered, very few in number. This may be accounted for by the fact that the lands of the district have been so long under cultivation, and that during a period when the study of archæology had practically no existence.

The deepening of the Clyde has led to several important discoveries of the craft in which our forefathers sailed and fished.

In 1854 the largest canoe hitherto recorded as excavated in the Clyde valley was discovered at Erskine Ferry by Mr. Gilbert Taylor, the tacksman of the ferry, and placed for inspection in the ferry-house garden. It was 33 feet in length, 4 feet in breadth, and of a depth of 3 feet 6 inches. The stern was flat and sloping, and the boards of oak fitted in a groove. The gunwale showed the appearance of iron locks on each side near the stern, and, judging from the distance between them, it would appear the craft had been propelled by 5 or 6 oars on each side. A visitor to Erskine Ferry, in 1856, records the almost entire disappearance of the canoe, it having been carried off in pieces by the curious. Some time later, about 1863, on the north side of the river, nearly opposite Renfrew, two canoes were laid bare, one of them being about 25 feet in length. In this connection it may be interesting to observe that the bones of a whale were discovered near Erskine Ferry in the year 1855. In 1868, in the river bend eastward from Dunglass Castle, Mr. Currie, then manager of the Little Mill Distillery, was instrumental in getting two canoes taken out of the river. They lay abreast of each other about two yards apart, their prows turned toward the south-west in a deposit of clay and sand. The larger canoe, composed merely of an undressed cylindrical hollow oak tree, of most uncouth aspect, measured 23½ feet in extreme length, and 11 feet in mean girth. Both ends had a truncated appearance, that which represented the prow having on the bottom side a formidable projection 2 feet in length, with a circular vertical perforation by which it might possibly be made fast to its moorings. The interior was well finished, being smoothed and carefully rounded, and capacious enough to have afforded room for 8 or 10 men. The lesser canoe measured 13 feet in length, 3 feet in breadth, and 2 feet in depth. It was neatly constructed, carefully finished, and must have originally been a tidy little craft. The sides had been fitted for row locks, and two unmistakeable foot-rests were in the bottom near the stern. A club was found lying in the bottom of the

canoe, similar in shape to the "pettle," which was in use up to the latest date by the local fishermen for stunning the newly caught salmon. These two canoes lay in a specially constructed shed at the distillery for many years; thereafter they were removed to the Kibble Palace, Botanic Gardens, Glasgow. In the same year a canoe, 22 feet long, was found a little below Milton Island, near Dunglass, in which it is said there were six stone axes, an oaken club, and a piece of deer's antler.

According to local report there are one or two canoes lying silted up on the Erskine shore opposite Bowling, it being the case that, many years ago, what was considered to be an inverted canoe, was partially laid bare there for some time.

In 1850 two unperforated spherical stones—one made of highly polished red granite, a species of rock unknown in the district—were shown to the late Sir Daniel Wilson, author of the "Prehistoric Annals of Scotland," as part of the contents of a cist, then recently opened in the course of farming operations on the estate of Cochno.

At New Kilpatrick, some years ago, a hammer of coarse-grained dolerite was found. It is 9⅝ inches in length, 4⅜ inches in maximum width, and 3½ inches in thickness. It is now in Kelvingrove Museum.

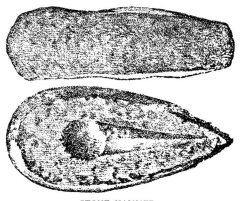

STONE HAMMER.

On the farm of Dawsholm, near Garscube, a barrow or tumulus was discovered about the year 1833, and in part opened up. Hitherto this mound, though sufficiently artificial, had attracted little observation, the curiosity of any chance inquirer being satisfied by the traditionary information of its being a court hill—one of those eminences on which Courts of Justice were held in the days of feudal jurisdiction. But the farmer, partly with the view of clearing his field of an incumbrance, and partly of obtaining soil to topdress other fields, set about removing the mound, and had not proceeded far in his operations when he came upon a narrow flight of steps leading upwards from the level of the field, not to the centre of the tumulus, but towards a point in the radius, distant about one-third of its length from the outer extremity. This stair being followed six or seven paces inward was found to terminate in a flagstone, on which some ashes and cinders lay, and which emitted a hollow sound on being struck with the tools of the workmen. It was removed, and beneath it was discovered a narrow oblong trough or cell, walled with stone on every side. In this several fragments of armour were found, among which were apparently the visor of a helmet, the head of a spear, and the blade of a sword, the first being of copper, and the last of iron. Besides these, there were what may have been a spade or shovel, much turned up at the edges, two picks of a small size, and several other articles, the purpose of which has not been guessed—all of iron. There were no bones discovered, and the stonework seemed to extend no further than has been described.*

A most interesting discovery was made in the year 1887, by the Rev. Mr. Harvey, Duntocher, of cup and ring markings on a rock surface, on the moor south of Cochno House, in a field of furze and bracken, known by the name of Craigpark, being the first of the kind

* New Statistical Account, vol. viii., page 36, Edinburgh, 1845.

discovered in Dumbartonshire. The rock is composed of the hard sandstone of the district, and dips westward for about 60 feet. There is a group of four series of concentric circles united by radial grooves. The most easterly series consists of seven perfect rings round a central cup, and the radius of the outmost ring measures 18 inches. From the innermost circle of the first moves

COCHNO CUP AND RING MARKINGS.

a duct, which passes to the innermost circle of the second, and is carried on to the outermost circle of the third. The second deviates from a circular to a rhomboidal appearance, with the same number of rings, but only a radius of 15 inches at the outside ; and the third has five rings with no radial grooves and 8½ inches for its greatest diameter. Sometimes there is a duct, oftener not, and it seems to have been cut both before and after the rings had been formed. An interesting feature occurs in a few with spiral volutes extending from the outermost circle, and with three cups enclosed by one ring. Numerous cups are distributed over this rock surface,

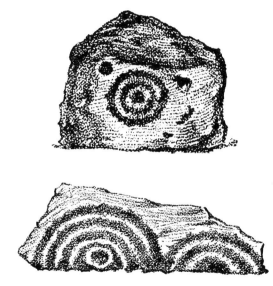

AUCHENTORLIE CUP AND RING MARKED STONES.

and some of them are from 3 to 4 inches in diameter, and from 2 to 2½ inches deep. These sculpturings are said to be much richer than usual.

Following the Cochno rock sculpturings, in the year 1889 two cup and ring marked stones were discovered in a dyke near the old farmhouse of Auchentorlie while the reservoir for the district water supply was being excavated close by. The sketches of both the Cochno and Auchentorlie sculptures are taken from the *Illustrated London News*.

In the spring of this year, 1893, a portion of a stone axe was found on the hill behind Carleith farm ; and some cup and ring markings have been recently discovered by Mr. William Smith, Post Office, Duntocher, on a rock surface a short distance east from the same farm steading. Lord Blantyre has a bronze hatchet, picked up on the shore of the Clyde near Kilpatrick. (See Appendix B.)

CHAPTER III.

ROMAN REMAINS

ON the approach of the summer of the year A.D. 80, Agricola marched into Scotland to push his conquests further north. Having penetrated into the country as far north as the Tay, and having surveyed the district extending between the Clyde and Forth, he employed his troops in completing a series of detached forts across the isthmus at intervals of from two to three miles, from Old Kilpatrick in the west to the shores of the Forth near Borrowstoness.

On the departure of Agricola, the Romans immediately lost much of what they had gained in Scotland through the indecision and inaction of the Lieutenants who were appointed his successors. In the year 120, the Emperor Hadrian, who had ascended the Imperial Throne A.D. 117, visited this island and erected a wall of defence between the river Tyne and the Solway Firth. Soon after this he was obliged to take his departure in consequence of some disturbance which had occurred in Egypt.

On the decease of Hadrian A.D. 138, Titus Antoninus succeeded to the Imperial purple, and soon after appointed Lollius Urbicus as his Lieutenant in Britain, the rapidity of whose conquests was such that in the year 140 he had taken re-possession of the country as far as the estuaries of the Forth and Clyde, and proceeded at once to retain and strengthen the detached forts left by Agricola, and to unite them by one continuous wall. This great work consisted of a large rampart of sods of turf, or *murus cespiticius*, and must have originally measured about 12 feet in height and 14 feet in breadth at the base, which is of stone with squared kerbs. It was surmounted by a parapet having a level platform behind it for the protection of its defenders. In the front there extended along its whole course an immense fosse averaging about 40 feet wide and 20 feet deep, and to the southward of the whole was a military road from 18 to 24 feet wide. The construction of this rampart was assigned to detachments of the three legions, the II., VI. and XX., the permanent Roman Guard of Britain. In spite of the wall, in the year 180 the Caledonians again forced their way southward, and were driven back later by the Roman soldiers. In the year A.D. 208 the aged Emperor Severus, determined to crush the bitter hostility of the Northern Britons, marched northwards with an immense force, but after concluding a treaty with the natives and losing 50,000 men in the expedition, returned with the remains of his army to the south of the Tyne.

Constantine the Great, who died in 337, is said to have so reduced the Caledonians, now called Picts, as to deprive them of the means of giving him any further annoyance. In 367, Theodosius came northwards, and after a series of victories again drove them beyond the wall of Antoninus, over which they had some time before made another incursion.

Early in the 5th century the Romans withdrew, and the knowledge of their departure became a signal of attack to the Scots and Picts, on the territories hitherto protected by them.

The Roman remains in this parish are of first importance, and I shall now proceed to describe these, and also refer to the various descriptions of the traces of the wall and remains as narrated in the works of those antiquarians and travellers who, last century, bestowed much learning and care on the subject. At this day the traces of the wall and ditch eastward to the farthest side of New Kilpatrick are few; in fact, to the casual observer the remains to the west of Duntocher may be said to be obliterated, but to the east, faint traces can be discerned at Cleddan burn, and at the Castle hill further east, in a wood there, the wall and ditch is in a fair state of preservation. The numerous houses at East Kilpatrick recently built has led to the almost total destruction of what was one of the best preserved portions of the vallum.

At Duntocher a section of the military way was laid bare recently, on the erection of the manse near the bridge.

From a very early date we find travellers carefully surveying the parish for traces of the Roman occupation, the first we read of being Dr. Irvine, who in 1686 was appointed historiographer royal of Scotland, and who travelled along the wall several times. As quoted by Sir Robert Sibbald, Dr. Irvine was of the opinion the wall began at Dumbarton, and states in his papers the following results of his investigations :—(1) At Dumbarton a great fort, (2) the Castle half a mile from it, (3) a mile thence at the foot of Dumbuck Hill a fort, (4) a mile thence at Dunglass a fort, (5) a mile thence to Chapelhill above the town of Kilpatrick a fort, and so on. Maitland, an acute and intelligent observer, the author of a History of Scotland, published in 1757, personally inspected the various places or forts referred to by Dr. Irvine, and says—"After the strictest search and inquiry, I could not learn that there was a fort at Dumbarton, and as to the fort at Dumbarton Castle it is only vestigia of certain trenches opened against the said Castle the last time it was besieged ; and the fort said to be at Dumbuck Hill seems rather to be the vestiges of an irregular sheepfold, and at Dunglass there is not the least appearance of a Roman work. That which has chiefly occasioned people to be of opinion that the wall ran to Dunglass is a small spot of ground at a place called the Dyke, about the length of 40 feet by 4 feet by 2 feet deep, representing part of a ditch, and from which the house* before it is denominated the Dyke, therefore it must have been part of the trench belonging to the Roman wall, whereas by its partly lying in and at the side of a garden, I take it to be part of a ditch formerly appertaining to a garden. Besides, as this small piece of trench is within a few feet of the flood mark in the estuary of the Clyde, there is not space left for the wall to have stood on, without mentioning the military way that would have lain within the same."

Bishop Pococke, who travelled in Scotland in 1760, had the supposed traces of the wall at Bowling Bay, referred to by Maitland, pointed out to him. In his journal he says:—"On inquiry here (at Dunglass) about the Roman wall, they showed me a mound in a garden, which they said they took to be part of it, and that a little further at a channel for water from the hill (Glenarbuck Burn), which is made under the road, they found part of the field very stony, which they thought was part of the foundation of the wall."

Maitland further says:—"That the Roman wall afore-

---

* This house stands on the north side of the road nearly opposite the Buchanan Institute, Bowling.

said began at Kinneil in the east and ended where the village called the Ferry Dyke is at present situated, about a furlong bewest the town of Old Kilpatrick, appears by a tradition amongst the people, which is confirmed by the great number of Roman antiquities found there, and as an additional proof that the wall came to this place, we have the word Dyke, the latter part of the compound Ferry Dyke, after the same manner as the whole fence is called Graham's Dyke,* and as this seems to have been one of the most considerable or principal stations on the wall, I am of opinion that the Roman trajectus or ferry across the Clyde was at this place, as was of late the Old Kilpatrick ferry, but within these few years a sand-bank being arisen in the river, the ferry was removed a quarter mile higher up; and that nothing may be wanting to show that the wall ended at this place, I shall only add another tradition that the wall in its way thither ran along where the church of Old Kilpatrick is at present situated."

Horsely,† in discussing this subject, says :—"The common opinion and tradition of the people is in favour of the wall terminating at Dunglass. They talk of striking sometimes upon the foundation of the Roman wall at

* Or Grimes Dyke.
† "Britannia Romana."

the Close not half a mile north-east from Old Kilpatrick, and then if the wall has proceeded in nearly the same line, it must have gone as far as Dunglass before it reaches the Firth. At Dunglass there is a fort, and the lands juts out into the Firth, which is deep here close to the shore; whereas near Old Kilpatrick the bottom is flat and the river shallow, so that at low water there would be room enough to pass by the end of the wall. Besides, the military way has certainly been continued as far as Dunglass, for it is very visible at Dunnerbuck.* This at least makes it evident that there has been a station there, whether we suppose the wall to have been so far continued or not. The principal arguments against the opinion of the wall being continued so far as Dunglass are these: that there are no visible remains of it further west than Old Kilpatrick, the seeming faint appearance of the ditch near Dunnerbuck not being such as can be depended on, and that the mountains on the north side along the skirts of which it must have been carried on to Dunglass would render the continuation of it almost entirely useless."

All authorities, inclusive of Gordon and General Roy, who minutely surveyed the district in the years 1724 and 1755 respectively, agree that the traces of the Roman

---

* The track across the field below Glenarbuck House, running parallel with the Dumbarton Road, referred to by both Maitland and Bishop Pococke.

PLATE 1.

occupation begins at the Chapel Hill * or Ferry Dyke, lying midway between Bowling and Kilpatrick and from thence eastward.

Two tabular stones were found on the Chapel Hill, and presented to the University of Glasgow, by Mr. Hamilton, of Orbiston, in the year 1695. Both bear legionary inscriptions, one of which is as follows (Fig. No. 3, Plate I.) :—

IMP · C · T · AELIO	*IMPERATORI CAESARI TITO AELIO*
HADRIANO · ANTO	*HADRIANO ANTONINO*
NINO · AVG · P . P ·	*AUGUSTO, PATRI PATRIAE*
VEX · LEG · VI · VIC ·	*VEXILLATIO LEGIONIS SEXTAE VICTRICIS*
P. F · OPVS · VALLI	*PERFECIT† OPUS VALLI (PER)*
P ∞ ∞ ∞ ∞ CXLI	*PASSUS, QUATOUR MILLE CENTUM*
	QUADRAGINTA UNUM

Announcing that the " Vexillation" of the sixth legion, surnamed "the Victorious," erected the said tablet in honour of the Emperor Titus Aelius Hadrianus Antoninus, the father of his country, having accomplished, in the formation of the wall, a portion of work to the extent of 4141 paces. A part of the other stone has been broken off and lost, but there is no difficulty in supplying the deficiency excepting the numerals which had preceded DXI in the concluding line. The interpretation is

---

* It is difficult to say how the name Chapel Hill has arisen, although the derivation perfectly obvious. There is a Chapel Hill on Hadrian's wall, where the remains of of a heathen place of worship have been discovered. Careful excavations might lead to a solution of the problem.

† Stuart suggests that instead of "carried on," as translated by Gordon, might it not rather read " perfected " or " finished."

similar to the former, with this difference, that the twentieth legion did the work instead of the sixth, and the fragmentary record of 511 paces of work completed. (Fig. No. 2, Plate I.). These inscriptions are engraved on slabs of common freestone.

Another stone, however, of much more artistic character, was likewise dug up on the Chapel Hill, and presented to the College of Glasgow by the Marquis of Montrose some time about the year 1695. This stone lay at Mugdock for some time (Fig. No. 1, Plate I.).

Stuart describes it as follows:—" There, within what may be called the mimic facade of a Corinthian portico, may be perceived the not inelegant form of a winged Victory, reclining with her left arm upon that emblem of empire, a globe ; while in the one hand she holds a palm branch, and with the other points to, or rather touches, an oaken wreath—the well-known *Corona Civica*, or Civic Crown. Within this wreath appears conspicuous the name of the twentieth legion, the " Valiant and Victorious," while crowding the tympanum of the pediment above, are inscribed the usual names and titles of the Emperor Antoninus. On the pedestal may be observed the figure of a wild boar, apparently escaping, as if he heard the shouts of the Damnian huntsman in pursuit, his course lying between the two divisions of the line, which records the number of paces accomplished in the formation of the wall. Instead of the peculiar figures formerly made use of, the miliary mark seems to be indicated in this instance by a transverse line which crosses above the four I's on the left side of the pedestal. Subjoined is a copy of the inscription, freed from the contractions, and accompanied by a literal translation :—

IMPERATORI CAESARI TITO AELIO HADRIANO ANTONINO AUGUSTO PIO, PATRI PATRIAE

To the Emperor Cæsar Titus Aelius Hadrianus Antoninus Augustus Pius, the father of his country.

VEXILLATIO LEGIONIS VICESIMAE VALENTIS VICTRICIS FECIT

The Vexillation of the Twentieth Legion, (surnamed) the Valiant and Victorious, performed

PER PASSUS, QUATOUR MILLE QUADRINGENTOS UNDECIM.

Four thousand four hundred and eleven paces.

Maitland, already quoted, says, after describing the above stone :—" Another stone I saw lying at the threshold of the door of the most eastern house of Ferrydyke, of 28 inches square, and 6 inches thick, had a border of 3½ inches, curiously wrought, but the inner part being greatly worn by people treading thereon, I could only discern there had been an inscription there, which then unintelligible. This stone, which was dug up at the eastward of the house where it lies, I take by its form to have been a legionary stone erected in the wall at or near the place where it was found, setting forth the name of the legion and other particulars." He further remarks—" There are many others of the same nation built in the walls of the houses of Old Kilpatrick and park walls in the neighbourhood."

In the year 1790, when the canal was being dug at the south end of the Sufield Park, between Portpatrick and the Ferrydyke drawbridge, a building constructed of freestone and lime was unearthed. In the inside were a considerable number of partitions about two feet apart, archedover with bricks about 9 inches long, and as many broad, while on the top of the arch were placed flat bricks about $1\frac{1}{2}$ inches thick, and of the same size. Inside the building several rows of urns were found about 2 feet deep and a foot and a half wide at the mouth, and made of burnt clay, and in them a number of silver coins were found covered over with earth. The writer [*] of this account then goes on to say :—" Mr. Davidson, then minister, and Sir Archibald Edmondstone, who was staying at the manse, got a number of the coins, as did also Mr. Colquhoun, superintendent of the canal. I got one of them which I gave to my uncle, the celebrated John Knox,[†] which he told me afterwards was deposited by him with the Scots' Antiquarian Society, London." Stuart mentions, in 1844, that several denarii of Trajan had then recently been found at the Chapelhill.

---

[*] MSS. John Millar Morrison.　　　　[†] See page 39.

These are all the recorded remains found in the vicinity of Kilpatrick, and it lies now with the Kilpatrick Naturalist and Antiquarian Society to prosecute an intelligent and diligent search by means of well considered excavations for further objects connected with the Roman occupation.

Eastward from Chapelhill or Ferrydyke, no trace of the wall has been found until beyond the village of Kilpatrick, and on the east side of Sandyford or Lusset Burn.

On the upper part of Sandyburn Hill, or North Dalnottar, * Maitland, and also General Roy, found traces of the ditch, and Maitland remarks that at this place the line of the wall points directly towards Ferrydyke. Between Carleith, on the north, and the Gateside of Auchentoshan on the south, both Gordon and Maitland found the ditch in great perfection, the public road to Duntocher being evidently on the line of the causeway or *via Militaris.* Horsely says that near Gateside, and about 3 chains north from the wall, was a small tumulus, and a pond, which, when drained by Mr. Buchanan, the owner of the estate, was found to be lined with hewn stones, and Mr. Buchanan was of opinion it had been a Roman bath. At Auchentoshan, an earthen vase and part of a stone bust were dug up,

---

* Formerly called by the country people Tittle Bog farm.

which seem entitled to claim a Roman origin; the latter resembles that of a Roman soldier, accoutred in his cuirass (Fig. No. 4, Plate IV.). A fibula of bronze, evidently Roman, in which were set some pieces of coloured glass, was discovered on this section. Close to Duntocher, Maitland found a few houses named the Dyke, so called (in this instance correctly) from being built on the wall, and also faint traces of the ditch to the north. Passing on eastward the wall crossed Duntocher burn to the north of the mill, and the military way to the south, and thence up the hill to the point known as the Golden Hill, on which was situated Duntocher Fort.

The so-called Roman bridge at the Duntocher mill was originally 8 feet wide; but, in 1772, Lord Blantyre made an addition of 6 feet to its width, as recorded on the memorial stone standing hard by. Maitland is of opinion that the original bridge was of wood, as the rock underneath has evidently been cut to receive beams of considerable thickness. The bridges of Hadrian's Wall were thus constructed. Stuart is inclined to think the bridge was built during the reign of King Robert the Bruce while he resided at Cardross; but, on the other hand, I would venture to suggest that the architects may have been the monks of Paisley Abbey, who thirled their numerous tenantry in the parish to the Duntocher

Mill adjoining. General Roy, in his "Military Antiquities," gives a view of this bridge.

In 1778, some fine fragments of Roman pottery were brought to light. They were of red colour, glazed on both sides, and in excellent preservation. The best specimen among them represents two centaurs at a gallop, with the figure of an armed soldier standing under a canopy between them. Another is ornamented by a succession of circles like small shields, with a female figure in the centre of each, and a row of dolphins gamboling underneath. A third, which seems part of the rim of a barn, has the words BRVSC. F., supposed to be the maker's name—Bruscus Fecit—stamped upon it. A bar of lead, covered with rust, has also been discovered in the neighbourhood of Duntocher.

A London Scot, John Knox by name, whose father was a vintner in Kilpatrick, published a book of travels in 1785, entitled "Knox's View of Scotland." In Vol. II., fol. 611, he writes :—" Upon the declivity of the Golden Hill, in the vicinity of the bridge, in the year 1775, a countryman, in digging a trench, turned up several tiles of uncommon form. The tiles were of seven different sizes, the smallest being seven, and the largest twenty-one inches square. They were from two to three inches in thickness, of a reddish colour, and in perfectly sound condition. The lesser ones composed

several rows of pillars, which formed a labyrinth of
passages of about 18 inches high, and the same in
width, the largest tiles being laid over these pillars,
served as a roof to support the earth on the surface,
which was two feet deep, and had been ploughed through
from time immemorial. The building was surrounded by
a subterranean wall of hewn stone. Some professors in
the University of Glasgow, and other gentlemen, having
unroofed the whole, discovered the appearance of a
Roman hot bath. The passages formed by rows of pillars
were strewed with bones and teeth of animals, and a sooty
kind of earth; in the bath was placed the figure of a
woman, cut in stone, which, with a set of tiles and other
curiosities found in this place, is deposited in the University." Knox remarks that he was returning from the
Highlands when the discovery was made, and that, with
threats and promises, he restrained the country people
from demolishing the structure until it had been examined
by those interested in such remains. He also says :—
" On the summit of the hill stood the Roman fort or
castella. The foundation was lately erased by a clerk or
overseer of an iron factory in the neighbourhood, who was,
however, disappointed in his expectation of finding treasure.
The same Goth expressed a strong desire to erase a fine
remain of the Roman *via* which is carried along the
base of the hill; but he hath not succeeded in his wishes, and

it rests with the family of Blantyre to prevent such practices in future upon the grounds of which they are superiors."

General Roy gives the dimensions of this fort at about 450 by 300 feet, measuring within the area of the ramparts, which, however, were so much dilapidated that the actual size and shape could with difficulty be ascertained. According to Gordon, one of the best executed legionary stones he had seen of all the Roman inscriptions discovered in Scotland was dug up at Duntocher some 160 years ago, and stood over the gateway of Cochno House, until Mr. Hamilton presented it to the University of Glasgow, where it now lies. (Fig. No. 3, Plate II.)

Stuart makes the following remarks on this particular piece of sculpture :—" On looking at it we might well be inclined to ask whence came the artist who rejoiced in the patronage of the Legio Secunda Augusta ? In what region of the globe did he acquire the style displayed before us—original though rude—and what can be the meaning which his emblems bear ? The present is but one specimen among many—all so much alike that we must either suppose some individual employé to have been an indefatigable workman, or else there existed a wide-spread partiality among the followers of Lollius Urbicus for the peculiar kind of decoration now referred to. There is nothing here like a reflection from the banks of the Nile, as little from those of the Tiber ; and, excepting the

really well executed Pegasus, which would be no disgrace
to a Vexillarius of ordinary taste, even had he mounted
guard for many a season on the steps of the Parthenon,
we can see nothing in the design but the stamp of an
original and self-taught genius. The winged horse and
sea goat are often found together on the Roman British
inscriptions. The semi-circular ornaments, something like
Parthian shields, terminating in rosettes, or eagles' heads,
are still more common. These last were, doubtless, mere
arbitrary decorations ; the two first must, however, have
had their signification ; what that signification was it is
difficult to determine."

The inscription on this stone is of similar import to
the three formerly mentioned. Instead, however, of having
been raised by its vexillation only, we find it dedicated to
the Emperor by the entire legion. A part of the legend
will be observed near the top, the remainder within the
interior border, some of the Imperial titles being omitted,
evidently for want of room. The whole may be read
thus :—

> TO THE EMPEROR ANTONINUS
> AUGUSTUS PIUS—FATHER OF HIS COUNTRY—
> THE SECOND LEGION (SURNAMED) AUGUSTA
> (DEDICATE THIS) HAVING EXECUTED 4270 PACES.

In the Hunterian Museum there is another stone
which might almost be called a fac-simile (Fig. No. 1,
Plate II.), but no record has been kept of where it

was discovered.   It is here introduced on account of its resemblance to the preceding slab.   The inscription comprises a few words:—

L E G	*LEGIO*	*The Second*
II	*SECUNDA*	*Legion Augusta*
AVG. F.	*AUGUSTA FECIT,*	*Executed*
P IIII CXI.	*PASSUS IIII CXI.*	4111 *Paces.*

While the Pegasus and sea goat appear on the tablets of the 2nd, the wild boar seems to have been the distinguishing feature on those of the 20th Legion. (See Fig. No. 1, Plate I.).   It is present, at all events, on a tablet found at Duntocher, and presented to the University of Glasgow by Mr. John Hamilton, of Barns. Stuart says the stone had met with a good deal of rough usage.   The inscription is as follows (see Fig. No. 2, Plate II.) :—

IMP. C.	*Imperatori Caesari*
T. AE. HADRIANO	*Tito Aelio Hadriano*
ANTONINO AVG	*Antonino Augusto*
PIO P.P. VEX . LEG˙	*Pio, Patri Patriae, Vexillatio Legionis*
XX VV F E C	*Vicesimae Valentis Victris Fesit*
P	*Passus*

Other and in some respects more important stones have been found in and near Duntocher fort, notably one found in the month of June, 1812, on the farm of Braidfield, about half a mile south-east from Duntocher Station, which Stuart considers to be the *chef d'œuvre* of the military artists who handled the chisel. It is a large slab of freestone, 42½ by 30 inches. (Fig. No. 4, Plate II.). The inscription is to the effect that the 6th Legion had erected 3240 paces of the wall, with the usual dedication.

At Duntocher a small votive altar has been found. It was discovered by Archibald Bulloch, son of the old miller of Duntocher, in the year 1829, while cutting drains in a marshy portion of the farm of Easter Duntiglennan, about half a mile north from the line of the wall, and in the vicinity of the fort. It was lying flat in the earth about two feet below the surface. The finder removed it from its hiding place, and put it upon the eaves of his father's antique cottage, where it was seen by the author of the "Caledonia Romana" in 1843. The cottage has since been demolished, but the altar was rescued, and fell into the possession of the late Mr. John Buchanan, Glasgow. When first found the letters I.O.M (which stand for Iovi Optimo Maximo—to Jove the best greatest) were visible, and recognised by the minister of a neighbouring parish, but they were obliterated by twenty years' exposure to the weather.

In the year 1775 some curious subterranean chambers were exposed in a field immediately to the north of where the fort stood, and not far from the church in the vicinity of Duntocher Bridge. Some labourers were at that time engaged in turning over the ground when they came upon a large stone, which was found to cover the mouth of a circular vault, about 4½ feet deep and 10 feet in diameter. The walls and floor were of hewn stone, the roof of bricks, and what says a great deal both for the skill of the builder and the strength of the cement employed, this roof was not arched but perfectly flat. No one would venture to enter until a young man of the neighbourhood offered his services and was lowered through the opening. This adventurous individual was alive in 1844, but died the following year at the age of 96 years, and was tenant in Duntocher Mill for 64 years. On descending he found that the vault was connected with two other chambers of the same size and identical in appearance. The passage from one to the other was by a narrow opening or doorway, having a neatly-executed groove on either side for the admission of a sliding panel, by means of which the communication between them might be cut off, as is shown on the accompanying plan:—

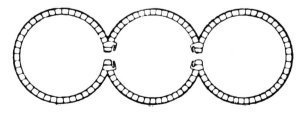

The only object of curiosity discovered within these vaults was an earthen jar standing in a niche of the wall, and containing a female figure, about 12 inches in height, formed of reddish clay. A few grains of wheat were likewise picked up, which renders it exceedingly probable that this subterranean building had been made use of as a granary. A drain for carrying off the water was found under the building. Bones of animals, and in particular the tusks apparently of boars, were found within the walls.

From Duntocher fort Gordon found the wall to be fairly visible for a quarter of a mile further east, passing to the left of a few houses called Cleddans and thence across a rivulet which goes by the same name. From it ascends a rising ground called Hutcheson Hill, on which the ditch is most visible, measuring about 33 feet in breadth and 8 or 10 feet in depth. From the rivulet called Cleddan Burn, he observes that the causeway takes a turn considerably southward from the ditch, keeping by the declivity or foot of the Hutcheson Hill, no doubt for the easier marching of the soldiers who travelled it.

In the spring of 1865 a legionary stone was found on the southern slope of the hill, at the depth of 3 feet below the surface. The slab measured 2 feet 10 inches by 2 feet 3 inches by 4 inches thick. (Fig. No. 3, Plate IV.). The inscription translated reads as follows;—

" To the Emperor Cæsar Titus Aelius Hadrianus
" Antoninus Augustus Pius, the Father of his Country,
" a vexillation of the 20th Legion, the valiant and
" victorious, constructed 3000 paces of the wall."

This stone was taken away to Chicago, U.S.A., where
all trace of it has been lost. A plaster cast is now in
the Hunterian Museum, from which the sketch has
been taken.

Gordon further says, "the vallum descends from the
above-mentioned hill to another brook called the burn of
the Peel Glen, at which place, where it crosses, the
foundation of a Roman bridge appears, consisting of large
square stones regularly cut and chequered, but most of
them are taken away for building the houses in the
neighbourhood, nor am I sure but that where the houses of
the Peel Glen are there might have been another fort, seeing
the foundations of stone buildings appear pretty visible
on this ground, though not so distinct as to afford me an
opportunity for taking their true dimensions and draught."

From this place a little further eastward the ditch
ascends a rising ground called Castlehill, where are to be
seen the vestiges of another castellum or fort upon the
wall. Here, on the Castlehill or third fort, a legionary
stone was discovered (Fig. 4, Plate III.), and in 1694
presented by Mr. Graham of Dougalston to the
University of Glasgow. The second stone found here

was a votive altar, the first we have met with along the course of the wall, with the exception of the one referred to as found at Duntocher. It is peculiarly interesting on account of the dedication, and somewhat singular combination of letters which it in some instances exhibits. (Fig. No. 2, Plate III.). It was discovered in 1826 and presented to the Hunterian Museum by the proprietor. It is rather above the average size, measuring 41 inches in height and 14 to 15 inches in breadth, and the shape of the letters are exactly similar to those which appear on the legionary inscriptions, showing it to have belonged most probably to the second century.

The dedication reads as follows :—

> To the Eternal Field Dieties
>   of Britain,
> Quintus Pisentius Justus,
> Praefect of The Fourth Cohort
> of the Gaulish Auxiliaries
>   (dedicates this)
> His vow (being) most willingly fulfilled.

Another legionary stone (Fig. No. 3, Plate III.), was n the spring of 1847 discovered near the Castlehill, and also the square base of a broken pillar (Fig. No. 1, Plate III.), and a tablet. Both were found lying on their edge, which seemed to warrant the inference that they were hid in the ground by the Romans on their departure from the spot. Stuart remarks "One motive for hiding them from the insults of the wild native after the soldiers left may be inferred from the circumstance that the Emperor Antoninus Pius, to whom the tablet is dedicated, was held in great veneration."

From the fort of Castlehill going eastward the vallum passes a little to the north of a place called the Mosshead of Ledcameroch, the causeway appearing again near the ditch, and both ascending the Cameroch Hill, the military way being about 18 paces south of the ditch on a parallel with it; both run down the higher ground to the village of New Kilpatrick, where, at one time, perhaps on the whole track of the wall from sea to sea, it is stated, the causeway could not be seen in greater perfection, measuring 20 feet in breadth.

The fort at New Kilpatrick was of an oblong form, rounded at the corners, the area enclosed measuring 480 by 330 feet. The military way passed directly through it, and its distance from the Castlehill was rather more than a mile and a third.

Two legionary stones were found here, and like those at Duntocher, shown on Plate II., Nos. 1 and 3, the one seems to be a copy of the other.

The first is a freestone slab, 5 feet long by 2½ broad, dedicated to the Emperor Antoninus Pius by the Vexillation of the Sixth Legion *Victrix* on their having completed 3665 paces of the wall. (See Fig. No. 1,

Plate IV.). The second stone (Fig. No. 2, Plate IV.), was found on the farm of Low Mullochan in the year 1803, a notice announcing the discovery, appearing in the *Glasgow Courier*, 5th March of that year.

See Appendix.

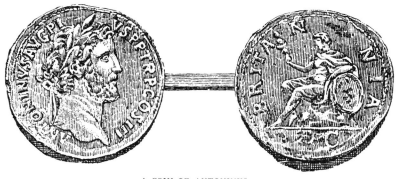

A COIN OF ANTONINUS.

CHAPTER IV.

ST. PATRICK.

THIS highly honoured and much revered saint—from whom the parish derives its name, and to whom the church was originally dedicated—is considered by the best authorities to have been born, if not at Kilpatrick at least in the vicinity, in the last quarter of the fourth century, whence he was carried off to Ireland, while yet a boy of 16 years, by Irish freebooters. There were at one time in the diocese of Glasgow six parishes deriving their name from St. Patrick, but we are told the most ancient and distinguished was Kilpatrick in the Lennox. Much controversy has arisen, and that for a long period, as to the birthplace of St. Patrick, Ireland and France having each their champions, Boulogne in the latter country claiming to be his natal place. As already mentioned the majority of critics now uphold the claim of Strathclyde. The Scotic freebooters from Antrim frequently ravaged the shores of the Firth of Clyde, and the Romans must have suffered much at their hands, as is evidenced by the numerous finds of Roman coins all along the Antrim coast. In the "Confession of St. Patrick,"* which, from the rude and ungrammatical character of its Latin, is a strong evidence of its genuineness, the writer says :—" I, Patrick, a sinner, the rudest and the least of all the faithful, and most contemptible to very many, had for my father Calpornius, a deacon, a son of Potitus, a presbyter, who dwelt in the village of Bannavem, Taberniae, for he had a small farm hard by the place where I was taken captive. I was then nearly 16 years of age. I·did not know the true God, and I was taken to Ireland in captivity with so many thousand men, in accordance with our deserts, because we departed from God, and we kept not His precepts, and were not obedient to our priests who admonished us for our salvation." In his "Epistle to Coroticus" St. Patrick further says :—" I was a freeman according to the flesh. I was born of a father who was a Decurio; for I bartered my noble birth—I do not blush or regret it—for the benefit of others." Decurians formed what might be called local Town Councils in every small town and village about the year 400.

While called Patrick, or Patricius, which was a common name among the Romans of Britain, he had, as Tirechan informs us, no less than three Celtic names—Succetus (Sucat), Magonus, and Cothraige (Cothrighe).

---

* "The Writings of Patrick the Apostle of Ireland," by Rev. C. H. H. Wright, D.D., London, N.D.

Patrick's place of captivity was close to the village of Broughshare, five miles from Ballymena, in the valley of the Braid, near the Hill of Slemish. There is a townland in the valley still called Bally-lig-Patrick, the townland of Patrick's Hollow. Here is a cave built with remarkable strength; it has had at least three compartments, and one of them is supplied with air by a chimney. The river Braid, originally called Braghad, a gullet or windpipe, and used to signify a gorge or deeply cut glen, forms the boundary between the parishes of Racavan, or Rathcavan, on the south and Skerry on the north of the river. There are in the district the ruins of a cluster of ancient buildings, formerly surrounded by a deep ditch and parapet, and the adjoining locality is known in the county as St. Patrick's Chapel. Patrick was employed by a chieftain, Milchu by name, son of Hua Bain, King of North Dalriada, to feed cattle, and served him six years. Escaping from slavery he reached his home again, after having been, as some think, a second time in captivity. His own words are:—"And again, after a few years, I was in the Britains with my parents, who received me as a son, and earnestly besought me that now at least, after the many hardships I had endured, I would never leave them again. And there I saw indeed, in the bosom of the night, a man coming as it were from Ireland, Victoricus by name, with innumerable letters, and he gave one of them to me, and

I read the beginning of the letter containing " The voice of the Irish."

The result of this vision was that Patrick returned to Ireland to preach the Gospel, having, as he again says, given up his "noble birth for the benefit of others."

God blessed his labours in Ireland above measure ; yet the modesty and humility exhibited by him in the account presented of his marvellous success is most remarkable. "There is, moreover," Dr. Wright says, "in his writings a display of genuine missionary spirit, which as it has roused many a Christian worker to action in the past, may well stir up many in our day also. Patrick everywhere displays an earnest trust and faith in the constant protection of a gracious Providence. His love for the souls of the men among whom he laboured, notwithstanding the ill-treatment he received at their hands, is remarkable. His honest simplicity and the contempt everywhere displayed for the riches of the world deserve far more general recognition than they have yet received. His acquaintance with the Holy Scripture, with the phraseology of which his Writings are thoroughly imbued, and his desire to conform his doctrine to their teaching, is significant. To him God and Satan, heaven and hell, were great realities ; 'he endured as seeing Him who is invisible' (Heb. xi. 27)."

The genuine writings of Patrick are three in number, namely, "Patrick's Hymn," "His Confession," and "His Epistle to Coroticus"; the doubtful remains are the "Dicta Patricii," the "Proverbs of Patrick," and the "Interview of Patrick with the daughters of King Loegaire." There are some other works attributed to Patrick which have been condemned as spurious by competent scholars.

What is considered by the best authors to be St. Patrick's copy of the Gospels is one of the most treasured possessions of the Royal Irish Academy. It is enclosed in a shrine called the "Domnach Airgid." The shrine is an oblong box, nine inches by seven, and five inches in height. It is composed of three distinct covers, in the ages of which there is obviously a great difference. The inner or first cover is of wood, apparently of yew, and may be coeval with the manuscript it is intended to preserve. The second, which is of copper plated with silver, is assigned to a period between the sixth and twelfth centuries, from the style of its scroll or interlaced ornaments. The figures in relief and letters on the third cover, which is of silver plated with gold, leave no doubt of its being the work of the fourteenth century.

St. Patrick's bell is also preserved in Dublin. It is rudely made of hammered iron, rivetted, and coated with bronze. Its height is 7¾ inches, including the handle, the width of the mouth 4⅞ by 3⅞ inches, and the entire weight 3 lbs. 11 oz. The case or shrine in which it is enclosed is of bronze, and richly ornamented in gold and silver, and is supposed to have been made between the years 1091 and 1105. The bell and shrine

St. Patrick's Bell

were in the custody of the family of Mulholland until the year 1798, when it was gifted by the then holder, a poor schoolmaster, Mulholland by name, to a former pupil, Mr. M'Lean of Belfast. They are now among the greatest treasures of the museum of the Royal Irish Academy*

Shrine of St. Patrick's Bell.

"The Hymn" is written in a very ancient dialect of Irish in the original, and the meaning of some of the

* Anderson's "Scotland in Early Christian Times," Edinburgh. 1881, page 203.

words and phrases is uncertain. It is one of those compositions termed by the Latin name of Lorica, or "breastplate," the repetition of which was supposed to guard a traveller like a breastplate from spiritual foes. The first two verses of the "Hymn," or "Breastplate," read as follows :—

> I bind myself to-day
> To a strong power, an invocation of the Trinity.
> I believe in a Threeness, with confession of a Oneness,
> In the Creator of Judgment.

> I bind myself to-day
> To the power of the birth of Christ, with His baptism ;
> To the power of the crucifixion, with His burial ;
> To the power of His resurrection, with His ascension ;
> To the power of His coming to the judgment of Doom.

The eleventh and last verse reads :—

> Salvation is the Lord's—
> Salvation is the Lord's—
> Salvation is Christ's :
> Let Thy salvation, O Lord, be ever with us.

This hymn has been set to music as a sacred cantata by Sir Robert Stewart, Professor of Music, in the University of Dublin, and was performed for the first time in St. Patrick's Cathedral, Dublin, on St. Patrick's Day, March 17, 1888.

The dedications to St. Patrick in the locality are numerous. In the castle of Dumbarton there was a chapel dedicated to him from a very ancient date. Adam, the chaplain of the castle, appears as a witness to a deed in 1271, and in the Exchequer Rolls of this period payments to the "capella sancti Patricii infra Castrum" frequently appear. Robert III., in 1390, granted this chapel 10 merks sterling yearly, out of the burrow mails of Dumbarton. The Parish Church of Dumbarton is sacred to his memory, as well as a collegiate church for a provost, and six prebendaries, which was founded by Isabel Dunbar, of Albany, and Countess of Lennox, in 1450, in the burgh town.

In Strathblane Parish there is "St. Patrick's Well," which used to be held sacred, and on the 1st of May, up to the beginning of this century, many a pilgrim drank its healing waters.

From the evidence led at a dispute about the lands of Kilpatrick, which will be referred to further on, there can be no doubt that, in the remote past, pilgrims came to worship at the shrine of St. Patrick in the village church, as the holder of the lands appears to have been under an obligation to receive and entertain those parties who came thither for that object. Duffgal, or Dougal, rector of the church about 1233, endowed the abbey with the land called Patrick's Seat, the locality of which it is now impossible to determine.

Besides the church dedicated to St. Patrick—which was said to be built on soil brought from Ireland in honour of its patron—we have St. Patrick's, or the Trees' Well, adjoining the church, which has been used until lately from time immemorial by the villagers, but now has been found unfit for use, and consequently ordered to be closed up. There is St. Patrick's Rock, near Erskine Ferry, on which, it is said, he was fishing as a boy when carried off to Ireland. Local tradition says erroneously, that St. Patrick was buried in his native place, but the Irish chroniclers tell us he lies buried in Downpatrick.

> "In Down three saints one tomb fill,
> Patrick, Bridget and Columkille."

CHAPTER V.

ECCLESIASTICAL HISTORY.

WHEN the Romans marched into Caledonia they found this part of the country peopled by a tribe whom they called the Damnonii or Damnii, a Cymric branch of the Celtic race. The district afterwards came to be called Cumbria or Strathclyde, the capital of which was Alcluith or Dumbarton. Under the civilising influence of the Romans, no doubt the inhabitants of this parish would, in their manners and customs, be far in advance of their wild neighbours the Picts, and that they were Christians we learn from St. Patrick's confession already referred to.

On the retiral of the Romans in the beginning of the 5th century, Strathclyde became a perfect battlefield. The Picts, Scots, and Saxons harassed the Britons; and latterly, the Danes in 870, under Ivan and Olave, having plundered Alcluith of all that was valuable, spread themselves over the surrounding country, and after twelve months' oppression, took their departure for Ireland. It was during these struggles that the great Cymric hero, Arthur the Faultless, King of the Poets, first saw the light,

Gildas in the 6th century, and Nennius in the 7th, relate the real Arthur's history; while Merlin, the poet of Tweedsdale, and Llywarch Hen and Taliesin, both poets of the Lennox, sing his praises. It has been thought that one of the battles of Arthur was fought in the neighbourhood of Duntocher, certainly in the neighbouring parish of Strathblane, where "Arthur's stone" bears witness to one of his victories.

About the year 900, Donald, the last of the Cymric or Brython Kings, died, and was succeeded by Donald, a brother of Constantine, King of the Scots. In 945, King Eadmund, who the year previous had harried all the Cumbrian kingdom, gave it all up to Malcolm, King of the Scots, on the condition that he should be his co-operator both on sea and land; and though there seems to have continued a line of Strathclyde kings, they were certainly subservient to the King of the Scots. Strathclyde was finally merged into Scotia or Scotland in 1038, when Duncan succeeded his grandfather Malcolm, son of Kenneth, as King of the united Scottish, Pictish, and Cymric Thrones.

The earldom of Lennox, which was also known as the Levanax or Leamhainach, derived its name from the river Leven, the principal stream in the earldom, so called from flowing through a forest of the Leamhan or elm tree. The inhabitants were known as the Leamhnaigh, and this name they retained till at least 1138, the date of the battle of the Standard. Shortly after 1174 the Lennox was formed by King William the Lion into an earldom, and bestowed upon his brother Prince David, from whom it passed shortly afterwards into the possession of Aluin, or Allan, the first of the old Earls of Lennox. The land tenure having become

SEAL OF EARL OF LENNOX, 1292 A.D.

feudalised, the Earls of Lennox bestowed estates great and small on the Church, and we now propose to give an account of the liberal endowments made by them to the Abbey of Paisley of the lands at their disposal in the parish.

Deriving its name from St Patrick, the church had in the remote and misty past been dedicated to that illustrious saint. Following the fashion of the times, the church of Kilpatrick, which had been built on the supposed birthplace of the saint, with the lands granted to it by the Earls of Lennox, was conveyed in 1227 by Maldowen, or Malcolm, the earl of the time, to the Monastery of Paisley, to God, St. James, St. Mirren, of Paisley, and for the soul of Alexander II., of himself, and all his race. " Lying on the northern bank of the Clyde," Dr. Cameron Lees writes,* "they formed a goodly possession, and probably on that account were difficult to retain. The wild Highlandmen who inhabited that part of the Lennox were continually seeking, by fair means and by foul, to obtain possession of the ground, and it took all the power of the Church to hold its own against their devices. The family of Lennox themselves seem no sooner to have parted with their fair lands than they sought to get them back. The eldest son of the Earl challenged the right of his father to bestow certain of the lands which he said belonged to him hereditarily, and the Abbot had to give him 60 merks to buy off his claim, or, as it is put, *pro bono pacis.* Duffgal, or Dougal, the brother of Earl Maldowen, made himself particularly obnoxious. He was at the time of his brother's gift rector of the Church of Kilpatrick, and probably thought the Abbot an intruder

* History of Paisley Abbey, 1878, page 60 *et seq.*

in his domains. Being a Churchman, and thus probably possessed of some skill in the drawing up of deeds, he forged charters, making himself out proprietor of the lands of Cochmanach, Dalevanach, Bachan, Fimbalach, Edenbernan, Drumcrew, Craigentalach, Monachkernan, Drumtechglenan, Cultebut and Losset, and entrenching himself behind these titles, he defied Abbot William and his convent to meddle with him. The Abbot, having found a former appeal to Rome successful, carried his grievance, June, 1232, to Pope Gregory IX., who issued a commission to his beloved sons the Deans of Cunningham and Carrick and the master of the School of Ayr to try the case between Duffgal and the Abbot. For a time the Kilpatrick rector kept to his own side of the river, and refused to answer the citations of the papal judges or to appear before them. At last, however, Duffgal's courage gave way before the threat of excommunication and consignment to the secular power, and in the Parish Church of Ayr, on the Sabbath following the Lord's Day on which is sung *Quasi modo geniti*, he appeared before the deputies. The charge was brought against him of having forged charters in order to obtain possession of certain lands contrary to his own salvation and the duty which he owed to the Church. Duffgal made no answer to this grave accusation, but, smitten by his own conscience, and seeing the imminent danger to his body and soul if the charges were proved against him, sought mercy instead of judgment, and placed himself in the hands of the Abbot and convent, who, on the advice of the judges, gave him the mercy he sought, and allowed him to hold his church and a caracute* of land at Cochmanach. Duffgal then made a formal resignation of his lands, endowed the Abbey with the land called Patrick's Seat,† and confessing in the most abject manner his wicked forgery, betook himself to his church and diminished acres, probably thankful to have got off so well. It has been said that the mass of evidence given by the large body of witnesses called in this dispute is worthy of a more advanced age, and the brief and retour of the inquest concerning the succession of Duffgal of Lennox carries back to the reign of Alexander II. a very peculiar form of procedure, altogether without that connection with church courts to which in general may be traced the early introduction of legal technicalities in a remote and otherwise barbarous country.

There were other lands in question before the judges besides those wrongly held by the Rector of Kilpatrick, and the name of one of them, that of Monach-kernan, appears constantly in the charters, inhibitions,

---

* A caracute of land—108 acres.
† Dennistoun MSS.

and agreements of the times. Monachkeneran, Cultebuthe, Drumtechglenan, and other lands lying to the east of the Church of Kilpatrick had been tenanted in the end of the 12th or beginning of the 13th century by a person named Beda Ferdan, who lived in a large house built of twigs, "*Habitantem in quaddam domo, magna fabricata de virgis*," * and who undertook for his holding the duty of receiving and feeding such pilgrims as came to the shrine of St. Patrick. A full account of this investigation is given in the Reg. de Passelet, from which we have drawn the narrative. The following are the names of some of the witnesses :—Anekol, Gilbethoc, Ressin, Nemias, Rotheric Beg, and Gillekonel Manthac. Beda Ferdan had not been allowed to retain peaceful possession of his lands, but had been slain in defence of the rights and liberty of the Church, and at the time of the Papal Commission which dispossessed the rector, Monachkeneran was held by a certain Gllbert, the son of Samuel of Renfrew, probably a follower of the house of Lennox, and Malcolm Begg had sold Cateconnen " prae timore." Dugald, the son of Cristinus, a former judge of Lennox, vindicated his right to the possession of Cultebuthe on the Clyde, and to a small piece of land which lay between the Church and the river on the east. †   With Gilbert, therefore, the

* Reg. de Pas., p. 166.
† Crawford's " History of Paisley, 1782," fol. 59-60,

Papal judges proceeded to deal, and summoned him to appear before them in the Parish Church of Irvine on the Monday preceding St. Matthews anniversary, 1233.*
Gilbert treated their citation very lightly, and merely sent them word that he would do what was right, taking no further notice of their summons. They proceeded, therefore, in his absence, to take proof, and to hear the witnesses brought forward by the convent. The evidence of these witnesses is taken in a manner that would do credit to any Court of Justice, and what they said is set down in a very terse and distinct style. Two diets of proof were held, and fourteen witnesses sworn and examined, all of whom testified to the lands in question having belonged to the Church of Kilpatrick. Some having been born and brought up in the neighbourhood remembered Beda Ferdan well; one, Alexander, son of Hugh, stated that when he was a boy, more than 60 years before, he and his father had been entertained as strangers by him; another, Anekol by name, swore that when Earl David of Lennox, in the time of King William, sought to raise men from the lands of Kilpatrick as from the other lands of his barony, the Church interfered in defence of her tenants, and proved their exemption from military service; Thomas Gaskel deponed to the same effect, and added that he afterwards

* See Appendix.

saw Cristinus, son of Beda, possessing these lands by
the same title as his father, and that the whole territory
of the Church of Kilpatrick was divided into four parts,
of which one was possessed by Beda Ferdan and the
other three by others, who also in the name of the Church
administered to such as chanced to come that way. The
judges held that the Abbot and convent had amply
proved their right to the lands in dispute, according
to their own judgment, and that of men skilled both
in canonical and civil law. They allowed them possession, and condemned Gilbert in expenses, namely, 'in
thirty pounds to be sworn to and taxed.' They then
asked execution of their sentence of the Bishop of
Glasgow. Gilbert was excommunicated for contumacy,
and King Alexander II. at the request of the Commissioners put in force against him the secular power.
This does not, however, appear to have been done with
sufficient energy, for sometime afterwards, we find they
again had recourse to His Majesty, wishing him 'salvation in that which gives salvation to kings,' and
asking him not to relax his efforts till the excommunicated Gilbert had obeyed the sentence and
satisfied his judges. Neither the secular nor the
sacred power appear to have been able, however,
to dispossess him, and it was not until two
years afterwards that his chief, the Earl, induced

him to resign his charters and the claim to his lands, by agreeing to pay him sixty merks of silver, in three portions of twenty merks at a time.

In 1250 the Earl repeated a general confirmation of all their lands within the Earldom, adding the right of pasturage formerly liferented by Ralph, the Chaplain Royal, to the north of Baccan, by the valley which slopes northward from Lochbeth to the waters of Corenade, thence westward along that water to the brook which flows northward from Salvari, where the men of his brother Dugald formerly had shielings, and thence to the march of Fimbelach.

From the great Bull of Pope Clement IV., 1265, we learn of the whole of the lands and churches owned by the Abbey of Paisley, and among them those in the County of Lennox, "which are commonly called Coupinanach, Edin-bernan, Bacchan, Finbelach, Cragbrectalach, Druncrene, Dallenneach, Drumtocher, Drumteyglenan, Drumdeynains, Cultbuy and Renfoyd; and the lands which they had had in the place called Monachkenran, with its pertinents." When Drumtocher and Duntiglenan were conveyed to the abbey by Earl Maldowen, they were burdened with the life rent of Ralph, Chaplain Royal, but he transferred to the abbey the annual payment due by the said Ralph of three silver merks, one chalder meal, and one chalder malt.*

---

* Dennistoun MSS.

The title of the abbey to the valuable lands in Kilpatrick, which had been disputed in the time of Abbot William, was again called in question. That energetic cleric had apparently brought all the matters in dispute to a satisfactory termination, but when his guiding hand was removed the old difficulties began afresh. So early as 1272, three persons—John de Wardroba, Bernard de Erth, or Airth, and Norinus de Monnorgund—who had married grand nieces and heiresses of Dugald, the contumacious rector whom Abbot William had so summarily silenced, renewed in right of their wives, the claim that he had abandoned, and were apparently inclined to prosecute it with vigour. A jury met at Dumbarton on Friday, before the feast of St. Dunstan Archbishop (15th May), and found that Maria, Elena and Forveleth, daughters of the late Finlay of Campsie, were the true lawful heirs of the deceasd Dugald, brother of Maldown, 3rd Earl of Lennox. The writ from Alexander III. to the Sheriff of Dumbarton is dated 24th April, 1271. The Abbot did not, however, go to law with them. Possibly there may have been dealings with Dugald that it would not have been convenient to bring to light. The claim was hushed up, and the claimants bought off by the payment on the part of the Abbot of 150 merks, "*pro bono pacis*," after which he received from each of them a separate resignation of all their claims, and in 1273 the Earl of

Lennox, when he received knighthood, wishing to be at peace with the Church before undergoing that ceremony, confirmed to the monastery all the lands which they held in his barony, and added a plenary exemption to the inhabitants of the territory from all subsidies and extortions. But in the time of the Abbot Walter, the old disputes broke out again. Taking advantage of the troubled state of Scotland, vigorous attempts were made in 1294 to strip the abbey of its Dumbartonshire possessions. They might have succeeded had not Walter found a firm friend and ally in his diocesan, Robert Wishart, the friend both of Wallace and of Bruce, and the determined foe of England, who entered into the contest between the abbey and its assailants with the vigour which history shows characterised all his actions, and who hurled against them the thunders of the Church. A certain Robert Reddehow, and Johanna, his wife, claimants like those already noticed, brought the abbot into the Court of the Earl of Lennox, who with his bailiff, under Royal Authority, proceeded to try the case, as his predecessor had done with the claimants of his time. The abbot, instead of giving these claimants a sum of money "*pro bono pacis*," refused to meet them in a secular court, or to acknowledge the right of the Earl, and those holding court with him, to interfere with the property of the Church, even under Royal Authority. The bishop, with whom the "Royal Authority" of John Baliol did not probably count for much, at once took the same view, and stood on the high ground of "spiritual independence." He issued a mandate requiring the Earl wholly to cease from the cognition of such causes as by Royal Authority he had caused to be dragged into his court, and ordered Reddehow and his wife to desist from their prosecution of the abbot under pain of the greater excommunication. The Earl and his bailiff disregarded these fulminations, and proceeded in his Court "against God and justice, and to the great prejudice of ecclesiastical liberty" to cognose upon the lands in dispute. Robert Reddehow and his wife, Johanna, fearless of the "greater excommuni- cation," also persisted in litigation, maintaining a protracted obduracy of mind, and irreverently contemning as sons of perdition the Keys of the Church. This was more than the bishop could endure, and he laid injunctions on five of his clergy—the Vicars of Cathcart, Pollok, Car- munnoc, Kilbarchan, and Kilmalcolm—to go, on the day on which the abbot was summoned to the Earl's Court, to the place of trial, and, taking with them "six or seven of their order, personally to advance to the said Earl, his baillies, and those holding court with them, and again warn them altogether to desist from the cognition of all such causes." He further enjoined them again to warn

Reddhow and his wife by name, and any others who might prosecute the said religious men in regard to their lands before said Court, wholly to cease from their prosecution. Should all this fail, the guilty parties were to be held as excommunicated, and their lands and chapels interdicted. The vicars, clothed in white sacerdotal vestments, in full Court, were further, if they thought expedient, publicly and by name, to denounce and cause to be denounced, the persons thus excommunicated in all the churches of the Deanery of Lennox, and Archdeanery of Glasgow, especially on each Lord's day and festal day, with candles burning and bells ringing, after offering of masses. They were to warn all the faithful in Christ to avoid them, and to place the lands and chapels of such as refused to obey under special interdict. The inhibition expressly warns Sir Patrick de Graham, Duncan, the son of Ameledy, Maurice, of Ardcapell, and twenty-four others, not to presume to intercommune with the excommunicated persons, or any one of them, in Court or out of Court, by assistance, favour, or counsel, by supplying them with food, drink, or fire, by grinding corn, or buying and selling. This terrible document is dated from Casteltaris, or Carstairs, 22nd August, 1294. Whether it had altogether the desired effect is doubtful, for we find the bishop two years afterwards returning to the contest, and commanding the Dean of the Christian

Jurisdiction of the Lennox to take with him four or five of his Order, and admonish the Earl and his bailiffs not to presume to drag the Abbot and Convent of Paisley before his Court in regard to the oft-disputed lands. The whole controversy furnishes a striking illustration of the struggle between the spiritual, or rather ecclesiastical, and secular powers, which, in some form or other, is constantly taking place even in modern times. *

The monks of Paisley, in common with other Scots ecclesiastics in those times, took the patriotic side. They were the good friends of Robert Wishart, the Bishop of Glasgow, who was so great a patriot that no oath could possibly bind him in allegiance to the English King, and who passed a great many years in an English prison. That the church lands of Kilpatrick furnished men who fought under the Earl of Lennox at Bannockburn is evident from the fact that in 1318 Malcolm, Earl of Lennox, admitted that the contingent furnished by the Abbot from the Kilpatrick lands was of free grace and favour.

The learned antiquary, George Chalmers, has justly observed that the Bruce won his crown mainly through the patriotism of the clergy, coupled with the devotion of the common people.

A charitable concession, which must have been

* Hist. of Paisley Abbey, page 166, *et seq.*

gratifying to the Abbot John and his brethren in their low estate (the Abbey having been burned in 1307 by the English), was made by Earl Malcolm of Lennox, 1329. He gave them all their lands in his country of Dumbartonshire. The contested properties of Monachkeneran, Bachan, and others, appear in his charters for the last time, all their rights, churches, and fishings being for ever secured, so that no person, clerical or lay, should interfere with them again. These properties had been an incessant cause of disquietude during nearly a century, and many of them, amid the confusion of the War of Independence, had in every likelihood been lost altogether. The Earl now confirmed them inalienably to the Monastery 'for the soul of the illustrious King Robert of Scotland,' who had died two years previously, In order that the Convent might hold their lands with a firm hand, he gave them power to have 'courts of life and members,' and escheat at the death of a man, in all their lands. These powers would enable them to keep all the wild Celts on their Dumbartonshire lands thoroughly in order, without help as formerly from the Bishop, of spiritual excommunication. For the latter, the rude marauders of the Lennox, as we have seen, cared but little, and the Bishop thundered at them in vain ; but the fear of execution and a short shrift could not fail to instil into them wholesome respect for their monastic superiors. The Earl, however, provided that when any were condemned to death, they should pay the penalty at his own gallows of Lennox.

In 1380, King Robert II. gave Abbot John a token of his goodwill by erecting into a barony all the Abbey lands of Lennox, with all the privileges which a barony usually possessed, assigning as the reason for this favour, that the Monastery had been founded by Walter, son of Alan Stewart of Scotland, of beloved memory, and liberally endowed by him and other of his ancestors, as well as by various other faithful Christians. In return for his concessions, the King asks the offering of their earnest prayers, and the only condition which he attaches to it is that they should continue to pay, as hitherto, five chalders of oatmeal to the watchmen of the Castle of Dumbarton. He reserved 'the four points of the Crown.'

To Abbot Tervas King James II. confirmed, in 1451, the regality into which Robert III. had erected the Abbey lands, granting even, in their Dumbartonshire lands, the four points of the Crown which that King had reserved—rape, rapine, murder and fire-raising.

Abbot Shaw, A.D 1478, like most of his predecessors, had to guard the possessions of his monastery against encroachments of various kinds. A certain Sir Hugh Fleming, of Dalnotter, gave him trouble about the pasturage lying between Bachan in Kilpatrick and his own property, Kynmunchayr. The Dean of Lennox was instructed by apostolic authority to assume with him chaplains and clerks, and going personally to the place of the king at Dumbarton, once, twice, and thrice, solemnly to warn Hugh, on the part of the Pope and the bishops of the Scottish church, that he was not under pain of excommunication, to draw the Abbot and convent before any lay tribunal, and to cite him to appear before apostolic delegates for the trial of his case. After this we hear no more of Hugh Fleming, who likely thought he would gain little by an appearance against the clergy in an ecclesiastical tribunal.

In the year 1275 an ecclesiastic, who is called Bagemont in the history and in the law of Scotland, but whose real name was Bayamond, came from the Pope to collect the tenth of all the benefices in North Britain, for the relief of the Holy Land. The clergy felt the oppression of paying truly one tenth of their real incomes, and induced Bayamond to repair to Rome in order to solicit some abatement of that burdensome imposition. The journey was unsuccessful, and Bayamond returned into Scotland, where he could not collect the tax, but found a grave.

In his tax-roll the value of the Kilpatrick vicarage is given at £53 6s. 8d., and it bears the same value in the books of the Collector-General of thirds of benefices, A.D. 1561 ; it also produced 28 chalders, 15 bolls, 2 firlots meal, and 7 chalders, 3 bolls, and 3 firlots barley.

In 1227, or before that date rather, when the Earl of Lennox, granted the church and lands to the Abbey, the vicarage was taxed at 12 merks of the altarage, or of the tithe of corn if the altarage was not sufficient. The procurations due the bishop of the diocese were taxed at one reception (*hospitum*) yearly.

CHAPTER VI.

THE ABBEY RENTAL BOOK.

M UCH valuable information regarding the Abbey
lands in the parish is contained in the Rental
Book, or Book of Leases, which was begun in the time
of Abbot Crichton, A.D. 1460 and, continued by his
successors. Dr. Cameron Lees, whom we again quote
freely, says—" It is beautifully written and neatly kept, and
perhaps, more than any other manuscript of this same kind
that has been published, gives us an idea of the conduct
of the monks in their capacity as landlords. The view
one takes of their government, after a study of this volume,
is a very kindly one, and corroborates all that historians
tell us regarding the lands of those ecclessiastics being
the best cultivated and the best managed in Scotland.
There were good reasons why they should be so. The
monks were not needy landlords, grinding out of their
tenants every penny they were able to pay. They were
proprietors whose own wants were few, and who had
education enabling them to adopt the best methods of
agriculture, and sense to encourage improvements. The
tenants were exempt from military service. The husbandman

EFFIGY.   WEST KILPATRICK CHURCHYARD.

on their lands was never called away like the retainer of
the neighbouring baron, to follow his master's banner,
and leave his field unploughed or his harvest unreaped.
He remained quietly cultivating the land, of which he
knew neither himself nor his children after him had any
likelihood of being dispossessed so long as they paid their
moderate rent to the bailiff or steward of the monastery.
The neighbourhood of a convent was always recognisable
by the well-cultivated land and happy tenantry which
surrounded it, and those of the Abbey of Paisley were
no exception to the general rule prevailing throughout the
rest of Scotland." A notable and patriotic exception to
the immunity enjoyed from being called to share in the
dangers of warfare arose during the war of Independence,
when, as already mentioned, the Kilpatrick lands furnished
a levy of men who fought at Bannockburn under the Earl
of Lennox, the fast friend of the Bruce.

> The men of Carrick and of Ayr,
> Lennox and Lanark too, were there,
> And all the western land.
> —*Lord of the Isles*, canto vi.

In looking over the list of tenants one is struck with
the familiar names to be found there, many of which are
still known in the parish, others again having disappeared
within the present century. We have Forsyth, Alanson
or Allison, Lang, Paterson, Houston, Fleming, Donald,

Brock, Bryson, Burnside, Morison, and many others. It is interesting to note that the surname of Brock, so common in the west-end of the parish in the early part of the century and still well and honourably known in the county, appears in the rental roll in the year 1460 as "de Strabrock." Henry Crichton, the Abbot of the time, was connected with the powerful family of the Crichtons who held large estates in the Lothians, and contemporary historians tell us that, about 1444, some fifteen years before, during the period of the struggles between the Douglas faction and the Livingstons and Crichtons, the barony of Strathbrock (the valley of brocks or badgers) in Linlithgowshire was overrun and plundered by the Crichtons, whose estates had been similarly dealt with by the Douglas some time before. It is difficult to account for the appearance in the rental roll of this Lothian name in these circumstances. The Livingstons of Drumry, whose lands were conterminous to those of the Abbey in the parish, were deeply involved in the troubles of the time, and it may be that de Strabrock, although bearing the name of a barony held by the Douglas family, was an ally of the Crichtons and Livingstons, and having suffered in the reprisals common to the times had been provided with a snug settlement on the lands of the Abbey. The sheriffdom of Renfrew formerly comprehended the barony and parish of Bathgate,

1

2

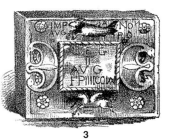

3

4

Robert I. having granted the said barony and sundry lands to Walter the Steward with his daughter Marjory. Thome de Strabrok is entered as tenant of the mill at Duntocher, at which the Kilpatrick tenants were bound to grind. These tenants were called "sukeners," and "thirled" or bound to the mill. If the dues chargeable by de Strabrock were the same as those payable at the Abbey mill, Paisley, he must have had a good thing of it. Any one grinding elsewhere than at the Abbey mill was fined in 100s. The rate of multure was each twenty-first peck besides the dues of the miller and his servants, namely—"Three fills of meal of a dish called 'angerem,' containing six pounds of Dutch weight, for fifteen bolls; two fills for ten bolls; and one fill for five bolls; and one streaked dish full of meal of the said dish for every boll of sheling."* These dues were very formidable, and it is supposed the curious name of "angerem" arose from the wrath of the tenants at seeing the miller thus securing so much of their meal. In addition to the mill, Thome de Strabrok is entered as one of the tenants in the Miltoun at the rent of 43s. 4d.; and also in Faifley, along with "John of Strabrok," the rent being 20s. "John of Strabrok" appears as one of the Duntiglennan tenants, paying 23s. 4d. of

---

* Dr. Cameron Lees, Hist. of Paisley Abbey, fol. 168.

rent, being by far the highest rent exigible from that
township, and he is entered, also, as tenant in Easter
Kilpatrick, jointly with Johanni Betone, paying annually
22s. 2d.   In a later rental roll the name appears as
Brock, and has come down as such to the present day.

In 1460, Hugh de Bronsyde or Burnside, and Andrew
Lang with Thome de Galbraith are entered as tenants in
Gavinburn or Wester Kilpatrick.   Simon de Bra, or of the
Brae, also appears as tenant in the same township.   A
portion of land valued at 26s. 8d. appears in the rental roll
as the Morislande and Huchonlande, that is, the moorland
and peatland, or bog.   Richardo Smale is first entered
as tenant, then John Fleming.   " Fynlay the merchant "
follows, who pays 13s. 4d. for his portion.   These lands
were burdened with what is termed " a lang carriage "—the
transportation of the peats to either the Barns of Clyde
or the monastery, as might be required.   Following Easter
Kilpatrick, with eight tenants, we have Auchintoshan, with
a similar number ; Duntiglennan, with six tenants—one of
whom, John Wilson, receives his mailing on condition
that he supports his father *pro toto tempore*, under
penalty of removal should he fail in his filial duty ;
Wester and Easter Cochnoch or Cochno, one of the
tenants in which is John Thomson, pleuchwricht ; Edin-
bernan or Edinbarnet, with six tenants ; Aschleck or Auchinleck, with eight tenants—one of whom is " ye colzar "

or collier, Johanni Brisane or Bryson. That coals were worked on this townland or in the neighbourhood we learn from the deed of confirmation, in 1587, of the Abbey lands to Claud Hamilton, in which Easter and Wester Cochno, *cum carbonaris*, is mentioned. Drumtocher, or Duntocher, *alias* Milton, with five tenants, is mentioned; also Le Bradfeld or Braidfield, with as many; then follows Litil and Mekil Culboye or Kilbowie; Mauchandran or Boquhanran; Ferchlay or Faifley; Le Bernis or Barns of Clyde, the head steading of the Abbey, on the north bank of the river Clyde, which is let to Thomas Hasty and Thomas Knock, paying annually 4 chalders flour, 8 bolls corn, and 8 bolls barley. Then we have Auchingre, held by the Abbot, and Craigbanzo, near Law—both muirs, the former being retained *pro suis equis siluestribus.* A house to the west of the church is let to Margaret Sclatar, widow, for the annual rent of 12 capons or fowls, and in a later rental roll we find "Fynlay the merchant" in possession with consent of the previous tenant. In 1548, "Schyr Wilyam Schawis house at ye est end of ye kyrk" is mentioned, and also "the smythis house for 13s. 4d. yearly is set to George Schaw, . . . of Schir James Denbe." These were Popes Knights—churchmen who were styled Sir.

By-names were not unknown amongst the Abbey tenants, as part of Auchentoshan is let to Robert Lang, *alias* "Cleme."

There were two chapels in the parish belonging to the Abbey, the lands of which were let :—"The land of the chapel of West Cochno or Warthill is let to William Anderson, paying annually 13s. 4d., and the said William shall maintain a bed at all times for the use of the poor, and shall keep the chapel in good repair," and "The chapel land of Boquhanran (now called N.-E. Boquhanran, but formerly Chapelyard) let to Wil Atkin (or Aitken), paying therefor yearly 13s. 4d., with one bed to travellers for Gods sake and our founders, with all freedoms usit of before." Descendants of Will Aitkin were farmers in the locality until some twenty or thirty years ago.

The monks were kind masters. No cases of eviction or deprivation are recorded. The same lands descended without rise of rent from father to son. Children, as we have seen, are held bound to maintain their parents in their old age, and widows are especially cared for, and are occasionally provided with another husband. "The 20s. land of Braidfield is let to Findlay Macgregor for Temple, widow of Robert Brison, and we give our consent to the said widow to contract matrimony with the said Findlay." There was in the bishopric of Glasgow a custom known as the custom of St. Mungo, by which the widow of a tenant on the bishop's rental was entitled, while she remained single, to hold her husband's lands for life.

PLATE 3.

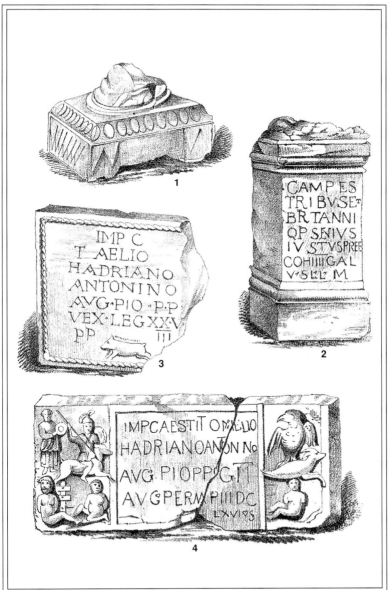

1

2

3

IMP C
T AELIO
HADRIANO
ANTONINO
AVG·PIO·P·P
VEX·LEG XX·V
P·P

4

CAMP·ES
TRIBVSE·
BR·TANNI
Q·P·SENIVS
IV·ST·VS·PREB
COH·IIII·GAL
V·S·L·L·M

IMPCAES·TITO·AELIO
HADRIANO·ANTON·No
AVG·PIO·PP·G·T·T·
AVG·PERM·P·II·DC
LXVI·85

The notorious and dissolute John Hamilton, the last abbot of Paisley, 1525-1544, who latterly became Bishop of Dunkeld and Archbishop of St. Andrews, forseeing the end of the old order of things, appointed the Master of Sempill, in 1545, bailie and justiciary over the whole lands of the abbey, and it is concurrently with Hamilton's tenure of the office of abbot that the name of his powerful and factious family appears on the rental roll. Robt. Hamilton, serjeant or baron officer, agrees to the letting of the "smythis house," 23rd April, 1548, and, some time later, he is entered as tenant in Duntiglenan in succession to his brother John, who had been located there from about the year 1538. In 1550 we find the first entry of the Hamiltons in connection with Cochno, an estate still in the possession of a branch of this family. On the 25th August of that year James Boyle and James Thomson both resigned their portions of Wester Cochnay in favour of Andrew Hamilton, Captain of Dumbarton Castle, and his son John. Later on, in 1551, William Nevin or Niven also resigned his holding in favour of Andrew Hamilton and his son John. At this date the rental roll contains the following short but suggestive entry:—" Estir Cochnay. In feu to Andro Hamylton, his airis." So numerous did the lairds or feuars of the name of Hamilton become, that no less than seven of that name—Cochno, Duntiglenan, Burnbrae, Kilbowie,

Drumry, and Auchenbarnet (Edenbarnet?)—fought on the side of Queen Mary at Langside, 13th May, 1568. John Alanson or Allison of Blackmailing, who had a daughter married to one of the Hamiltons before-mentioned, possibly he of Burnbrae, the farms being in touch with each other, lost his life in that battle. It is said by Dennistoun * that the Alansons were descended from Alan, Lord Cathcart, but his authority for this is not given. There were quite a number of Alansons on the rent roll of the Abbey at this period on both sides of the Clyde.

There were other families besides the Hamiltons who secured portions of the Abbey lands. The Spreulls, who held the Dalmuir lands for many centuries, appear as tenants in 1512 of the lands of Edenbarnet, Robert Spreull paying therefor yearly 43s. 4d. In 1549 we find most of the Edenbarnet lands in the possession of Stephen Spreull, son of Robert. Craigbanzeoch, being always held by the tenants of Edenbarnet, is found included in a charter dated 13th July, 1569, in which Stephen Spreull of Edenbarnet conveyed to Andrew Stirling, son of the late William Stirling and Margaret Houston, the lands of Edenbarnet and Craigbanzeoch, in the lordship of Kilpatrick and regality of Paisley.

---

* Dennistoun MSS., Advocates' Library.

PLATE 4.

1

2

3   4

William Edmeston became tenant in Moquhanray or Boquhanran and the muir attached called Auchingre, and these lands, having been let to him, were, at the expiry of his lease of nineteen years, turned into a feu. Edmeston appears to have been connected with the Duntreath family, as Margaret, second daughter of Sir John Colquhoun of Luss, was infeft in the £8 lands of Boquhanran and Auchingre on 12th and 13th February, 1585, in which year she married Sir James Edmonston of Duntreath.* Like the Hamiltons, the Edmonstons appear on the rental roll, when the Abbot of the time was apparently not averse to doing his relations a good turn. Janet, sister of George Shaw, Abbot, 1472-1498, son of Sir James Shaw of Sauchie, being the wife of Sir Archibald Edmonston, third of Duntreath. The change from the old order of things was soon experienced by the Abbey tenants. Andrew Hamilton of Cochno was attacked on the High Street of Dumbarton on the 18th of March, 1564, by nine individuals of the name of Houston, who, being fully armed for the fray, would have in all probability taken his life had he not escaped to a friend's house in the neighbourhood. The names of the Houstons were Patrick of that ilk; Peter, William, John, and William,

---

* Hist. of Parish of Strathblane, J. Guthrie Smith, fol. 119.

his brothers german; William, burgess of Dumbarton; John in Kilpatrick; John the elder in Dumbarton; and John his son. It is very significant that there is a John Houston mentioned in the rental roll in connection with Easter Cochno, of which Hamilton had obtained the feu. The Houstons were tenants long before the advent of the Hamiltons.

On 24th April, 1579, the "puir tennentis within the lordschip and parochin of Kilpatrick pertening to the Abbey of Paisley" complained to the Privy Council that they had been charged by two different parties for payment of their "ferme and tiend meill"; while in the year 1594 Archibald Bruce of Powfoulis became cautioner for Claud Hamilton that Archibald Paterson of Auchenleck should be harmless of him. Caution to same effect was given by the said Claud for James Hamilton of Cochno that the following should be harmless :—

Robert Shearer, Cochno.	William Bryson, West Cochno.	
James Paul, do.	Umpra Lang, do.	
John Paul, do.	James Slaiter, do.	
Gilbert Mories, do.	James M'Rae, Hutcheson.	
John Burnside Elder, Fachla or Faifley.	William M'Rae, do.	
	James Logan Smith, do.	
John Burnside, West Cochno.	Gilbert Mathew, do.	*
James Burnside, do.		

The seal of the Abbey † has been lost, but its form is

* Reg. Privy Seal, vol. v., fol. 165.
† See Gordon's "Monasticon," page 556.

well-known from the impressions attached to the charters
still in existence.

On the seal is a figure of St. James, with pilgrim's
staff and scrip. At each side is a shield; the dexter

PAISLEY ABBEY SEAL.

bearing a fess cheque for the Stewart, the founder of the
monastery; and the sinister, a saltire cantoned with four
roses, the armorial bearings of the Earls of Lennox, the
grantors of the Kilpatrick and other lands. Above the
dexter shield is a saltire, crescent, and star. The back-
ground is ornamented with foliage, interspersed with
crosses fleury and fleur-de-lis.

On the counter seal is the figure of a bishop vested,

his right hand raised, and his left holding a crosier. The shields on each side are charged as on the seal; above the dexter shield is a saltire and crescent,

PAISLEY ABBEY SEAL.

and above the sinister, a saltire and star. At the dexter side of the bishop's head is a fleur-de-lis; at his feet, two sprigs of foliage.

The last notice of the common seal of the Abbey is in 1574, when Claud Hamilton, the commendator, brought a successful action against Lord Sempill for its recovery.

CHAPTER VII.

WATCH MEAL OF KILPATRICK.

IN the Paisley Abbey rental roll there is the following entry :—

"Memorandum. As ye land of lordschip of Kilpatrick pertenand to ye Abbay of Paslay pais na cane foullis becaus yai ar thryllyt to fyff chalder of wache meil to ye castell of Dumbertane, to quhilk towne pais elik."

This refers to a very ancient tax payable to the governor of Dumbarton castle by the fourteen towns of Kilpatrick, of 5 chalders of meal, known as the watch meal of Kilpatrick.

In Fraser's "Lennox," a full account is given, of which we extract the following particulars :—"As one mode of sustaining a garrison in the castle of Dumbarton, the proprietors of certain lands in the parish of Kilpatrick were bound by their feudal charters, originally derived from the Earls of Lennox, to pay certain quantities of meal to the governor of the castle. This payment was called the watch meal of Kilpatrick. It was payable from the lands of—

Kilpatrick,
Cochinanach (Cochno),
Edynbarnan (Edenbarnet),
Backan (Auchentoshan ?),
Fymbaloe (Faifley ?),
Cragbrecholan (Craigban-
    zeoch ?),
Monakeran (Lusset ?),

Drumtglunan (Dunti-
    glennan),
Cultenfuthe (Kilbowie),
Drumthouter (Duntocher?),
Drumcrewe,
Dalfearn,
Renfode, and
Drumdyvanis
} (Barns?)."

The lands with such uncouth names were all embraced in the grant to Paisley Abbey by Maldoven, and it is difficult, if not impossible, to identify them with the names of the farms given in the rental roll of 1460. David II. and his lieutenant, Robert Stewart, successively interfered regarding this tax in 1335 and 1348. In the year 1329 we find the Abbot paying 10 chalders, being probably an arrear of two years.

Robert II., on succeeding to the throne, confirmed to the convent, 7th October, 1381, its various possessions, the reddendo clause mentioning the 5 chalders oatmeal, " which were wont to be paid to the Crown, for the support of those who for the time were the watch in the castle of Dumbarton."

On 4th August, 1455, this payment was annexed by the Crown. The clause in the Act of Parliament referring to the same reads as follows :—" Item, the castell of Dumbertane, with ye lands of Cardross, Rosnette, ande ye pensione of Cadyow, with ye pensione of the ferme meill of Kilpatrick."

In 1579, on the 24th of April, the Privy Council sat at Stirling, on which day, among other business, the "complaint of the puir tennentis within the lordschip and parochin of Kilpatrick pertening to the Abbey of Paisley" was heard. The complaint being that Adam, Commendator of Cambuskenneth, had charged them to make payment to him of their "ferme and tiend meill," while, on the other hand, John Cunningham of Drumquhassil, captain of the castle of Dumbarton, had also claimed payment. The Council referred the matter to the Lords of Session, ordering Adam and Drumquhassil to desist and cease from troubling the said "puir tennentis" pending the decision of the Court.*

Some years after, in 1584, Parliament decreed "that the money and victualles assigned in tyme bypast for keping of ye castle of . . . Dumbartane . . . sall remaine and abyd wth ye captaine and keipar thairof." †

Again, in 1606, we find Parliament confirming the Act of 1584. "Act in fauoris of the captain and keparis of the castell of Dumbartane. Our soveraine Lord and Estaittis of this present Parliament considering how necessar it is for the weill of Scotland that the castell of

---

* Acts of the Scottish Parliament, vol. iii., page 142.
† Acts of the Scottish Parliament, vol. iv., page 313.

Dumbartane qlk is the key and special hold of that pairt of our country be entertenyit—confirm the Pensioun ferme meill of Kilpatrick."

The Dukes of Lennox became in time hereditary keepers of the castle, and, during their long residence in England, the chamberlains or factors had been accustomed from time to time to make easy agreements with the heritors for payment in ready money instead of meal. But James, fourth Marquis of Montrose, as having right by progress to the whole estate of Lennox, comprehending the heritable keeping of the castle of Dumbarton, and the maills and duties payable to the castle, and as having been infefted upon that right, pursued the heritors and tenants of the parish of Kilpatrick before the Sheriff of Dumbarton, as being liable to pay the said castle 5 chalders and half a boll of oatmeal yearly, commonly called the watch meal of Kilpatrick, and craved decreet against them for the enforcement of the payment of the *ipsa corpora*.   The vassals contended that they were not bound to pay the *ipsa corpora*, but a liquidation such as they had been wont to pay, and alleged that what was urged by the Duke of Montrose had no foundation in truth, and that the said pension meal was nothing but dog meal, for the maintenance of dogs kept in the castle of Dumbarton for securing the country from wolves and other ravenous beasts.   The Duke of Montrose

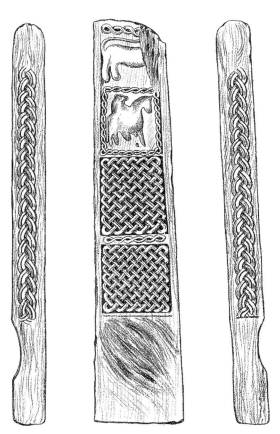

· SANDYFORD STONE ·

· FRONT · AND · SIDE · VIEWS ·

obtained a decreet, 13th July, 1706, against the vassals
of the fourteen towns of Kilpatrick decerning them to
deliver 5 chalders and a half boll of meal, being 5 bolls
and 3 firlots for each of the foresaid fourteen towns, and
likewise decerning them to carry the same to the port of
Kilpatrick or waterside of Clyde.

   The heritors and tenants, however, appealed to the Court
of Session, and on 15th July, 1712, "Walter, Lord Blantyre;
Archd. Edmonston of Duntreath; Claud Hamilton of Barns;
Alex. and James Lang in Edenbarnet; John Spreull of
Milntoun; Walter Buchanan of Auchintoshan; Elizabeth
Colquhoun of Auchintorlie, and James Colquhoun, one
of the captains of Her Majesty's Foot Guards, her hus-
band, for his interest; John M'Crae of Hole; Margaret
Alexander, relict of umquhile Robt. Shaw in Wester
Duntiglenan; Wm. and John Johnstone and James Finlay,
portioners in Auchinleck; John Johnstone, portioner, of
Auchintoshan; James Lang, Nethercloss; James Finlay
of Closs; Robert Brock of Burnbrae; Robert Brock, called
Swordum, portioner of Easter Kilpatrick; John Hunter,
John Morison, Robt. Lang, and the heirs of umquhile John
Boyle, portioners of Kilbowie; James Donald and Alexander Douglas of Easter Milntoun; heritors and portioners
of the fourteen tounes within the royalty of Kilpatrick,
lyable in payment of the watch meal of Kilpatrick," brought
an action of suspension against James, Duke of Montrose,

and James Grahame, his factor, and endeavoured to establish, amongst other things, that the tax was payable by Linlithgow measure, and not by that of Dunbarton, which was more favourable to the Duke. The following witnesses were called on behalf of the Duke:—Robert Bruce, in Woodside of Cambusdeane, who had formerly lived on Colgrain, Ardencaple, Kilmahew, and Ardoch lands; John Chalmers, Dalquhurn; James Donald, Auchinsail*; Robt. Steuart, Mains of Cardross; James Colquhoun, miller, in Colquhoun, who testified that the laird of Luss received for the Barony of Colquhoun by a measure which weighed 9 stones and 3 or 6 pounds, and if the meal was very good it weighed 9½ stones per boll; Nicol Bain, miller, mill of Cardross; John Mitchell, Chapeltoun (of Colquhoun); Robt. Lang, Duntocher; John Miller, Garscube; Wm. Campbell of Succoth, John Stobo, miller, in Douglas of Mains mill, &c., &c. On the other hand, the suspendors brought forward in support of their contention —Robt. Douglas, tenant in Barns; Robt. Knox, tenant in Thirdpart of Kilpatrick; Walter Aitkin, tenant in Dalmuir, who deponed he had been thirty years tenant to the laird of Barns, in Barns of Clyde; Andrew Paterson, Townfoot of Boquhanran; Wm. Brock, in Netherton of Boquhanran; and James Donald, Braidfield. After considering the

---

* Mentioned in Dr. Murray's Old Cardross, page 84.

evidence led, and the pleadings and cross-pleadings, decree was finally given in favour of the Duke as aforesaid.

At the beginning of this century a portion of the watch meal tax was valued at £30 19s. 8d. sterling, or 32 bolls 1 firlot 1 peck and 1 lippey of farm meal, and was payable on the last week of January.

The following is a note of the assessment on some of the farms for this tax:—

Gavinburn, ... about	14 bolls.
Blackmailing, ... ,,	1 boll.
Hole, ... ,,	2 firlots.
Wester Duntiglennan, ... ,,	3 bolls.
Golden Hill, ... ,,	3 firlots.
Cowbreggan, ... ,,	3 ,,
Wester Milton (3 bolls) and Easter do. (1 firlot), ,,	3 bolls 1 firlot.
Edenbarnet, ... ,,	6 bolls.

This tax is now held by the proprietors of the various lands from which it is payable, with the exception of the proportion payable from Lord Blantyre's lands, which now belongs, through purchase, to David Murray, LL.D., Cardross.

CHAPTER VIII.

THE PARISH CHURCH AND CHURCHYARD.

SESSION RECORDS AND SUCCESSION OF CLERGY.

THE present church was built in the year 1812 on the site of the old edifice, which appears to have been an ancient and interesting building. A strong feeling was manifested by the parishioners against its demolition, but to no purpose, and the then minister, the Rev. Mr. M'Cartney, having refused to preach in the church on the grounds that it had become, by age, unfit for such a purpose, the heritors were compelled to provide proper accommodation. The dilapidated condition of the church at that time is borne out by an entry in the Kilpatrick Society's books. On 10th May, 1811, it is minuted as follows:—" The meeting think it necessary to record, that on account of the bad situation (*sic*) of the church there appeared no persons to take the seats in their loft for the ensuing year."— Signed, Peter M'Lintock, preses.

It is said to have been the oldest church of the time in the west country,* and, in 1790, the Old Statistical

---

* Richardson's Guide to Lochlomond : Paisley, 1825.

Account says it was considered to be "a very ancient edifice." The date of its erection is now purely a matter of conjecture.

The drawing of the church, which we have much pleasure in introducing to the notice of our readers, was copied by Miss Cross Buchanan, Helensburgh, from a sketch by the late Miss Hamilton of Cochno, taken previous to its demolition. This copy is now in the possession of Miss Buchanan, Edinburgh, aunt to the present laird of Auchentorlie, but the original has disappeared.

The architecture is apparently of the Norman period, and points to the early part of the 12th century. A similar date has been given for the Govan church which was removed in 1762.

Heron, in his "Journey through Scotland,"* says, "The church of this parish has been anciently dedicated to St. Patrick. It seems to have been an edifice of some extent and consequence in the times when the parish churches of Scotland had little stateliness or magnificence to recommend them."

In entering the old church, one ascended two or three steps, where, in front, appeared a stone font which had been used in pre-Reformation times. It is recorded in the "Book of Colquhoun" that John Colqu-

---

* Vol. i., fol. 380 : Edinburgh, 1793.

houn of Garscadden was the first to be baptised in this church according to the rites of the reformed faith. There was a loft or gallery in the church, erected by the kirk session in 1770, the seat rents of which went for the support of the poor. In 1767, the Kilpatrick Society were allowed to erect a loft, the seats in which were let for the benefit of the Society's funds. The Cochno seat was in the area of the church, and had over it a 17th century date carved in bold relief; this panel, which is of oak, is still in the possession of the Hamilton family.

In 1773, James Houston, wright, received 1s., as the kirk session records inform us, for a new couple for the porch. The bell, as will be seen, was suspended from the west gable, and many tricks were played by the village boys in having it rung at unseemly hours, thus alarming the sleeping denizens of the Kirktown. The following curious entry regarding the bells appears in the Reg. Privy Seal :—" The Bellis of Kirkpatrick : to my Lord Sempil. August 5, 1568. The quhilk day my Lord Regents grace with dvise of the Lordis of Secrit Counsall, ordains the bellis of Kirkpatrick to be delivered to my Lord Sempil to be employed be him in the further setting of the King's service as he sall think expedient." In 1776 the kirk session records show the sum of 1s. being disbursed for a cord for the bell.

There was an altar dedicated to St. Ninian in the church, mention of which is made about the year 1520.*

On clearing the foundations a medal or coin of an unknown date was found. The remains of the old church are few but important. Last year the writer unearthed what appears to be the stone lid of a coffin, which, from the moulding, looks like 13th or 14th century work. When the Auchentorlie tomb was opened, in 1886, to admit of the burial of the late Andrew Buchanan, Esq., a portion of an early Christian sculptured stone of date previous to the year 1100 was discovered, and also a portion of a grave slab of true West Highland type of perhaps ·some two or three centuries later. The first stone mentioned is being embraced in the list of Sculptured Stones of Scotland now being prepared by J. Romilly Allan, Esq., F.S.A.Scot., for the Society of Antiquaries of Scotland. It is of red sandstone, and similar in style of carving to the Inchinnan and Arthurlie stones; it measures 33 × 15 × 8 in. The portion of the grave slab, which measures 32 × 13 × 6 in., is interesting from the fact that the reversed sword guard is almost identical with that on the stone effigy, a print of which, as well as of the forementioned, is given here.

---

* Dennistoun MSS.

This effigy is said to have at one time lain in the church. In whose honour it was designed cannot now be determined ; but possibly it may have been that of a predecessor of the Earl of Lennox, who granted the lands and church of Kilpatrick to Paisley Abbey, and at the same time stipulated for a place of interment therein ; or perchance that of Somerled, or his son, who were both slain at Renfrew in 1164 ; or may be one of his chieftains. In 1238, the early part of the 13th century, the grant above referred to is witnessed by "Isaac Capellano Sumerlede." *

A knocking stone, used for the preparation of barley for the pot, was also found in the Buchanan tomb, á probable relic of "ye hostilar house at⁻ ye west end of ye kirk." †

During the building of the present church the congregation met frequently under the now magnificent plane tree on the glebe in front of the manse.

The oldest family burying vault is that of the Hamiltons of Barns and Cochno, whose possessions in the parish date from the Reformation times. It has no architectural pretensions whatever. A mural tablet in Stirling of Law's tomb gives the date of 1658 as time of erection, while over the doorway is carved the

* Reg. de Passlet, page 161.
† Page 85.

OLD KILPATRICK PRE-REFORMATION CHURCH.

DEMOLISHED A.D. 1812.

arms of Stirling and Maxwell per pale with the initials
W S & M M. 1659.

Adjoining the Law tomb stands a mural tablet dedicated
to the memory of the MacNair family, who were feuars
at Kilbowie in the 17th century. In 1657, Robert and
John M'Nair in Kilbowie had their lands valued at
£116 13s. 4d. Scots.

The Auchentoshan enclosure contains two fine old
gravestones. Here lies John Cross Buchanan, the last

laird of Auchentoshan of that name, whose sudden and
premature decease in 1839 was universally lamented.

There are few traces of the Colquhouns now visible in the churchyard, that of Carcaston, the old name for Mains of Dumbuck, being almost the only stone left.

Not many years ago the tombstone of Colquhoun of Auchentorlie, with its Latin inscription, could be seen, but it, with many others, has been swept away.

The oldest tombstone now extant is one bearing the date 1616, with the initials T P & I P.

The tombstone of my maternal ancestors, the Patersons of Auchentorlie, is still to be seen with this inscription round the border —" Burial place apoynted 1683 to James Paterson." On an adjacent stone there can still be read " Here lyes the corps of James Peterson and his spouse Marion M'Lintock who died anno 1726." This couple were married at Dumbarton in February, 1690, having been duly cried in Kilpatrick church on the 7th of that month. They gifted two dollars to the poor's box.

Robert Whitworth, who completed the construction of the Forth and Clyde Canal, was buried here. He died, at the age of 32 years, on 23rd July, 1802, and his wife, Jane Fleming of Dalnotter, died 1st August, 1807, aged 33 years.

A great many of the older and unclaimed tombstones have been removed from time to time within the last few years, consequent on the great increase of the population at Clydebank. In order to keep pace with the demand for lair accommodation an extension of the churchyard was made in the year 1878, a piece of land adjoining having been acquired by purchase from Lord Blantyre.

Nothing shows the increase of wealth in the parish more than the tasteful and expensive monuments which have been recently erected by sorrowing friends over their loved ones.

Jamie Brock, who was gravedigger many years ago, was in his younger days tenant in Gavinburn farm. There were then few passenger steamers on the Clyde, and it was before the time when the late Mr. Bell of Bowling inn ran his stage-coach to and from Glasgow, so that travellers to the city had to be content with "shanks' nag." Some of Brock's neighbours coming home from Glasgow one afternoon found him working in a field by the roadside, and, knowing his thirst for information, resolved to have some fun with him. When they came up, the first question was : "Whit news frae the toon the day, men?" The great news—"The Dutch ha'e ta'en Holland, and burnt ten mile of the sea!" "There'll be anither war about that, feth," quoth Brock.

Not many years ago the large ash trees which graced the churchyard were cut down, their excessive size threatening to ruin the wall skirting the highway. Some fifty years earlier the heritors proposed to remove them, but the proposal met with considerable opposition from the parishoners, and William Galloway, poet, wrote a few verses in defence of the trees, entitled "The Old Ash Tree in the Churchyard."

The session records begin in 1745 with the ordination of the Rev. John Davidson on the 7th May of that year. The previous records are said to have been purposely destroyed by Mr. Davidson's predecessor, as several of the entries were prejudicial to his character. When Mr. Davidson was ordained, the following were members of the kirk session :—

John Morison, session clerk.	John Donald.
John Hamilton of Barns.	Robert Lang.
John Stirling of Law.	John Park.
John Miller.	Alexr. Aitken.
Ninian Hill.	Walter Brock.

PORTION GRAVE SLAB.
(West Highland Type.)

PORTION EARLY CHRISTIAN
SCULPTURED STONE.

OLD KILPATRICK CHURCHYARD.

Feb. 5, 1745. The which day John Miller Treas presented his accompts. The session having inspected the accompts anent the poor's money found that the clerks and treasurers books did agree. And that there had been collected from June 29th, 1740, till the date hereof the sum of £634 9s., and that there had been distributed out of that sum to the poor conform to the clerks books and by precepts £609, so that there remained £25 9s. Scots money in the treasurers hands which sum with that he had received from the Lairds of Barns and Law amounted to £85 3s. Scots, which he immediately paid into the session. John Morison also gave in £2 11s. Scots money as a part of the annual rent due by John Spreul of Milton.

June 1, 1746. Sederunt—Minister, James Hamilton of Barns, John Stirling of Law, Ninian Hill, John Millar, John Donald, John Park, and Walter Brock, elders.

The which day the minister acquainted the session that God willing he resolved to celebrate the sacrament of the Lords Supper in this place upon the last Sabbath of the month.

June 22. Tokens handed to elders for distribution.

July 13, 1746. Session found there was collected during the days of the last sacramtal occasion the sum of £51 1s. Scots money which was distributed in part as under—

Three poor strangers well recommended £3 10s.

The Schoolmaster for a man to present in the tent £3.

This day the treasurer reported—"That he had sold the bad brass which was lodged in his hands by the session Decbr. 5, 1745, and that he got for the same £1 11s. Scots money which sum with 17s. he had given in exchanging the two flagons and bason belonging to the session.

July 10, 1748. The session considering that their number was decreasing and that there was a necessity for having some new elders chosen; thought John Buchanan in Kilbowie, Wm. Park, there, Robt. Brock in Barns of Clyde, John Miller, younger, in Dunglass, Wm. Donald in Spittle, and Robt. Brock in Braes, proper persons for that office.

Augt. 6, 1748. The which day Robt. Govan, Kirk Officer, having, by order of the session, passed to the most patent doors of the church, and made due and lawful intimation three several times that Robt. Brock, above the Brae, and Wm. Donald were instantly to be admitted as elders if no objections were offered, and, none being made, the session resolved immediately to proceed to receive them into the office of elders and members of the kirk session.

July 8, 1750. John Brock in Balquhanran, Robt. Donald in Dumerbuck, Wm. Donald in Auchentorlie,

John M'Murrich in Auchenleck, Wm. Paul in Chapelton, and Jas. Latta in Mains, among others, were considered proper persons for the eldership.

Augt. 4, 1756. The session granted to Wm. Anderson £7 Scots to help him to buy a horse.

May 31, 1752. John Brock in Over Dalnotter, John Donald in Over Gavinburn, amongst others, were eligible persons for the office of eldership.

Feb. 1, 1756. In which day Agnes Weir, relict of the deceased Claud Lang, in dwelling at Miln of Duntocher, gave in a petition to the session praying that they would settle something weekly on her to support her poor family, who were in the greatest straits. The sum of 10s. Scots money was ordered to be paid.

Sept. 30, 1759. The which day Robert Govan, Kirk Officer, having, by order of the session, passed to the most patent door of the church and made due and lawful intimation three several times that Mr. Islay Campbell, Advocate, heritor of Nether Dalnotter, was instantly to be admitted an elder of this session, and no objections were offered.

June 2, 1765. John Paterson, tenant in Barns of Clyde; Wm. Donald, tenant in Meikle Overton; and James Houston were proposed as elders.

Oct. 27, 1765. This day John Colquhoun of Milton gave in a signed report to this session—"That Alex.

Caldwell of Nether Closs died the 15th of Sept., 1765, and, by his will and testament, left 300 merks Scots money to the manager of the funds of the kirk session of the parish of Old Kilpatrick for the behoof of the poor of said parish on this express condition—That a board be put up in the said church denoting the grant and the name of me the granter, and keeped up in all time thereafter, and that a year's interest of the said sum be given to any poor person in the parish, they having a horse or cow dead, and they apply for the same."

Novb. 10, 1765. Jas. Houston, wright in Kilpatrick, one of the session appontid to prepare a board to be put up in the said church narrating the said legacy of 300 merks Scots (£16 13s. 4d.) to the poor of the parish by the said Alex. Caldwell, agreeable to his desire in his last will.

Jan, 9, 1766. This day 9s. of bad brass found amongst the poor money amounting to fuly £25.

Feb. 12, 1770. Session agreed with James Houston, wright, to erect a loft in the east end of the church according to plan agreed upon for the sum of £22, and at same time agreed with Wm. Galbraith, mason, to build and erect a stair at the east end of the kirk, and to strike out a door in the east end of the kirk for an entry to said loft, for the sum of £5 15s.

The cost of the loft was defrayed out of the poor's fund, and the seat rents went to the good of the poor.

Mar. 1, 1771. Treasurer reported 9s. 8d. having been paid for repairs to church and schoolhouse.

May 24th, 1771. The which day after prayer, minister and elders Wm. Donald, John Brock, Robt. Brock, and Jas. Houston being present.

The session did set the loft belonging to the poor for the ensuing year at the sum of £5 5s. 8d. stg., which was paid into the treasurer.

The which day Mr. Davidson, minister of this parish, paid into the session £33 6s. 8d., being the principal sum contained in a Bond granted by the deceased Jas. Hamilton of Barns to the kirk session of Old Kilpatrick, dated at Cochnay the first day of February . . . and forty-two years, with seven Pounds ten shillings stg. as four years and one half years interest due on the said bond, viz., from Martinmas 1766 to Whitsunday 1771. The which day the minister did likewise pay into the session £27 15s. 6d. and ⅔ of a penny stg. as principal sum contained in a Bond granted by the deceast Claud Hamilton of Barns, dated at Kilpatrick the last day of April, 1685, in which bond it is expressly provided and declared that the interest of the said principal sum shall always be paid to the schoolmaster of the parish, and when there is none exercising that function, the said interest to be applyed for repairing the kirk, as more fully appears by the Bond itself, whereof follows :—(but here a large blank occurs, evidently left so for the insertion of the terms of the bond).

March 5, 1773. Treasurer reported to the kirk session that in £10 13s. 4d. of a balance remaining in his hands, £3 4s. 6d. thereof consisted of bad brass or not current coin. He was ordered to hand the bad brass to John Paterson, elder, in Barns of Clyde, to be melted doon and sold by him for the benefit of the poor.

Sept. 21, 1783. The which day, after prayer. Sederunt —Minister and elders John M'Murrich, John Brock, John Donald, John Patterson, James Houston, and Robert Paul.

The said day the minister acquainted the session that he had received a letter from the Sheriff of Dumbarton-shire acquainting him that the Barons of Exchequer had ordered a supply of meal for the poor of this parish, viz., 11 bolls 2 firlots 2 pecks, gratis, and a further supply of 24 bolls 3 firlots is likewise ordered, but for which last quantity they were to pay at the rate of 8s. 6d. per boll at receiving. The session then ordered their clerk to write to John Hamilton of Barns, Esq., desiring him to advance the sum of £15 stg. out of the £140 due by him to the session in order to pay the said meal and expenses thereof.

In explanation of this it may be said that the weather during the whole of the spring and summer was the most unfavourable that had occurred within the memory of any person then living. Owing to the snow continuing on the ground so long, sowing of every kind of grain was postponed at least a month beyond the usual time. The summer was uncommonly wet and cold, and most of the crop was not cut down till October, a great part in November, and no small proportion in the high grounds never ripened.*

June 16, 1789. At meeting of kirk session appontid to inspect and balance the accounts relating to the poor, it was reported that a meeting of heritors held in the kirk, the 9th June, 1786, for the purpose of assessing themselves for repairs of manse, kirk and schoolhouse, at which meeting there were present, Sir Arch. Edmonstone of Duntreath, Bart.; John Hamilton of Barns, Esq.; Mr. Jas. Dickson, factor for Lord Blantyre; Mr. James Davidson, factor for the Lord Advocate, and others, and it being proposed at the said meeting that a part of the poor's money should be laid out for the purpose of buying mortcloths for the use of the parish. John Donald, treasurer, was enjoined to lay out in the

---

* Somerville's Life and Times, 1741-1814: Edinburgh, 1861.

most frugal and beneficial manner as much of the poor's money as would purchase a proper set of mortcloths, the hire of same to go to the benefit of the poor's fund.

20th Augt., 1804. The session being duly met and constituted proceeded to the election of Mr. Shirra, the parochial schoolmaster, as their session clerk, and to enjoy all the emoluments, and perform all the duties of that office during the pleasure of the session.

They proceeded next to consider the dues of proclamation and baptism, and as not being altered for many years the session came to the determination of following the practice of the neighbouring parishes and they fixed proclamation dues—three days at 4s. stg., for two days at 7s. 6d., and for one day 25s., to be divided in the following manner—for three days, 2s. 9d. to the clerk, 9d. to kirk officer.

SUCCESSION OF THE CLERGY IN THE KILPATRICK CHURCH HAS THUS FAR BEEN ASCERTAINED.

1232. Dugald, brother of Maldowen, Earl of Lennox, was rector.*

1238. Patrick, Capellano de Kylpatrick, is witness to

---

* Dennistoun MSS.

the grant of the lands of Duncrew, Craginbreatalach, and Drumlosset.

1298. Walter de Bedewynde presented to the church of Kilpatrick by Edward I., 26th July.

1316. Sir Pat. Floker, curate, had dispensation from residence on being appointed master of the hospital of Polmadie.

1409. Sir W. Bruce, vicar.

1418. Sir John de Loudon, perpetual vicar.

1440. Sir Thomas Wyschard, vicar.

1507. Sir George Blair, perpetual vicar. Presentation objected to by the Archbishop on the ground that this had been conferred on himself by Pope Innocent VIII. of happy memory. And in virtue thereof he had already presented another fit person to the cure, but he expressed himself willing to hear parties and do what was just.*

1527. Sir George Langmure, vicar, clerk of the King's closet for life, with a salary of 40 lib.

1548. Sir Wm. Schaw is mentioned.

1550. Robt. Douglas, curate.

1560. Jno. Archibald Barry, vicar. In this year, on 17th August, Parliament adopted the confession of Knox as expressing the religion of the land, and on the 24th

---

* Vol. i. Dio. Reg. of Glasgow, fol. 392.

of the same month the Pope's jurisdiction was abolished. To say or hear mass was made a criminal offence—on the first occasion to be punished with confiscation of goods, on the second with banishment, and on the third with death.*

Barry reported the revenue of the vicarage to be 80 merks yearly, out of which he paid the curate of the church 24 merks.

In 1587, the patronage and the titles of the church of Kilpatrick, which belonged to Lord Claud Hamilton for life as commendator of Paisley, were vested heritably in him and his heirs. They were inherited by his grandson James, Earl of Abercorn, from whom they passed by purchase in 1638 † to Hamilton of Orbiston, whose family in turn disposed of same to Lord Blantyre.

The patronage of the church was held for some time by the Earl of Dundonald.

Some time after 1636 the Earl of Eglinton sold "that part of the bayliare of the regality of Paisley within the barony of Kilpatrick beyond upon the north side of the river Clyde to William Hamilton of Orbiston." ‡

---

* Hist. of P. A. Cameron Lees, page 197.

† Hamilton's Sheriffdom of Lanark and Renfrew gives 1653 as the date of transfer.

‡ Hamilton's Sheriffdom of Lanark and Renfrew, page 72.

SUCCESSION OF CLERGY AFTER THE REFORMATION
24TH AUGUST, 1560.

1563. Robt. Johnston, exhorter, with 40 m.

1568. Wm. Hunter, reader; his stipend, "the haill vicarage thereof."

1572. Robert Houston, exhorter, "now unabill," and to get xx li. ; former salary, 40 m. ; died after Cxmas same year.

1575. John Anderson, minister; his stipend, lxxj lib. xiij iiijd., with the kirkland of Kirkpatrick, etc.

1577. Matthew Douglas, reader, was presented to the vicarage by James VI. 18th Feby., 1577, and is said to have been minister, and deposed about ten years later. In 1583, Robt. Semple, feuar, Foulwood, became cautioner for Douglas' portion of a tax on vicarages, the amount payable by him being £6 9s.

1585. Walter Stewart was presented to the vicarage by James VI., and was ordained 24th June, 1587. This minister testified that Alex. Colquhoun of Luss was unable to attend Edinburgh, through sickness, at an assize held on the Earl of Orkney, who was executed that year. W. Stewart was alive in 1628.

In 1590 John Colquhoun held the living. On 7th September, 1602, we find him witnessing a deed at Auchentoshan.

1635. James Forsyth, A.M., was appointed minister, but was deposed by the General Assembly 10th December, 1838, it having been proved that upon a communion Sabbath, betwixt the sermon and serving the first table, he brought a mesenger-at-arms to the end of the communion table, and caused him to read letters of horning in the presence of 1600 communicants, charging them for his teinds, etc. ; that he taught the lawfulness of bowing at the name of Jesus, and that those who kneeled not at the receiving of the elements received no good by the communion ; that he accused the covenant as seditious, treasonable, and jesuitical ; that he gave money for being admitted to his place ; and that he was a decliner of his Presbytery and of the Assembly.*

1640. James Wood, son of Sir David Wood of Craig, was admitted. He was imprisoned 23rd September, 1645, in Dumbarton Castle for visiting James, Marquis of Montrose, though excommunicated, reading the papers of said James in his pulpit, pressing a messenger-at-arms to read said papers at the Cross of Dumbarton, accompanying enemies to the castle and demanding its surrender, using opprobrious speeches, and calling Mr. Robert Pollock, minister of Murroes, a loon minister. In the Dennistoun MSS. we find the following information :—" I have extracted

---

* Stevenson's Church Hist., vol. ii., fol. 631.

the minutes as a curious instance of the lengths to which party spirit was carried during the civil wars. On the 23rd September, 1645, the Presbytery, after ordering a public thanksgiving for the defeat of Montrose at Philiphaugh, understanding Mr. James Wood, minister at Kilpatrick, imprisoned in the castle of Dumbarton, appoints Mr. David Elphingstone and Mr. Robert Watson to repair presently to the castle and to enquire of John Semple, present captain there, of the said Mr. James his offence, that thereafter the Presbytery may do what is incumbent to them.

"They report from the said captain that the said Mr. James did accompaine the charge sent from James Grahame, sometyme Earl of Montrose, for surrendering the castle. As by . . . it was openly report that the said Mr. James had hoasted an messenger-of-arms to read the said enemies papers at the Cross of Dumbarton, and that the said Mr. James himself did read these papers out of pulpit to his parishoners and had dealt with them to join with the said enemy, and also that the said Mr. James had haunted familiarly with the said enemy communicat, and blessed his table at Bodwell. Whereupon the said Mr. James is ordained to be summoned by literal citatioune to compeir before the Presbytery against this day twenty days in the kirk of Dumbarton to answer the particulars aforesaid.

"On the 14th October compeared Mr. James Wood, and acknowledged he received a literal citation to compear before the Presbytery this day, and in obedience thereto does present himself to answer.

"1. The said Mr. James being interrogated if he went to that excommunicat enemie, James Grahame, and conversed familiarly with him and blessed his table at Bodwel?—Answered he went to the said James Graham against wholsom counsell given him to the contrary, and did communicat familiarly with him and bless his table.

"2. Being interrogated if he did read publicly in his pulpit before the congregation the said excommunicat enemies papers, and if he used persuasions to his people to follow and embrace the traitor's terms?—Answered he read his declarations, urged persuasions to his people as is contained in the interrogaterie.

"3. Being interrogated if he did press the messenger to read the said enemies papers at the Cross of Dumbarton?—Confessed he did so.

"4 Being interrogated if he did accompaine the said enemie his charge to the captain of the castle for surrendering thereof, and if he used persuasions to that captain for that effect?—Confessed that he did so.

"5. Being asked if he used any opprobrious speeches against the captain refusing to render?—Confessed that when the captain had replied to the said Mr. James his dealing with him to surrender the castle—'That there was no loon to a loon minister as Robert Pollock said of old,' he answered that there was no loun to a loun provost who keeped the King's castle against those who were sent by the King to recover it. The Presbytery finding the points full of gross malignancy and fearful breaches of the league and covenant, and a reall joining with the unatural enemie, and that therefore the said Mr. James deserves the censure of deposition. Do all in one voice depose him from the office of the ministrie, and declare his place vacant; lyk as the moderator in the name of God and of the Presbytery did pronounce the sentence of deposition judicially in his own presence."

In 1648, Matt. Ramsay, A.M., was admitted, after Mr. Alex. Dunlop at Paisley, Mr. Hugh Blair at Glasgow, and Mr. John Durie had been severally presented by the Earl of Dundonald, and had all successively refused. Mr. Ramsay is characterised by Woodrow as "a person of the most shining piety, staid gravity, of great eminency of gifts, extraordinary sweetness of temper, and most peaceable." In 1665, he was deposed for nonconformity upon charges for refusing to attend church courts, and of irregularly marrying and baptising; but four years after was indulged to preach at Paisley, whenever his health required an associate in his labours. On the establishment of Episcopacy he was asked by Lord Glencairn to accept the Archbishopric of Glasgow, which he declined.

In 1667, Thos. Allan succeeded, and is stated to have been outed by a rabble as a scandalous drunken sot; but as no such charge was ever made against him to the Presbytery his punishment was probably one of the inflictions of mob law, not uncommon during "the glorious revolution." In 1674 and 1675, he reported to the Presbytery that conventicles were being held at Drumry, Garscadden, and Boquhanran.

In 1689, Mr. John Ritchie was ordained, and died 11th December, 1726, aged upwards of 70 years. He was a faithful and useful minister, had a great regard for the judicatories of the church, and attended them while in health, was well versed in scholastic learning, and because he was a good philosopher had the by-name of Aristotle. He was present at Bargarran when Christina Shaw was troubled by witches. On March 10th, 1679, El. Anderson confessed before Lord Blantyre that she was at a meeting of witches with the devil above the town of Kilpatrick, and that she went to the ferryboat of Erskine, where the devil, with the rest of the band, overturned the boat and drowned the Laird of Brighouse and the ferryman. It is recorded that Hamilton of Barns was bewitched in the year 1677, and in the end of this century a woman was burned for witchcraft at Sandyford, the bones being found fully a century later when the road between Kilpatrick and Dumbarton was being improved. Agnes Naismith, one of the persons burnt for the crime of witchcraft at Paisley, 10th June, 1697, is said to have belonged to Kilpatrick.

1728. John Miller was presented to the church by Thomas, Earl of Dundonald, and died in 1738.

1739. Robert Yeats, a native of England, was ordained, and deposed on 7th March, 1744, for profaning the Lord's day and other irregularities.

Mr. John Davidson was ordained in 1745, and died 1793. He married a daughter of Hamilton of Barns, and was brother of Principal Davidson of Glasgow University. Mr. Davidson wrote the account of the parish for Sir John Sinclair's Statistical Returns, published 1793.

His successor, William M'Cartney, son of a farmer at Mains of Penninghame, born in 1762, was ordained 10th April, 1794, the elders on that date being Alex. Bell, Clerk ; John Donald, James Houston, William Donald, William Brock, Robert Paul. He got a new church built in 1812, and died October 6th, 1828, in his 66th year and 35th of his ministry. He mixed much with political affairs, so that proceedings were instituted against him in 1820 for violent language in the pulpit, which, not being proved against him, fell to the ground. Mr.

M'Cartney translated the Treatise of Cicero, and it is said to be the best translation which has yet appeared. He was somewhat eccentric. He would not allow a collection to be taken at the church doors, so the elders had the plates removed to the stone porches at each side of the kirkyard gate, where he found them one Sabbath morning on crossing over from the manse to the church. Without a moment's hesitation, with the toe of his boot, sent first one and then the other birling in the air, scattering their contents round. Alexander Rankin, my informant Mr. Jas. Lauder told me, an itinerant fiddler and dancing master, better known as "Hing a wing," was passing home at the time from one of his country rambles, and, in stooping down to pick up some of the coppers, knocked his breadwinner, which he had stuck up the back of his coat, all to pieces.

His reverence, like "Rab of the Jail," Robert Donald, whose fame was sung by the late Andrew Galloway, poet and teacher, "was mair than a match for the best on the braes." Once upon a time two sturdy lairds from that quarter primed themselves with *aqua vitæ* to go and give the minister a thrashing for some real or fancied wrong he had done them. He was walking in the glebe when the pair forced themselves through a hole in the hedge just beside where he was walking; and, when asked what had brought them that way instead of by the gate, they at once declared their errand. "Well, gentlemen," said the minister, buttoning up his coat, "you could not have taken me at a better time." He turned to and gave them both a sound thrashing. There is very often two ways of telling a story, but it is said that Mr. M'Cartney was presented to the living by Lord Blantyre on condition that he was to marry his patron's housekeeper. Time went on, and being reminded of the bargain, he said that he was quite willing to marry her at any time she and her intended husband came before him.

Mr. M'Cartney was the means of closing up Messrs. Edington's Ironworks at Dalnotter. These works turned out hoes, billhooks, and other implements, which were largely exported to the West Indies.

1829. William Fleming, D.D., was admitted in 1829, and resigned in 1832 on being elected Professor of Oriental Languages in Glasgow University.

1833. Matt. Barclay was ordained 18th April, 1833. In 1841, the following were members of the kirk session :—

Moses Shirra, Session Clerk, ordained 1804.
John Stark, . . .   ,,   1804.
A. M'Phie, . . .   ,,   1833.
John Conner, . . .   ,,   1833.
Samuel M'Dougall, . .   ,,   1840.
Frederick Hope Pattison,   ,,   1841.
Michael Pottie, . .   ,,   1841.

Mr. Barclay was declared no longer minister, 20th June 1840, having joined the Free Church secession.

PARISH CHURCH COMMUNION TOKEN.

1843. Rev. John Reid, M.A., was ordained 21st September, and died, universally respected, 3rd May, 1867.

1867. Rev. John Barclay was inducted the same year, and translated to Dunblane, 1869.

1869. Rev. Robert Henderson, M.A., formerly of Kirkurd, Peeblesshire, was inducted the same year, and died 11th May, 1893. He was unmarried.

1893. The Rev. William Swan, from Toward Point, was inducted 26th September, 1893.

The members of the kirk session at present are as follows :—

> William Sewell, Session Clerk, Old Kilpatrick.
> Samuel Stevenson, Dalmuir.
> William Moore, Dalmuir.
> William Webster, Dalmuir.
> Thomas Woodbridge, Bowling.
> Matthew Dickson, Bowling.
> Peter Moreland, Kilbowie.

CHAPTER IX.

BURGH OF BARONY.

IN the rental roll of the Abbey relating to the Kilpatrick lands we find the "hostilar house at ye west end of ye kirk" is let, with part of the Morisland, to Fynlay, the merchant, and the smyth's house to George Schaw, both under date of 23rd April, 1568, showing that the nucleus of a village had sprung up in the vicinity of the church. That such is the case may be inferred from the fact that the village finds a place in Mercator's map of Scotland, dated 1595.

In 1607,* Robert Mure, son of Thomas Mure, burgess of Glasgow, and Alexander Dunlop, merchant there, made complaint as follows:—"In August last they were returning from the burgh of Dunbertane to Glasgow, Arch[d.] Cunynghame, bailie of Dunbertane, 'convocat the haill inhabitantis' of said burgh, including W[m.] Cunningham, messenger, also his son W[m.,] John Patirsoun, y[r.,] with others, all armed with jacks, corslets, steelbonnets, picks, lances, halberts, swords, and other weapons, followed

---

* Reg. Privy Council, A.D. 1607, fol. 437.

complainers and overtook them at the town of Kilpatrick, where they 'maist fearslie' set upon them, and would have slain them 'wer not be the providence of God and help of the cuntrey people they were fred.'"

Cunningham and his associates, not appearing after having been duly cited, were denounced as rebels. A more serious affair took place near the village so early as the year 1445, when the faction of Douglas had spread the horrors of civil strife throughout Scotland, the murder perpetrated exciting universal detestation at a period when such deeds were almost of daily occurrence. The incident referred to is thus narrated in the Asloan MS., Advocates' Library.*

"The yer of God MCCCCXLV. the last dai of Mai Sir James Stewart of Auchingoun was slane, and ane with him at Drumglass (Dunglass) besyd Kirkpatrick be the Lard of Duchall (Robert Boyd, captain of Dumbarton Castle) and Alexander the Lyle † and their childer, and erdit in the kirk of Dunbartane. And that samyn time Robyn Boyd send Schir Alexander Cunnynghame, Chaplane to Robyn Kalender, to the Kirk of Cardros to Sir James' wyf and bad her cum to the castell efter that he had cummyn fra the slauchter of hir husband, and said

---

* Scot. Antiq., vol. iv., page 25.

† At this time the lands of Auchintorlie and Dunerbuck were held by the Lyles of Duchall, who forfeited them later for insurrection.

thai suld send her hame in a bait and warand her, for the gart hir trew (believe) thar was men waitand hir on hors and fut to tak her. And schortlie throu Schir Alexanderis fair language and hechtis, sche passit with him, and sone within vi dayis efter, for diseis sche toke her childill and was deliverit before hir tyme of ane knaif child, that leffit nocht ane hour, and was erdid besyd his fader in the kirk aforesaid."

This Sir James Stewart is supposed to be the son or grandson of Sir John Stewart of Auchingoun, Blackhall and Ardgowan, natural son of King Robert III., born about the middle of the 14th century, 1350-1360.*

From Dumbarton burgh records we learn that the town of Renfrew had interfered in the collection of customs dues at Kilpatrick to the loss of the burgh town. The entry reads—" October 20th 1631. Forasmeikle as the toun of Renfrew hes intercept them in the taking up of customes at Kilpatrick a man is to ryd to Ed^r· anent this, and also Grinok's plea, this burgh being evir in possession of the haill customes in Clyd." †

Fully one hundred years earlier trouble had arisen between the burghs of Dumbarton and Renfrew regarding

---

* In Lindsay's Hist. of Scotland, 1436 to 1565, Edinburgh 1628, it is mentioned that Sir James "was but 16 men in train" when attacked. See also Buchanan's Hist. of Scotland, vol. ii., page 137.

† Irving's Hist. of Dumbartonshire, fol. 499.

this same question of dues, and a conference on the matter in dispute was held in "ye parrisch kirk of Kilpatrick," 18th May, 1524. The following document gives a full record of the business then transacted. The original orthography has been retained.

1524.—PRO BALLIVIS DE DUNBERTANE, &C.

"Die xviij mensis maii, anno domini millesimo quingentesimo xxiiij : the quhilk day comperit rycht honorable mene, viz. : Johnne Smolet & Johnne Palmer balzeis of ye burgh of Dunbertane, wyth tene of ye honorable & wirschipfull mene of yar nychtbowris burgessis of ye said burgh, in ye parrisch kirk of Kilpatrick ; and in lykwiise comperit honourable mene, viz. : Johnne Robisoune and Adame of Haw, balzeis of ye burgh of Renfrew, as was allegit, wyth tene of ye honorable & wirschipfull mene of yar nychtbowris of ye said burgh of Renfrew, in ye said parrisch kirk of Kilpatrick. And ye forsadis xxiiij personis aboune vrityne chesit xij of yaim, to sit desyde determine, & to end all queralis debatible materris and contraverciis menit betwix ye forsadis borrowis, & inhabitaris of ye samyng, efter ye forme & tenor of ane auld band and lege, maid betwixt ye forsadis borrowis onder yar commoun selis. The personis chosying be ye forsaid burgh of Dunbertane, in ye fyrst, ye said Johne Smolet balze, Maister Robert

Barre ersdene of Ergile, Thomas Dowglas, Johne Lyndissay, Thomas Fallisdail and Colyne Porterfyld : and ye personis chosyng for ye burgh of Renfrew, in ye fyrst, John Robisone & Adame of Haw balzies, Robert Langomwre, Niniane Jaksone, Johne of Knok and Findillaw Crawfurd. And yan ye said John Smolet balze, in ye nayme and behalf of his nychtbouris, conburgensis of ye said burgh of Dunbertane, askyt & alse requirit at ye forsaides balzeis of Renfrew, quhare one yai war plaintwes upone ye forsaides nychtbouris of ye said burgh of Dunbertane. And yai allegit at ye balzies & burgese of Dunbertane had faltyt to yem diuerse wiise : in ye fyrst, at yai had maid ane band & confederatione wyth ye cita of Glasgw wythout yare leif : secundlay, at the said Johne Palmer balze had intrommettit wyth ye custum and toll of ane scheip of Franse, wythin yare boundis & fredoundis, &c. And yan ye forsaid Johne Smolet balze, & his nycht-bouris aboune exprimit, askyt quhat rycht and euidentis yai had, for yaim to schaw yaim before ye fornamit personis and jugis aboune virtyne. And yan ye forsadis balzeis of Renfrew schow ane lettir wyth diverse selis, and, as he allegit, ane testimoniale ; ane instrument of ye transumpt of ye samyng, as yai allegit. And yarefter, ye said Johne Smolet & his nychtbouris requirit ye saidis balzeis & nychtbouris gif yai haid ony uther letteris or documentis to schaw for yaim. Ye said John Robisone balzie answert at yai wald schaw na uther euidentis to ye saidis at yat time.

"Item yar efter, ye said John Smolet requirit ye saidis balzeis of Renfrew, at ye forsadis xij personis aboune exprimit suld [desyd] & determine ye debatis & querelis betwix ye saidis bowrrowis, and gif yai culd nocht determine & desyde yaim, yat yai suld chese & aggre upone a place, quhar bath ye saidis borrowis might haif hastyest expedicione, efter, ye tenor and forme of yar auld band. Item efternoune, ye said John Smolet balze, in ye nayme & behalf of ye said burgh of Dunbertane, passit to ye forsadis balzies & burgese of Renfrew, and requirit yaim yat yai wald put fra yaim all personis, excep ye six personis at war chosying for Dunbertane, & to brying before yaim yar euidentis at yai wil vise for yaim. And gif ye sadis xij personis culd nocht aggre upone ye debatis & querelis, that ye saidis xij personis suld chese new jugis and set ane new day, efter ye forme and tenor of ye indentor and band maid betwix ye saidis bowrrowis, as he allegit; ye quhilkis ye saidis balzeis and nychtbowris of Renfrew refusit. Upone all gir thyngis aboune vritine, ye said John Smolet, in nayme & behalf of ye said burgh of Dunbertane, suld nocht hurt ye said burgh or privelegis of ye samyng, & for remede of law, solempniter protestyd.

"'Acta erant hec in ecclesia parochiali de Kilpatrik, et circa cimeterium eiusdem, horis xj et secunda ante meridiem et post meridiem, presentibus ibidem honestis viris Johanne Culquhoun, Gilberto Makcartor, Georgio Abernathy, Willielmo Cunynghame, Waltero Robisone et Johanne Houston cum diuersis aliis.'"

On 7th September, 1633, a merchant of the Kirktown, William Colquhoun by name, had to be dealt with at the instance of the procurator-fiscal for the burgh of Dumbarton "for forstalling and regratting of cornes and aitts cumand in be sey wth the river of Clyde; specialle at Kilpatrick, be buying of dyuers and sindrie barks and boitfulls of aits be him and his p'ners, be giving arles and goodis pennies, and thairefter befoir recevit or delyuerie, or missiring the said corne, selling the same over again to others in that same plaice an wth the said veschels, taking sex shillings or thairby of vantage of ilk boll." * Colquhoun was interned in the Tolbooth, Dumbarton, till he could find caution to "byde the issue of ae assize."

The great plague which ravaged Scotland in 1647-1648 attacked Kilpatrick, as we learn from the following excerpt from the session records of Kilmaronock parish, 30th

---

* Irving's Hist. of Dumbartonshire, fol. 503.

January, 1648. The entry reads as follows :—" This day publick intimatione was maid to the peopill that they sould watche over themselves diligentlie and be earnest with the Lord that he wold protect them from the plague of pestilence quhilk is raging in Kilpatrick, and also that they should bewar of receaving strangers and especially of hieland beggars seeing they know quhat inconvenience they have already receavit by them and how wonderfullie the Lord hes delyverit us quhi it was in the middest of us." *

In Tucker's report to the English Parliament under the Protectorate, dated 1655, he says, " there is in this port (Glasgow) a collector, a checque, and four wayters who look to this place, Renfrew, Arskin on the south, and Kilpatrick on north bank of the Clyde, with Dumbarton, a small and very poor burgh, at the head of the Firth."

As already mentioned, the Kilpatrick lands were acquired by Hamilton of Orbiston from the Abercorn family, and in response to a petition presented to the Scottish Parliament which sat at Edinburgh on 28th July, 1681, during the reign of Charles II., an Act was passed ratifying in favour of William Hamilton of Orbiston the erection of the said lands into the Barony and Regality

---

* " Glasgow Herald," 9th Sept., 1893.

of Kilpatrick, with the privilege of having a weekly market on Thursdays, and also two fairs during the year, to be held on the 27th day of June and 28th day of October, and each of them to continue for the space of eight days (see Appendix).

There appears to be a discrepancy in the date of the erection of the burgh, a burgess ticket, still extant, reading as follows :—" I John Farquharson, Bayley of the Burgh of the Barony of Kilpatrick In virtue of a charter under the Great Seal the 27th day of January 1679, declaring the village of Kilpatrick to be the head Burgh of the Barony of Kilpatrick and also erecting the same a free burgh of Barony with power to name Bailies to create admit and receive burgesses in and to all the freedoms liberties and immunities allowed by law, and known to appertain to any such burgh within the kingdom, and discharging the molesting and disturbing the said burgesses in the enjoyment thereof. They created admitted and received Malcolm McFarlane in Old Kilpatrick, Burgess of the said Burgh, and the whole privileges, liberties and immunities thereof, and hereby granted to him, he always performing the duties incumbent on him as a Burgess of the same who gives his oath of fidelity as use is. Given under my hand at Kilpatrick this 24th November 1763.—Signed John Ferguson."

These " wickid thevis and lymaris," the M'Gregors,

were not unknown in the parish. In the month of September, 1680, there were taken away from the moor of Dumbarton and Kilpatrick a number of cattle, for which theft some members of that clan were summoned to appear at Crieff in 1684, but, failing to appear, decree was given in absence, and Colquhoun of Luss was empowered to make reprisals to the value of the cattle stolen.

In 1685, the tide of war rolled through the recently formed burgh, which, no doubt, excited the hopes and fears of the burgesses as their sympathies lay. On 18th June of that year, the Earl of Argyll's ill-fated expedition was dispersed on the moor of Kilpatrick. In M'Crie's Memoirs of Veitch and Bryson * we are told that on Tuesday, 16th June, the expedition left the Gareloch and crossed the water of Leven at night, three miles above Dumbarton. Then wandering over the moors by way of Kilmaronock, an attempt was made to reach Glasgow via Kilpatrick, the narrator further says :—" I do not mind what regiment took the leading, but, however, they led us all wrong, for they brought us into a moss which broke us all from one another; and, although we were a very good army at night, we were so dispersed that there was not above 500 of us together on the

---

* From M'Crie's Memoirs of Veitch and Bryson, fol. 318, *et seq.*

morrow. All people, being wonderfully discouraged, took the opportunity to leave us in the night, but those that came together on the morrow came to Kilpatrick. For, indeed, we lost many brave men by reason of the darkness of the night, who have been loath to have left us, especially one Rumbold, an Englishman, who came from Holland with us."

[Sir Patrick Hume, who followed Argyle, says in his narrative:—"Next morning, being Thursday, 18th June, wee came back to Kilpatrick, not above 500 men in all, sadly wearied; soone as I got downe the hill, very faint and weary, I tooke the first alehouse, and quickly ate a bit of bread and took a drink, and immediately went to search out the erle; but I met Sir John (Cochrane) with others accompaniaing him, who, taking mee by the hand, turned mee, saying, 'My heart goe you with mee.' 'Whither goe you?' said I. 'Over Clide by boate,' said he. I.—'Where is Argyle? I must see him.' He.— 'He is gone to his owne countrey, you cannot see him.' I.—'How comes this change of resolution, and that we went not together to Glasgow.' He.—'It is no time to answer questions, but I shall satisfy you afterwards.'"]

"We resolved then to cross the Clyde. But, behold, there was a troop of horse lying on the other side of the water, which made our passage most difficult. However, Sir John Cochrane said, 'Gentlemen, it is not time for us to delay, for, whenever the enemy does miss us in the morning, they will pursue; therefore let us force our passage across the water.' There were two boats. Sir John entered the one with about 10 or 12 men. Polwart got into the other with as many men. The troop sent down 4 or 5 of their men on foot to the side of an old boat that lay at the side of the river. Our men would have fired at them, but Sir John would not suffer them, because they had the old boat to be a defence to them, but desired them to forbear till they were nearer the side of the water, and then said, 'I think our shot will now reach the body of their troop; so fire at them,' which was accordingly done, and one of their horses being shot dead, and some wounded, the 5 men that lay at the side of the boat firing at us, made haste to get to their horses, and so the whole troop fled; and we got ashore as fast as we could, and pursued them. They rode more than a mile before they stunted, and so drew up on the top of a hill. So we sent the boats to and again till we had brought over 150 men. The Earl of Argyle and the rest refused to come over."

"There was a gentleman whose house stood upon the waterside (probably Erskine House) who had provided a brewing of good ale and a batch of oat loaves to serve the King's forces, as we were informed. The gentleman, being with the forces himself, we went in and refreshed ourselves; and, indeed, we had great need, for some of us had eaten very little for three days, being still pursued by the enemy, and had slept none all that time. I tied up three loaves in my napkin, thinking to keep myself from such a strait again for sometime as I had been in before, and I tied them to my belt, but, through sleeplessness and weariness, I lost all."

Argyle escaped over the Clyde in the garb of a yeoman, but was captured at Inchinnan, conveyed to Edinburgh, and there beheaded. The Earl's body was brought back some years after to Dunglass, and there shipped to Kilmun, the burying place of the Argyle family.

The house in which the Earl is said to have taken refuge, when in Kilpatrick, stands immediately opposite the churchyard. From its style of architecture it would appear to have been built early in the 17th century.

The persecution arising out of the restoration of Episcopacy did not assume such serious importance or produce such baneful effects as in the neighbouring parishes. So far as records go, the landed gentry were the only sufferers.

Among those in the Presbytery of Dumbarton who remained faithful to Presbyterianism were Matthew Ramsay, Old Kilpatrick, and Robert Law, New Kilpatrick. In 1671, Thomas Nelson, in Drumry, was proved, with others, to have held a conventicle in his house during the hours of divine service, whereby so many were drawn away from their several churches that kirk sessions could not be held.

Hamilton of Orbiston, who at this time was a considerable proprietor in the parish, was sheriff of the County, and on 19th February, 1685, among those cited to appear before him for attending conventicles and non-attendance at the parish church were Claud Hamilton of Barns and . . . Stewart, his wife; John Douglas of Mains and Elizabeth Hamilton, his wife; and William Colquhoun of Craigton and . . . Stirling, his wife.

Claud Hamilton of Barns had his innings later. William, Prince of Orange, landed at Torbay, 5th November, 1688, and in February of the following year the magistrates of Dumbarton and Council appointed "Thursday next as the day for proclamation of King William and Queen Mary to be King and Queen of Scotland, at the public place for such solemnitie, and ordains intimation thairof to be made to the burgesses and inhabitants' to provyd themselves against the said day for putting on thair bonfyres."

On 23rd September of same year, the Provost and Town Council of Dumbarton took the oath of allegiance to King William and Queen Mary in presence of "Claud Hamilton of Barns ane of the com$^{ms.}$ of the shyre of

Dunbritane to the Parlia^t and George Maxwell sheriff deput of the s^d sheriffdom." *

The Episcopal minister in Kilpatrick, Thomas• Allan, is mentioned as having been "deprived by the people for scandalous conduct" about this date.

Even after the Revolution was an accomplished fact, the county was still exposed to danger from the adherents of the expelled King.

Under date of May 6th, 1692, it is recorded in the burgh records of Dumbarton that Hamilton of Orbiston "and severall others had a meeting hard by Dumbarton, and all their horses with them, which they have sent to some places in the Highlands ; and that it is said their design was upon the castle of Dumbarton." †

In December, 1696, a Shire muster was held at Kilpatrick of the fencible men from the different parishes.

In 1699, Kilpatrick was assessed in a small sum, it being agreed in Council that the "surface traders in the burghs (of Regality) should pay a share of the taxation formerly levied on the Royal Burghs. The apportionment for the burghs of Regality in Dumbartonshire being 1s. 6d., it was divided as follows ·—Kirkintilloch, 10d. ; Cumbernauld, 6d. ; Kilpatrick, 2d."

Although elevated into a Burgh of Barony the trade

---

* Dumbarton Burgh Records.
† Irving's History of Dumbartonshire.

of the village can never have been of much importance, in spite of the fairs provided for under the the Royal Charter. From the Friendly Society's books the inhabitants of the Kirktown, as it was called, were chiefly weavers, wrights, nailmakers, vintners, and tailors.

The election of a bailie and other officials required for the due exercise of the duties of the burgh seems to have fallen into disuse in the beginning of this century.

In the year 1793, the managers of the Relief Church were infefted in due legal form into possession of the parcel of ground on which the church and manse is built, John Lang, weaver, being named as bailie.

On the abolition of Heritable Jurisdictions, in 1748, Lord Blantyre received a small sum in compensation for the burgh of Kilpatrick.

The burgh possessed a tolbooth, built in the early part of the 18th century, which stood in the centre of the village. It was removed by Lord Blantyre in the year 1855, and on its site he erected the block of buildings now known as Blantyre's Land. Latterly the jail had been tenanted as a dwelling-house, the last occupant being Robert Donald, who rejoiced in the soubriquet, "Rab o' the Jail." William Galloway, teacher, composed a ballad of some length on this worthy, a few verses of which read as follows :—

RAB O' THE JAIL.

Ye'll no fin the equal o' Rab o' the Jail,
Ye'll no fin the equal o' Rab o' the Jail,
Ye may search the hale kintra frae Clyde tae Carlisle,
An' no fin the equal o' Rab o' the Jail.

The strongest that tried him he held them in scorn ;
For nane could come near him at cudgelling corn,
He'd soon sen' them aff the floor winning the flail,
For a long-winded thresher was Rab o' the Jail.

He ken's a' about farming, 'bout craps, and 'bout kye,
Frae the parlour down tae where Grumphie did lie,
An' what parks wud fit stane-drains and what wud fit tile,
A great ingle-neuk farmer was Rab o' the Jail.

What a notable fisher, his match he ne'er met,
At wester, at angling, at stake, or dragnet ;
Ilk fish o' ilk river frae Cart to the Nile,
Could a' be described by Rab o' the Jail.

He kent how the moon made the tide rise an' fa',
The natural causes o' frost and o' snaw,
An' what weather wad happen frae May tae April,
Could a' be predicted by Rab o' the Jail.

When tun'd like a fiddle he sweetly could sing,
As cheery's the blackbird that welcome's the spring ;
For dancing he'd challenge the hail clan o' Argyle,
For my feet gang like drumsticks, quo' Rab o' the Jail.

The Kilpatrick weavers and some of the other trades folks were strong politicians, and took an active part in the troubles of the time. Alexander Hart, who was the worst wounded of all the men taken prisoners at Bonnymuir on 5th April, 1820, was a native of Kilpatrick, being born there, 3rd February, 1794. He was a man of some education, and had a great influence amongst his comrades. Being expatriated to New South Wales, he died there, March, 1876, in his 83rd year.

Robert M'Kinlay, tailor, assumed to be Dictator in the troublous times we speak of. Some wags, who knew of this, knocked him up one night at twelve o'clock and informed him the insurrection had broken out, and that they had got Laird Lang, a well-known Tory, with them as a prisoner, and were anxious to know what to do with him. M'Kinlay instantly called out without opening the door, "Behead the d--l, and I'll sanction it the morn!" On one occasion, this same character, while "whipping the cat" at the house of James Hamilton, a very worthy man, a haulage contractor on the canal, gravely informed the inmates that he and the other members of his party had had a meeting one night lately to divide the lands and houses aright, and that he was going to take Cochno house and grounds for his share, etc. Hamilton was clannish enough to resent such a proceeding, and discharged M'Kinlay on the spot. Shortly after this, Mr. Hamilton, the laird of Cochno, met M'Kinlay, and mentioned having heard of the proposal of the Radicals to divide out the lands, and inquired how much had been allotted to him. M'Kinlay, scratching his head, replied, "Deed, Cochno, to tell you the truth, we clean forgot you a' thegither."

When the " Dictator " heard that the soldiers were on the track, he said to his son, " Wullie, tak' shipping and flee tae Leith, or some ither foreign port." It having been reported to the authorities that the Radicals of Duntocher had designs upon the Castle of Dumbarton, a detachment of the Dumbartonshire Fencibles was despatched to nip the insurrection in the bud. Two or three of the would-be insurgents were captured, and one of them, called Munro, was tried before the judges of the Court of Session at a Court held in the Parish Church of Dumbarton, 1819. The case against Munro having broken down, he and the other prisoners were set at liberty. This incident was termed the battle of the bellows, from the fact that two pairs of bellows were captured which had been used in the manufacture of pikes, a few of which are still exhibited in the armoury at Dumbarton Castle.

In 1836, the use of the privileges of being a Burgh of Barony had ceased, although, as is remarked in the New Statistical Account, there was then as much need as ever for bailies and their officers to restrain the bad and encourage the good.

About the year 1841 there were thirty-one public-houses in the parish, and the population was 7020; in 1891, with a population of 17,715, there were twenty-three public-houses, inclusive of one hotel and nine licensed grocers. The village used to be very well off for public-houses, but very few of them had any distinctive sign. Duncan M'Coll, at the Storegate, had the picture of a sloop being tracked along the canal by two horses, and his house was dignified by the name of the "Ship Tavern." Further down the village, William M'Lintock, or "Pinkie," as he was called from his partiality to the tune of "Pinkie House," had the sign of the "Salmon"; and one, opposite the old Jail, had Sir William Wallace's bust painted on his signboard. Further down, there was the "Red Lion"; and opposite that, Andrew White, tailor, opened a "pub." with a picture of Burns on his sign, which gave rise to the couplet—

> "The like was never seen before,
> Burns abune a tailor's door."

Galloway, the village poet, dubbed this house "Poosie Nancy's."

About forty-five years ago an attempt was made to revive Kilpatrick Fair. Races were started, and Joseph Boyd, known as "Vittoria" from having served as artilleryman in that memorable battle, acted as starter, dressed in a cocked hat and military coat.

As showing the style of the accommodation of the county inns of the period, the following extract from Bristead's Pedestrian Tour in Scotland, 1801, is of interest:—"At 9 o'clock in the morning we came to an inn, and were shown into a room, not very cleanly to be sure, for the floor was of soft dirt which stuck to our shoes, and the ceiling was boarded and plentifully hung with cobwebs; the chairs, table, and windows not too much accustomed to the pail and cloth. However, they got us an abundant breakfast of tea, eggs, milk, and bread, all very good of their kind. During our repast we were amused by hearing the people of the house in the next room singing psalms and reading portions of the scriptures. Some of the tones indeed were not very melodious, but there seemed to be a sincerity and an earnestness of devotion in their manner that surpass all the efforts of art. I was particularly delighted to find that the Sunday morning, before the places of worship were opened, was passed in a way so calculated to keep up and to increase that noble spirit of religion and of morality among the Scottish people which has so long made them loved at home and revered abroad. I could not but call to mind these exquisite lines of Burns in his "Cottar's Saturday Night"—

"They chant their artless notes in simple grace," etc.

As soon as we had breakfasted, and a pause in their devotions allowed us an opportunity, we paid our bill, which was more moderate than any charge that had hitherto been made upon us, and departed."

THE KILPATRICK SOCIETY.

The minutes of the Kilpatrick Friendly Society, constituted in the year 1756, contain some interesting information regarding the social life of the burgh. The book is intact, with exception of the first leaf which has disappeared, and the entries are made with unfailing regularity from 7th August, 1756, to 29th November, 1861. The career of the society has been very chequered, but it has, through the careful management of the late Mr. Michael Findlay, been brought into a very sound position, both as regards funds and members. Mr. James Struthers, the present manager, reported last year that the accumulated funds amounted to close on £1000. The members of the society originally were burgesses of the barony, and the bailie of the burgh was the bailie of the society as well. At present there are some sixty-four members on the roll.

CHAPTER X.

PARISH REGISTERS OF BIRTHS AND MARRIAGES.

THERE are three volumes in the Register House, Edinburgh—

1st.—Births, 1688-1743 ; Marriages, 1689-1743.

2nd.—Births and Marriages, 1743-1801.

3rd.—Births and Marriages, 1802-1819.

The record of births, previous to 1750, has suffered from damp. There is a modern copy of the portion prior to August, 1696. There is a leaf wanting of the marriages, May, 1693, to January, 1694. From 1762-86, inclusive, the fact of marriage is very seldom added to the entry of booking for proclamation, and only in a few instances, 1795-1811, inclusive, but more frequently after 1812.

The following entries are extracted from these interesting volumes :—

BIRTHS.

1688. May 15. This day was baptized John son lawful of Wm. Colquhoun of Craigton and Mary Stirling his spouse. Witnesses Wm. Stirling of Law and Hum. Colquhoun of Lawmuir.

1688. Feby. 14. This day was baptised Mary daughter lawful of Major Adam Colquhoun and Janet Stewart both in this parish. Witnesses W^m. Stirling of Law and James Knox in Barns.

1688. Feb. 21. Was baptised James son lawful to James Knox and Janet Brock both in Easter parish. Andrew Paul and James Finlay witnesses.

1688. Novb^r. 29. This day was baptised Walter son lawful to John Brock and Janet Colquhoun both in this parish. Witnesses Cornelius Lang and James Houston.

1689. May 19. Was baptised Robert son lawful to John Colquhoun and Margery Colquhoun both in this parish. Witnesses John Colquhoun of Garshake and John Colquhoun of Dunglass.

1689. June 30. This day was baptised Margaret daughter lawful to W^m. Donald and Isobel Hanna, both in this parish. Witnesses Robt. Donald and James Patersoun.

1689. Oct. 27. This day was baptised Elizabeth d. l. to Robt. Donald and Janet Filshie both in this parish. Witnesses James Donald and Patrick Lang.

1689. Novb. 17. This day was baptised Anne daughter lawful to W^m. Shaw and Janet Smith both in the parish of Erskine. W. Claud Hamilton of Barns and John Shaw of Bargarran.

1689. Decb. 15. On the qk day was baptised William son lawful to W^m. Paul and Margaret Filshie both in this parish. Witnesses Finlay Lang and Robt. Finlay.

1690. Feb. 9. This day was baptised John son lawful to Robt. Martine and Katherine Campbell both in this parish. Witnesses James Patersoune and James Lattay.

1690. Oct. 12th. Was baptised Margaret d. l. to Jno. Colquhoun and Margaret Colquhoun both in this parish. Witnesses John Colquhoun in Dunnotter and Pat. Colquhoun in Milton.

1690. Novbr. ye 23. The quhilk day was baptised Agnes d. l. to James Petersoune and Marion M'Lintock both in this parish. Witnesses Robt. M'Lintock and Robt. Lang.

1692. Feb. 21. Was b. Agnes d. l. to James Donald and Agnes Filshie both in this parish. W. James and Robert Lang.

1692. Feb. 21. Was b. James s. l. to James Petersoun and Marion M'Lintock.

1692. Augt. 11. On quhilk day was b. James s. l. to Jno. Filshie and Janet Wood. W^t. W^m. Johnstone and W^m. Robine.

1693. Sept. 26. Was b. James s. l. to James Donald and Agnes Filshie both in this parish. W^t. Robert Donald and Robert Filshie.

1694. Jan. 22. Was b.   son lawful to James Petersoune and Joan Allan both in this parish. W$^{t.}$ Jno. M'Indoe and W$^{m.}$ Brock.

1694. Novb. 18. Was b. Isobel d. l. to Alex$^{r.}$ Filshie and Joan Spreull both in this parish. W$^{t.}$ John Lang, schoolmaster, and Malcolm Johnstone.

1697. June 22. The quhilk day w. b. James s. l. to James Hamilton of Hutchesone and Agnes Stirling his wife. W$^{t.}$ Jno. Maxwell of Dargavel, and W$^{m.}$ Campbell, Garscube etc.

1698. May 20. The quhilk day was b. W$^{m.}$ Anderson s. l. to W$^{m.}$ Andersoune, Bailie in Kilpatrick, and Janet Burdie his spouse.

1698. July 17. The quhilk day was baptised Janet d. l. to John Filshie and Janet Wood. W$^{t.}$ Robert Filshie and Matt. Crawford.

1745.   This day w. b. Janet d. l. to James Donald and Janet Stewart his spouse, in Heads of Connalton.

1747. Augt. 2. Was b. Ann d. l. to W$^{m.}$ Findlay and Agnes Glen in Bowland. Wit. Jno. Donald and Jno. Findlay. (Here we have the origin of the name of Bowling. In an entry 1752 the place is designated Bowland of Spittle.)

1749. Feb. 4. Was b. Jean d. l. to James and Janet Stewart in Riddingower. Witnesses James Paterson and

Wm. Donald. (Riddingower or Riggengower was situated on the hill behind Auchentorlie House.)

1752. May 25. Was b. Arch^{d.} s. l. to Robt. Denny and Ann Paterson in town end of Balquhanran. W^{t.} Jno. Brock and Alex^{r.} Clerk.

1752. May 25. Was b. Thomas s. l. to Jno. Miller and Margt. M'Farlane in Dunglass. W^{t.} Thomas Yuile of Darlieth Esq. and John Morison.

1752. Novb. 19. Was b. Mary d. l. to John Donald and Janet Scott in Spittle. W^{t.} Jas. Donald and Wm. Findlay. (Spittle was the name of the farm where Glenarbuck House now stands.)

1754. Feb. 3. Was b. W^{m.} s. l. to James Donald and Janet Stewart in Riddengower. W^{t.} Walter Stewart and Alexr. Clark.

1756. June 20. Was b. John Donald s. l. to Jas. Donald and Janet Stewart in Riddengower. Wt. Alexr. Clark and Wm. Donald.

1756. Augt. 22. Was b. James s. l. to James Forsyth and Jean Scott in Connalton. W^{t.} Peter Scott and John Donald.

1757. Jan. 19. Was b. John s. l. to James Smith and Mar^{t.} Mair at Waulkmiln (Faifley). W^{t.} Robt. Smith and John M'Murrich.

1757. April 3. Was b. Agnes d. l. to James Craig and Agnes Walker in Bowland. W^{t.} Arch^{d.} M'Intyre and James Donald.

1757. Sept. 20. Was b. John Miller son l. to Jno.

Morrison and Cath. Knox in Kirkton. W^t. Arch^d. Davidson and John Knox.

1758. Jan. 8. Was b. Isobel d. l. to Walter Colquhoun of Holl and Elizabeth Campbell. W^t. James Donald and John Paul.

1758. Mar. 17. Was b. Mary d. l. to Thos. Woodhouse and Elizabeth Campbell at Paper Mill of Balquhanran. W^t. E. Collins and Richard Garnet.

1760. Augt. . . . Was b. Ann d. l. to James Scott and Mary Chalmers at the Toll Bar.

1761. June 19. Was b. Thomas s. l. to Robert Aiken and Agnes Findlay in Chapelyeard (now N. E. Boquhanran).

1761. Decb. 6. Was b. George s. l. to Robt. Ronnel and Janet Scletar in Brecan Lie of Edinbarnet.

1762. July 7. Was b. Janet d. l. to W^m. Donald and Mary M'Goan in Bowling.

1772. July 23. Was b. William s. l. to Bernard Buchanan and Janet Ewing in Cohabbuck.

1784. 5th Septbr. Was bap^d. William s. l. to George Hutchinson and Mary Forsyth in Meikle Overtoun.

1785. 11th Decb^r Was bap^d Robert son lawful to Jno. Brock and Elizabeth Hart in High Gavinburn.

1786. 25th Jany. Was born Alexander son lawful to Robt. Gardner and Agnes Brock in High Drum of Edenbarnet. Bap^d. 3rd Feb.

1786. 11th Novbr. Was born James s. l. to John Fletcher and Janet Leitch in Cobbraggan (Cowbreggan). Bap^{d.} 12th Novb.

27th Feby. 1787. Was b. Arch^{d.} son lawful to Robt. Glen and Janet Buchanan in Cohabbuck. Bap^{d.} 4th March.

25th April 1787. Was b. Marjory d. l. to Robert Paul and Mary Scott in Mattockhill. Bap^{d.} 29th April.

14th October 1787. Was b. Helen d. l. to Robert Hanna and Janet Matthie in Back of the Craigs. Bap^{d.} 16th October.

19th Feby. 1788. Was b. Johanna d. l. to Wm. Hervie and Eleonora Garrey in Yockker. Bap^{d.} 20th Feby.

16th April 1788. Was b. John s. l. to John McGowan and Jean Marshall in Dukslin. Bap^{d.} 29th April.

25th July 1788. Was b. Agnes d. l. to Jno. Donald and Mary Govan in Burnbrae. Bap^{d.} 26th.

3rd Jany 1789. Was b. John son lawful to Daniel Grant and Elizabeth Pittulloch in Moss Mallon. Bap^{d.} 6th Jan.

27th October 1789. Was b. Jean d. l. to James Paterson and Janet McDonald in Auchentorlie. Bap^{d.} 30th.

21st Decbr. 1790. Was b. Arch^{d.} s. l. to Robt. Kinloch and Ann McLaren in Snab. Bap^{td.} 26th.

11th June 1791. Was b. Mary d. l. to Robt. Smith and Elizabeth Gardner in Faifley. Bapt^{d.} . . .

20th Decb. 1791. Was b. W^{m.} son l. to Wm. Brock and Agnes Paterson in Barns of Clyde. Bapt^{d.} . . .

19th May 1794. Was b. John s. l. to Wm. Brock and Katherine McKellar in Little Overtoun. Bapt^{d.} 25th.

31st Oct. 1794. Was b. Robert s. l. to Thomas Baird and Agnes Knox in Dalmuir. Bapt^{d.} 2nd Novbr.

11th August 1795. Was b. James s. l. to James Paterson and Janet McDonald in Auchentorly. Bap^{td.} 14th.

19th August 1795. Was b. John s. l. to Matt. Clark and Elizabeth Houstoun in Smallburn (Little Mill).

6th May 1796. Was b. Jean d. l. to Walter McLean and Jean Brock in Balquhanran. Bapt^{d.} 8th.

20th Decb. 1796. Was b. Peter s. l. to James Scott and Jean M'Learn in Dyke of Dunerbuck. Bapt. 25th.

6th April 1797. Was b. Grace d. l. to James Hamilton and Helenora Dunn in Cochney. Bapt^{d.} 19th May.

6th July 1797. Was b. Agnes and Ann l. children to John Filshy and Janet Lang in Dalnotter or Toddal Bog. Bab^{d.} 18th.

28th Sept. 1797. Was b. Robert s. l. to John Walker and Katherine Miller in Gowkston. Bapt^{d.} 24th.

N.B.—There are many children's names not inserted in this book. The reason is that since the secession took place at the Faifley and the Relief at Kilpatrick, many parents, to save the booking money, have not registered their children nor paid the clerk's dues. Is attested at Old Kilpatrick by Alexander Bell, session clerk, this 15th May, 1796.

21st Feb. 1799. Was born James s. l. to John McIlquham and Jean Schullar in Whitecrook. Bap[d.] 28[th.]

23rd June 1799. W. b. Bonaparte alias Andrew s. l. to Wm. Melrose and Barbara Harper in Dalmuir. Bap[d.] 30[th.]

Dec. 17 1799. Was b. Mary d. l. to James Walker and Magdalene Campbell in Mount Pleasant. Bap[d.] 22[nd.]

June 22. 1800. Was b. Marion d. l. to Wm. Cross Esq. of Auchintoshan and Ann Buchanan. Bap[d.] 5th July.

April 17. 1803. Was b. Alison d. l. to Thomas Macgill and Jean Scott in Dyke. Bap[d.] same day.

Decb. 29. 1806. Was b. David s. l. to Thomas Macgill and Jean Scott in Dyke, Bap[d.] 4th Jan. 1807.

MARRIAGES.

Feb. 7th 1690. The quhilk day James Petersoun and Marion McLintock both in this parish were booked in order to proclamation of marriage, consigned 2 Loggdolors (dollars for poor's box) and married the . . . of the foresaid month at Dumbartane.

August ye 5th 1691. On quhilk day John Fillshy in that parish and Janet Wood in the paroch of Eister Kilpatrick were booked in order to proclamation of marriage consigned one logdolor and were married . . . foresaid month at Eister Kilpatrick.

4th Sept. 1711. The quhilk day Master James Spittal, Paisley, to Margaret Wilson lawful daughter to Mr. Adam Wilson clerk to the Regality of Kilpatrick were booked in order to proclam. of marr. and consigned a crown. Married 19th Oct.

6th Novbr. 1747. Were booked John Morison Schoolmaster in Kilpatrick and Catherine Knox daughter lawful to John Knox Innkeeper in said Parish and were married the 16th day of the said month.

30th Sept. 1748. There were booked in order to proclam. of marriage John Millar lawful son to the deceased John Millar maltman in Dunglass and Margaret M'Farlane granddaughter to the Laird of Camstrodden, and were married the 6th October.

4th Decb. 1761. The which day were booked in order to marriage W^{m.} McCrae weaver in the city of Paisley and Margaret McMurrich daughter lawful to Alexr. McMurrich Taylor in Auchinleck and was proclaimed 3 several Sabbaths and did give 10^{d.} stg. to the poor in this Parish and the clerk's dues besides. Were married 25th Decb.

Nov. 3, 1769. The said day were booked in order for proclamation of marr. Walter Allan in this parish and Jean Findlay in the city of Glasgow.

PARISH CHURCH, OLD KILPATRICK.

June . . . 1785. The said day were booked in order for proclamation of marr. James Paterson and Janet McDonald both in this parish.

July . . . 1785. The said day were booked in order for proclamation of marr. Richard Collins in Dalmuir and Miss Ann Sword in the city of Glasgow. Married 14th July.

July 20, 1793. The said day were booked in order for proclamation of marr. Robert Whitworth and Miss Jane Fleming daughter lawful to John Fleming in Dalnotter. Married 24th July.

CHAPTER XI

UNITED PRESBYTERIAN CHURCH, FREE CHURCH, AND EDUCATIONAL MATTERS.

OLD KILPATRICK UNITED PRESBYTERIAN CHURCH.

THE increased interest in religious questions which manifested itself in the last half of the eighteenth century had for one of its results a demand upon behalf of the people for a larger share of church government. It was a widespread feeling, and our parish shared in the movement. On the death of the parish minister, Rev. John Davidson, after an incumbency of 48 years, an agitation was begun to protest against patronage. The minute book has the following :—" A respectable number of the inhabitants of the parish met at Dalmuir on 17th September, 1793, to consult together about a minister, the church being vacant by the death of the Rev. John Davidson, who had been ordained in the year 1745. Being afraid of an intrusion, the following resolutions were agreed to." These were :—

" 1. That it is the opinion of this meeting that the church is a society distinct from any other, and has a right, from her Head and Lawgiver, to choose her own office-bearers, especially her pastors, and that to force a minister upon a congregation, contrary to their inclinations, is to deprive them of their liberty, in which the Scriptures invite them to stand fast; and that these ministers, thus intruded, do not preach the gospel in its purity.

" 2. That an advice should be given the elders to oppose the intrusion by giving in their demission at the first meeting of Presbytery.

" 3. That, if the elders stand out against the people and comply with the imposition, or if their endeavours can not prevent the intrusion, that application be made to the Relief Presbytery for sermon."

This minute is signed by John M'Laren, farmer, Boquhanran, Dalmuir, a steading which was pulled down in the year 1884.

The elders not having demitted office, and the presentation being given, and the presentee, the Rev. Wm. Macartney, having accepted the charge without ever having been heard or seen in the place, it was resolved at a meeting held in Kilpatrick on 24th September, 1793, to petition the Relief Presbytery for pulpit supply, which appears to have been granted at once. At a meeting on 28th December, 1793, James Morrison, farmer, Kilbowie, was chosen preses, and John M'Laren, Walter Aitken, John Stark, and Robert and John Donald a committee, with John Houston, schoolmaster, Dalmuir, as clerk.

With a view to building a church, this committee printed subscription papers with an appropriate heading. The introductory appeal winds up rather naïvely—" It is hoped the friends of truth will see the propriety and necessity of above (referring to what had been already said) and will honour their Redeemer with part of their substance, according to their several abilities, by subscribing any sum not below 5s. sterling, and when the seats are set those who subscribe highest shall be preferred in their choice."

At a later meeting it was resolved not to lodge in public houses the ministers who supplied the pulpit, the members in turn providing for their accommodation.

On March 28th, 1794, the granary still standing and now called Bankside was leased from James Donald for a year at the rent of £10, and used as a meeting-place before the church was built.

On June 11th of same year, the ground on which the church now stands was bought from Mr. Lang, merchant, Glasgow, at the price of £80 per acre, and the same month saw the contracts for the different kinds of work required fixed—Robert Miller, Partick, being contractor for the mason work.

In addition to their subscriptions, the sum of £200

was advanced on loan by eighteen individuals, of whom thirteen were farmers. Dalmuir heads the list with £20 from Walter M'Laren, Balquhanran ; John Paterson, Auchentorlie, £10 ; John Donald, wright, Bowling, £10 ; Robert Lang, Braes of Kilpatrick, £10 ; Robert Paul, Mattockhill, £10 ; Peter Scott, Greenland, £10 ; and John Scott, farmer, Dyke, £10.

The subscriptions for the church came from every part of the parish, and many places beyond, such as Kilbowie, Duntocher, Glenhead, Glasgow, Anderston, Dalnotter, Dalmuir, Boquhanran—there are over ten individual subscribers from this place alone—Little Mill, Milton, Bowling, Auchentorlie, Dunerbuck, Mattockhill, Inchinnan, Kilpatrick Braes and village, Greenland, Threepart, Glenshinnon, Yoker, Cleddans, Carleith, Cochno, Faifley, Whitecrook, Partick, Drumry, &c.

On 29th February, 1796, the minutes of a meeting held that day record—"That after an excellent sermon

COMMUNICANT'S TOKEN—OLD KILPATRICK RELIEF CHURCH, 1796.

by the Rev. Mr. Dunn, who was appointed to preside on the occasion, the call turned almost unanimously in favour of the Rev. James Smith of East Kilbride, there being only two members in favour of another candidate, and it was agreed to offer £80 sterling per annum as stipend, and a free house or £7 10s.; stipend payable half-yearly; also 50s. at each sacrament to defray expenses, and the ministers' horses to be entertained by the congregation."

The first elders were, on 17th July, 1796, chosen by the members—they were five in number, as the minutes record—Robert Paul, farmer at Mattockhill, Milton, was chosen by the people in the west end of the parish; James Houston, by the people in the town of Kilpatrick and the Braes; James Colquhoun at the Law, by the people about Duntocher, Cochno, Law, &c.; John Houston, by the people at Dalmuir; and James Denny by those in Boquhanran.

The intimations were read by the precentor, and, in accordance with one which, as the minutes say, was "advertised from the precentor's desk," the following parties were added to the list of managers, 16th August, 1798 :—

> James Duncan, Boquhanran.
> Allan Paul, Milton of Colquhoun.
> Wm. M'Ilwham, Milton of Colquhoun.
> A. Langwill, Duntocher.

John Walker, Gowkstone, had been put on the list some time before.

On 7th January, 1799, convinced of the necessity of building a manse for the accommodation of the minister, a committee was appointed to float the scheme, and John Houston, precentor and clerk (the secretary in those days must have been a good all-round man), was asked to draw out a plan of a house similar to one recently built for the minister of the Relief congregation at Dumbarton.

On 3rd May the offer of John M'Murrich, wright, Faifley, to erect and complete the house for £279 was accepted.

In 1808, Mr. Smith had his stipend raised to £120, but towards the end of the year he accepted a call from College Street congregation, Edinburgh. Rev. John Watt of Blairlogie was called, 12th January, 1809, and inducted 1st April, 1809; stipend to be £120 with manse. At a meeting with a deputation from the church to arrange matters before he entered on his duties, Mr. Watt hinted that he would require a bond for his stipend. Duncan M'Coll, one of the number, speaking very bad English, said, "We'll give you no bones at all, sir, but when you'll come, you'll get good beefs and muttons." Mr. Watt was a short little man, and wore a black frock coat, knee breeches, and black silk stockings.

Mr. Watt died 1st September, 1840, and was succeeded by Rev. James Russell from Strathaven, who had been called as his colleague and successor, and ordained 20th

February, 1834; he died 4th October, 1876. Rev. James Lamb, Perth, who still retains the charge, was called 5th November, 1866, and ordained 5th February, 1867, as colleague and successor.

COMMUNICANT'S TOKEN—OLD KILPATRICK UNITED PRESBYTERIAN CHURCH.

The kirk session is composed as follows :—

Alex. Stark, Old Kilpatrick, session clerk; ordained 3rd November, 1844.

John Walker, Dalmuir; ordained 1st February, 1874.

John M'K. Thompson, Bowling; ordained 8th March, 1885.

James Scott, Littlemill, Bowling; ordained 12th June, 1887.

Alex. D. P. M'Corkindale, Clydebank; ordained 12th June, 1887.

Charles W. Scott, Bowling; ordained 4th Sept., 1892.

William Macaulay, Bowling; ordained 4th Sept., 1892.

FREE CHURCH.

The old grievance of patronage was still a difficulty, and culminated in the Disruption of 1843, when the Rev.

Matt. Barclay demitted the charge of the parish church on 20th June. On leaving the parish church the congregation worshipped in a tent, pitched on the ground where the gasworks now stand, until the erection of the present church was arranged for and completed. The first sermon preached by Mr. Barclay after leaving the Establishment was from 1 John iii. 19—"They went out from us," etc.

The first recorded meeting of the Deacons' Court was held on 24th April, 1844. Sederunt—Rev. Matt. Barclay, Messrs. Fred. Hope Pattison, Samuel M'Dougall, David Russell, Walter Scott, George M'Gown, —— Buchanan, and —— Smith, elders ; Duncan Taylor, Alex. Stark,

COMMUNICANT'S TOKEN—OLD KILPATRICK FREE CHURCH.

Andrew M'Gown, Wm. Robertson, James Comrie, George Scott, —— Bell, —— Lennox, Duntocher ; —— Leckie, Milton ; —— Kennedy, Milton, deacons.

The new church was opened on the third Sunday of June, 1844, by the late Rev. Dr. Begg. During the laying of the foundation stone (at which Lieutenant Fred.

Hope Pattison of Mount Blow assisted) Mr. Barclay was reminded that he had not given it the customary knocks, when he replied in his homely way, "Oh, never mind, I'll chap it weel afterwards."

Mr. Barclay, who, later on in life, received the honour of D.D., was deservedly popular in the parish, and was followed at the Disruption by the large majority of his congregation. He was wealthy, and spent money freely amongst the poor and needy, and had been heard to say shortly before the Disruption that he had not pocketed one farthing of his stipend since he came to the parish. In early life a merchant, he, from high motives, became a clergyman; in mature years taking his seat in the Junior Latin Class, Glasgow University, where he was distinguished by his juvenile associates unanimously awarding to him the prize for "the best behaved boy during the session." Several of his sermons on Temperance were printed in pamphlet form. On his decease, in 1865, he left a sum for educational purposes, which at the present time amounts to £1,400, and is administered under the Educational Endowments Act by three members of the Deacons' Court and two members of the School Board. The income is given for bursaries to be competed for by pupils attending the Board schools in the parish. The successful candidates must attend a secondary or technical school in Glasgow, the Dumbarton academy,

Clydebank school, or any such school as the governors may think fit. Chairman of the Barclay Trust, Rev. Mr. Munro ; clerk, John A. Ross, Dalmuir.

In 1861, the Rev. John Stewart, now of Dennistoun, Glasgow, was ordained colleague and successor to Dr. Barclay. In May, 1866, Mr. Stewart accepted a call to South Shields, and the same year the Rev. George M'Aulay, Stockwell Free Church, Glasgow, was inducted. In 1874, Mr. M'Aulay was called to the Roxburgh Church, Edinburgh, and the Rev. D. D. Robertson, M.A., Dudley, was chosen minister. A church having been erected at Bowling in 1869, Mr. Robertson was chosen as minister, May, 1877 ; and on 28th November, 1878, the Rev. Robert Munro, B.D., F.S.A.Scot., F.R.S.E., was ordained to the charge at Kilpatrick.

The present Deacons' Court consists of the following members :— Rev. Robert Munro, chairman ; Messrs. Duncan Breingan, James Fairley, George Lang, Thomas Edgar, John A. Ross, James M'Nab, Murdoch M'Ivor, Peter M'Aulay, elders ; and Messrs. T. L. Carswell, James Filshie, Duncan Fraser, Hugh M'Nab, William Mercer, Duncan M'Innes, Robert Hillhouse, William M'Millan, deacons.

THE PARISH SCHOOL.

The information to be found in the session records extant regarding educational matters is of the most meagre description. From these we learn that in the year 1684 Claud Hamilton of Cochno had bequeathed the sum of £27 15s. sterling, the interest of which was to be paid to the schoolmaster of the parish for the time being, and when there was none exercising that office the interest was to be applied to the repairing of the church. The capital sum, which had been retained in the Hamilton family, was paid to the kirk session on 24th March, 1774.

From 1692 John Lang, schoolmaster, witnesses some of the entries in the register of births. In 1747 John Morison appears as schoolmaster; he was married on 16th November of this year, and in 1761 he was elected clerk to the then recently formed Kilpatrick Benefit Society.

There was a school at Law, and also at Kilbowie, in the year 1773, James Arroll being mentioned as teacher in the former in the year 1779. In 1771 John Arroll, schoolmaster, is entered as a member of the Kilpatrick Society.

In 1762 Alexander Bell appears to have succeeded John Morison, and the same year was appointed clerk to the Kilpatrick Society. In fact, up to the decease of Mr. Findlay, the post of clerk to the Society was always held by the parochial schoolmaster.

The following receipt of Alexander Bell is still extant :—
" Old Kilpatrick May 24, 1764. Received by me Alexr.

Bell schoolmr. in Old Kilpatrick from Mr. John Farquharson * factor for Lord Blantyre the sum of seventeen shillings and fourpence as schoolm. salary payable by Lord Blantyre out of his land in this parish the which salary is from Whitsunday 1763 to Whitsunday 1764 and the same is discharged by—Alex. Bell."

A certificate of character issued by Mr. Bell, as session clerk, reads as follows :—" These certify the bearer Katharine Maxwel unmarried hath her residence in this parish several years bypast having always behaved soberly and honestly free of public scandal or ground of church censure known to us and therefore may be admitted into any christian congregation or society where God in his providence shall order her lot. Given at Old Kilpatrick this 22nd May 1763."

In 1802 the heritors determined to appoint an assistant to Mr. Bell, who had, through age, become unqualified to teach, but it was not until 1804 that Mr. Moses Shirra was appointed colleague and successor at a salary of 300 merks yearly during the life of Mr. Bell, and on his decease 400 merks yearly. On the appointment of Mr. Shirra the school fees were fixed as follows :— Reading, 2s. per quarter ; English grammar, with or without reading, 2s. 6d. per quarter ; writing, with or

---

* See page 137.

without the foregoing, 3s. per quarter; Arithmetic, with or without all the preceding branches, 3s. per quarter.

In 1772 Robert Brock was paid 10d. for thatching the school-house. Before the year 1803, when a new one was built, the school-house would appear to have adjoined the church, most likely the old building at the north-east corner of the churchyard, now used as a tool-house. Lord Blantyre offered the heritors the choice of two pieces of ground—one, called the jail-yard, and the other, part of M'Crae's park at the east-end of the village. The Rev. Mr. M'Cartney was empowered to obtain a plan and estimate for a suitable building, the dimensions not to exceed those of the school-house in New Kilpatrick, the dwelling-house to be above the school; Mr. William Cross of Auchentoshan and Mr. Douglas of Milton-Douglas being appointed as a committee to act with the minister. M'Crae's park was selected as the site, Lord Blantyre guaranteeing the heritors against all questions with the villagers, and tenders having been called for, that of John and Robert Stark was accepted, and the house now occupied by Mr. Sewell, session clerk, was built and used as school and dwelling-house until the year 1851, when the present more commodious school-room was erected.

Mr. Shirra died in 1845, and the same year Mr. Michael Findlay was appointed parochial schoolmaster and session clerk. He retained the former office until the school was absorbed by the School Board in 1873, and in 1875 he retired on a well-earned pension. Mr. Findlay was the beau-ideal of a parochial schoolmaster. Thoroughly versed in Greek, Latin, and Mathematics, he held his position with dignity and success, and was yearly congratulated by the Dumbarton Presbytery on the care bestowed in teaching the scholars. Mr. Findlay died on the 2nd of February, 1887.

A school in connection with the Free Church, liberally supported and endowed by the Rev. Dr. Barclay, was carried on in the village with success until it was taken over by the School Board along with the parochial and other schools in the parish.

A noted character in the village was William Galloway, teacher, born, 1789, and died, February, 1858. He was a rhymer of no mean order, and several of his ballads are still well remembered in the district. In his lifetime, St. Patrick or the Trees Well, now unfit for use, fell into a ruinous state, and this circumstance drew from him the following lines :—

PETITION OF THE TREES WELL.

> Ye men o' Auld Kilpatrick a',
> To you I now compleen ;
> Ye wives and bonnie lassies braw,
> In hopes ye'll me befreen.

Lang, lang indeed I served you weel,
  And ne'er before did grumble ;
My spring's the same, but yet I feel
  My bigging's like to tumble.

I served you, and at little cost ;
  Ye ken I ne'er gaed dry ;
Through summer's drought and winter's frost
  I did you aye supply.

O dinna let my wa's fa' doun
  To shun a wee expense,
Or bring discredit on your toun
  For sake o' twa three pence.

Do a' my bigging soon repair,
  A fence aroun' me lay,
And train my water clear and fair
  To in a fountain play.

Kilpatrick men, now hear my prayer.
  For credit to yoursel' ;
And wives and bonnie lassies fair,
  A' join and mend your well.

The first election under Lord Young's Education Act
was held on 5th April, 1873, the members elected
being—

Andrew Buchanan, Auchentorlie.

N. C. Campbell, Barnhill.

Rev. Francis Danaher, Duntocher.

Andrew Muter, Milton.

Rev. John Stark, Duntocher.

E. W. McCormick.

OLD HOUSES, DUNTOCHER ROAD, WEST KILPATRICK.

James Thomson, Dalmuir House.

James White, Overtoun, Chairman.

Clerk and Treasurer, . Robert Barr.

Officer, ... Donald M'Murphy.

As shewing the rapid rise in the population it may be stated that in April, 1873, there were, in ten schools with as many teachers, 800 pupils on the roll, with an average attendance of 660, the population of the parish being computed at 6,247 persons; whereas in 1893 there were 3,086 pupils on the roll, with an average attendance of 2,644 in five schools with 58 teachers, the population of the parish being about 19,000 persons.

The schools which are situated at Clydebank, Dalmuir, Duntocher, Gavinburn, and Milton are splendidly equipped, and that of Clydebank will rank as one of the finest in Scotland.

Last year (1893) the following gentlemen comprised the School Board :—

E. C. C. Stanford, Esq., chairman, Glenwood, Dalmuir.

Alexander Aitken, Esq., Barnes Place, Clydebank.

John Cumming, Esq., The Tower, Dalmuir.

James Filshie, Esq., Mount Pleasant, Old Kilpatrick.

James Harvie, Esq., Erskine Villa, Duntocher.

Rev. John Montgomery, Our Holy Redeemer's, Kilbowie Road, Clydebank.

Robert Campbell Mackenzie, Esq., Edinbarnet, by Duntocher.

Rev. Robert James M'Clusky, St. Mary's, Duntocher.

Hugh Wallace, Esq., Bloomfield, Dalmuir.

Clerk and Treasurer—Mr. George Smith, Union Bank of Scotland, Limited, Partick.

Officer—Mr. James Simpson, Clydebank.

MASON MARK ON HOUSE IN OLD KILPATRICK.

CHAPTER XII.

THE LANDS OF KILPATRICK.

LORD CLAUD HAMILTON, commendator of Paisley Abbey, was, in 1587, granted heritably all the Abbey lands in the parish, and they passed, by purchase, in 1638, to Hamilton of Orbiston, who sold them to Lord Blantyre in 1703. Some of the farms seem to have come into the possession of people who were tenants under the Abbot. The farms included in the Abbey rental roll as Easter and Wester Kilpatrick were bounded on the west by the Hawcraig and the small rivulet which runs into the river known as the Gavinburn; and on the east by the Dalnottar or Lusset Burn, which runs in a direct line from the Kilpatrick hills to the river, having the Dalnottar lands on its eastern side. The farms now embraced in this area are Gavinburn, Mount Pleasant, Blackmailing, Closs, Hole, Craigleith, and Burnbrae. Gavinburn is presently tenanted by Mrs. James Filshie, widow of the late James Filshie, distiller, Auchentoshan, and was, last century, divided into High and Low Gavinburn. As already mentioned,* Hugh

* Page 85.

de Bronsyde or Burnside was a rentaller of the Abbey in this farm in 1460, and as late as 1585 we learn from the Privy Council Register that caution was given in £200 by Bontein, yr., of Ardoch, for Allan Macaulay of Ardincaple, and Patrick Macaulay, Allister Dewar's son, "that Peter Burnsyde in Gowaineburne, his wife, bairns, and servants shall not be troubled or molested by them." In 1657 James Burnside was tenant in the adjoining farm of Closs.   There are traces of ancient tillage on the hill slope behind Gavinburn farm-house such as has been observed in other parts of the country.

Mount Pleasant farm, which lies east of Gavinburn, and is formed out of the smaller portion of lands which were known formerly as the Closs, Hole, and Craigleith, received its name towards the end of last century. Blackmailing farm, latterly held by the Langs and sold some years ago to Lord Blantyre, and Burnbrae farm, last tenanted by the late Matthew Forsyth, are all rented by Mr. James Filshie, C.C., who also farms that part of the Lusset lands belonging to Lord Blantyre.

The part of the Lusset lands now belonging to Gilbert Scott, Esq., Grangemouth, were, in 1780, possessed by James Brock, son of James Brock of Little Overtoun, who sold them in that year to James M'Lintock, merchant in Kilpatrick, from whose descendants Gabriel Scott acquired them in 1839.

In the year 1866 Walter Scott, master mariner, took possession as the nearest lawful heir, and having died without issue, Mr. G. Scott succeeded to the titles on the death of Mrs. Walter Scott, his aunt. Captain Walter Scott laid out the Lusset on a feuing plan, and the first villa, built in the year 1868, is owned at present by D. C. Paton, Esq., whose ancestors, for centuries, were farmers in East Kilpatrick parish. The feudal superiority of the Lusset lands is still held by the Campbells of Succoth and Garscube, formerly the lairds of Dalnottar. The only portion of the lands of Easter and Wester Kilpatrick not in the possession of Lord Blantyre is the house and lands of the Drums, tenanted at present by James A. Napier, Esq., formerly in the possession of James M'Crae of Craigleith. William Donald, late in Braehead of Closs, and merchant in Glasgow, was, on 13th October, 1784, infeft in "all and haill that part of the lands of Craigleith called the High and Low Drums, bounded by the lands of Closs on the east, west, and south parts, the property of Lord Blantyre, with liberty of carting peats in the moss for the use of his family, and freeish and entry for leading the same home—the said lands being a 12th part of the lands of Easter Kilpatrick extending to an 11/3d. land of old extent lying above the wall commonly called the Beardike, and now commonly called Craigleith, and bringing the whole corn growing upon the said lands to the mill of Duntocher to be grinded thereat and paying and performing thereat the whole mill dues and services used and accustomed."

On the demise of William Donald, his brother Robert fell heir to these lands, and, in the month of May, 1858, he conveyed them, "with the special advice and consent of Robert Scott, residing at Drums," to Thomas Barr, Esq., railway contractor, then residing at Mount Pleasant. Mr. Barr died in the year 1859, and his son James now possesses the property.

KILPATRICK JAIL—TAKEN DOWN, 1855.

CHAPTER XIII.

LANDS OF GLENARBUCK, EAST AND WEST DYKE, AND LITTLE MILL.

TAKING the highway westward from Kilpatrick, and passing the lands of Gavinburn, we at once skirt the beautifully wooded policies of Glenarbuck (the glen of the roebucks), whose trees afford a grateful shelter to the passing wayfarer. From this point westward to the extreme boundary of the parish the lands were at one time, for a shorter or longer period, in the possession of the Colquhouns of Luss. The mansion house of Glenarbuck was built by Gilbert Hamilton on his acquisition, by purchase, of the lands, the grounds and garden being laid out under his superintendence. He was Lord Provost of Glasgow in 1792, and has been eulogised as a most useful and energetic chief magistrate, and a man of extraordinary and varied public activities. On his decease, Glenarbuck was acquired by Robert Glasgow, Esq., of Mountgreenan, Ayrshire, whose daughter Anne married, in 1804, Robert Robertson of Prenderguest, Brownsbank, and Gumgreen, who assumed the name of Glasgow.

The family of Robertson Glasgow of Mountgreenan traditionally claims descent from the Robertsons of Strowan, Perthshire, and in the female line represents the Setons of Monkmylne, Haddingtonshire, lineally descended from Sir Christopher Seton and Christian Bruce, sister of Robert I.

Lord Blantyre having married, in 1843, the second daughter of George Granville, second Duke of Sutherland, the lands of Glenarbuck were conveyed to him by his father-in-law, who had purchased them from Sheriff Robertson Glasgow, son of Robert Robertson Glasgow.

The original designation of the Glenarbuck lands was the Spittal of Dunnerbuck. The remains of the farm-house known as the Spittal may still be seen behind the coach-house. The last tenant was of the name of * Donald (common amongst the Abbey tenants), the last representative of whom, known as William Donald of the Spittal, a seaman, who sailed with the late Captain James Scott˙ in the locally built and owned sloop "The Brothers," died at Little Mill many years ago.

Mention † has been made of what appears to have been a road, 25 feet or so wide and bordered on either side by fine old trees, across the field below Glenarbuck house, considered by Horsely to be the

---

* See page 155.

† See pages 30 and 32.

Roman Military way. This year Mr. H. M. Napier of Milton House, whose mother is tenant of Glenarbuck, had trenches cut across the supposed road in several places, but discovered no traces of a regular causeway such as is found on the Roman made roads; it is possible, however, that the stones used might have been removed when the field was brought under tillage, as Bishop Pocoke says, "they found part of the field very stony."

The Glenarbuck lands stretch down to the river and are intersected by the highway, the North British Railway, the Canal, and the new Lanarkshire and Dumbartonshire Railway, all being within a stone's throw of each other.

Passing the Sutherland Arms Hotel on the left, and on the right what was formerly the Bowling Toll Bar, we have on the north side of the road the lands of East Dyke, now acquired by the Lanarkshire and Dumbartonshire Railway Company. These lands, with those contiguous on the west belonging to John Scott, Esq., Cardross, and John Scott, Esq., Woodside, belonged formerly to Dunerbuck estate, and, as mentioned before,* received the appellation of the Dyke from the tradition that the Roman Wall ran that way westward to Dunglass.

---

* See page 30.

The river formed the southern boundary to the Dyke lands, and the houses forming the present village are built on ground feued off from time to time by the Scotts, who were the original proprietors. William Scott of East Dyke died some years ago, and on his demise the lands were sold. The farm-house attached was pulled down some years ago, and at the time of its demolition was the only thatched building in the vicinity.

EAST DYKE HOUSE.
(From a Photo. in possession of Matthew Clark, Esq.)

The village of Bowling, or, as it was known many years ago, Bowling Bay, appears last century in the parish registers as the Bowland of Spittal,* evidently deriving its appellation from the curve of the bay, which has been greatly and repeatedly altered since

* See page 154.

the formation of the Canal in 1790 down to the present day. The present harbour and canal basin was constructed by the Canal Company in the year 1850, and a considerable extension of the canal basin is now in progress consequent on the alterations rendered necessary by the new railway. The western portion of the harbour belonging to the Clyde Trustees was constructed in the year 1840, and altered as it now appears in 1857, after the great gale in February of that year.

When the Canal was completed a graving dock was constructed suitable for the repair of vessels passing

HARBOUR MASTER'S OFFICE, BROOMIELAW, 1819.
(From Pen and Ink Sketch of that date.)

through the Navigation. In the year 1800 this dock was let to Thomas Macgill, who is styled in the lease as shipbuilder, Broomielaw,* where he had built the

---

* It is from Mr. Macgill's yard that Wood Lane, close to Jamaica Street, took its name.

now almost extinct craft known as "gabberts," and repaired the Highland wherries which in those days formed the bulk of the shipping in the harbour of Glasgow. The Macgills have been long shipbuilders on the Clyde. On 6th August, 1780, Thomas Macgill, cousin of the forementioned, launched from his building yard, Port-Glasgow, as the *Glasgow Mercury* informs us, a fine ship for the Jamaica trade, pierced for 18 guns. This vessel, called the "Jessie," sailed on 14th November of that year for Kingston, Jamaica, and outports, having on board 900 barrels beef and a quantity of dry goods. On 1st May, 1781, she was reported at Lloyd's, London, as having been captured by the U.S. Frigates "Deane" and "Protector," and carried into Martinico.

The rent paid by Mr. Macgill for the Canal graving dock was £25 for the first year, rising to £40 at the seventh year. For several years repairs only were executed, but in 1804 the sloop "Active" was built for and sailed by Captain John Scott, who was the first of the Dunerbuck family to become a shipowner. It is said this vessel was the first that was advertised to take cargo direct from Liverpool to Glasgow without transhipping whole or part cargo at Greenock; the average passage at this time from Greenock to Glasgow being about a fortnight for vessels of her class. On one occasion the "Active" and a coal gabbert were the only vessels in the harbour of Glasgow. She once made the passage from Belfast Loch to Greenock in twelve hours.

The first schooner built on the Clyde, and named the "Osprey," was launched at Bowling, and owned by Captain Walter Scott, her model being taken from the sloop "Glasgow" which had undergone an overhaul at the dock. In 1812 the sloop "Acorn," latterly masted as a schooner, was launched, and was partly built out of the wood from the old parish church. She was owned by Captain Gabriel Scott. In 1825 the schooner "Eagle," of 95 tons register, was launched for Captain Peter Scott, who had the "Rainbow" built some time after, and in 1827 the brig "Amity," of 116 tons register, for Captain Roy, was built, and report has it she was the first that loaded for Montreal direct from Glasgow. The loading berth was at the foot of Robertson Street. Although not over 70 feet long, she had 'tween decks which were planked underneath the beams to give a greater height to the passengers there accommodated. She carried 200 emigrants. In 1834 ten journeymen and six apprentice carpenters were employed by Mr. Macgill. The largest vessel built at the dock was the "Bowling," of 253 tons register, launched in 1842, and barque rigged. She was 93 feet long, 22 feet beam, and 14 feet deep. Being built with full lines, as was the fashion in these days, she was a good carrier. She traded to the West Coast of South America and the East Indies. Captain Robert Gentle, a native of Kincardine-on-Forth, was master, and sailed her for many years; he was one of the old school salts now giving place to more scientific masters, though not bolder sailors; there was scarcely a seaport that he was not acquainted with in every ocean and every climate. He died, March, 1863, and lies buried in Old Kilpatrick churchyard. When this vessel was projected there was no floor large enough in the village on which to lay down her lines. At Milton, however, the necessary floorage space was arranged for and granted on condition that no nails were to be used, the batons had therefore to be kept in their places with 56 lb. weights.

In late years Mr. Thomas Macgill was assisted in his business by his sons David and Thomas. When the Canal Company extended the harbour, necessitating the removal of the dock, a slip was constructed at Little Mill in 1851, and the business carried on under the style of Scott & Macgill. Mr. Thomas Macgill retired in the year 1880. The business is now carried on by Messrs. Scott & Sons, the partners being Mr. James Scott, Orchard Cottage, and his two sons, Charles Wood and James.

Bowling Bay at one time was a health resort for the

citizens of Glasgow, and a story is told of Sandy Cameron, who kept the public house at Little Mill, locally known as the " Dunters," that on one occasion some of his customers having become noisy in their cups, he shouted into the room, " Dinna, lads, mak' sic a din, there's saut water folk abin," referring to visitors who had taken rooms for the summer in the flat above.

In the Clyde Trustees' harbour for many years lay the " Industry," the oldest steamer then in existence. Built at Fairlie by the Fyfes in 1814, she was at the time of her launch the seventh steamer which had been constructed on the Clyde. Her dimensions were 65 feet keel, 16 feet breadth of beam, and measurement 55 tons. In 1862 the " Industry " got seriously damaged through collision, and as she was not considered by her owners, Messrs. Steel & M'Caskill, worth repairing they presented her to the Clyde Trustees, who had her removed to Bowling. In the year 1888 the engines, which were fitted with spur gearing, were taken out and re-erected at the Museum, Kelvingrove Park, where they are still to be seen. The hull and paddle-boxes were for many a day the favourite bathing box for the village youths.

The Free Church, built in the early English Gothic style, was erected in 1869, and for several years was used

as a mission station in connection with the Kilpatrick
Free Church. In the year 1878 it was created a regular
charge, and the Rev. D. D. Robertson was inducted
in the month of May. Mr. Robertson having resigned
the charge, the Rev. George M'Aulay, M'Crie-Roxburgh
Church, Edinburgh, and formerly in the Kilpatrick
Church, was inducted 1st April, 1886 ; owing to his
failing health, Mr. M'Aulay applied for a colleague
and successor, and the Rev. Daniel Georgeson, M.A.,
was ordained 5th August, 1890.

MASON MARK ON HOUSES AT LITTLE MILL, OLD KILPATRICK, AND KILBOWIE.

LITTLE MILL.

This tiny village, which forms the western part of
Bowling, derives it name from the mill of Auchentorlie
which stood on the site now occupied by the distillery
of Messrs. Hay, Fairman & Co.

A receipt is still extant, dated Auchentorlie, 15th August,
1769, acknowledging receipt from "Wm. Glen, Jr., in
Mill poffle and croft of Auchentorlie of the just and

CANAL BASIN, BOWLING.

equal half of his rent for crop 1768." In 1775 Sir Archibald Edmonstone of Duntreath granted a tack of 5 acres of the Little Miln lands to John Clark, who erected thereon a calico printing work. He failed in business in 1781, when the plant was purchased by James Provand & Co., Glasgow, who carried on the business of calico printers and bleachers for a few years, employing some fifty persons, and then closed the premises.

From Lettice's "Tour in Scotland," 1792, folio 188, we make the following interesting extract :—

"Sept. 4, 1792. Turning on our left (having crossed Erskine ferry), we proceeded, and came to Bowling Bay, about 11 miles north-west of Glasgow, where the Grand Junction Canal enters the Clyde. This bay is about a quarter of a mile wide, and 14 feet deep at high water.

"At a small distance from it, the busy scene of a bleachery tempted us to dismount. We were first shown some capacious boiling vats, constructed of wood above, and metal below, sufficiently large to receive fifteen hundred yards of linen or cotton; which here undergo their first operation of being boiled with soap and ashes. Contiguous to these vats is placed the washing machinery contrived to despatch as much work in an hour as almost the whole host of washwomen at Glasgow could finish in a day. Several broad-headed beetles, of massive wood, or stocks, as they are technically called, being put into the action of hammering, by a large water wheel, beat and press the cloths, which a rapid stream of cold water, passing continually beneath them, keeps turning on every side, till they have discharged their impurities. They are then thrown into a great vat, filled in a few minutes with cold water by means of copper tubes suspended above it. Being thus perfectly cleared of the soap, they are removed from hence into a wringing machine made on much the same principle with that in Beetham's patent washer. They are now entirely prepared for the bleaching field, of which there are several in this corner of Dumbartonshire of great extent and consideration.

"These cloths which are intended to be dyed or printed are, when taken up from the field, steeped immediately in water having an infusion of vitriol, and dried in spacious rooms constructed for the purpose with an infinity of apertures, to draw a constant current of air."

In the *Glasgow Courier* of June 18th, 1795, the following advertisement appears :—

"To be sold upon the premises, by public roup, upon Friday, the 21st August next, the following property which belonged to the deceased William Findlay at Little Miln of Auchentorlie. The roup to begin at Kilpatrick or Frisky, as may suit intending purchasers, at 11 o'clock forenoon, and continued till all are sold off.

"Lot 1. That house and yard in the town of Old Kilpatrick presently occupied by A. Hart and others.

"Lot 2. The eastmost half of that front house, back houses and yards, built on the site of Cunningham's land in the town of Old Kilpatrick.

"Lot 3. The westmost half of the last mentioned tenement and lands.

"Lot 4. The lands called Corse Delph adjoining the lands of Frisky, consisting of 2 acres or thereby, with the dwelling house and barn at Little Mill, possessed by Widow Findlay and others.

"Lot 5. The said William Findlay's interest in the property of that elegant villa called Frisky Hall, under lease to the late Ronald Crawford, Esq., for 91 years after Martinmas, 1784, at the yearly rent of £10 3s. 4½d. ; and the property of that triangular piece of ground situated immediately to the eastward of Frisky Hall, let to Mr. Crawford for the period of the former tack yet to run at £1 15s. yearly. Upon the property in the first-mentioned tack, the substantial and elegant house of Frisky Hall and offices, pleasure grounds, etc., are situated, and the whole having cost several thousand pounds sterling in finishing, is not only an eligible security for the price, but notwithstanding the length of the tack, from the substantial manner of the houses, these must be of considerable value to the purchaser. William Findlay's interest, exclusive of the triangular piece of ground, is - - - - - £10 3 4 and James M'Ilwham, the only other pro- prietor, his interest is   - . - -   4 17 6 and by these proportions this valuable property will fall ultimately to be divided.

"Lot 6. That dwelling house * and yard at Little Miln presently possessed by Duncan Cameron and others.

"Lot 7. That park, consisting of 3 acres or thereby, at Little Miln, lying on the south side of the highway, presently occupied by James Provand & Co. as a bleachfield, the lease whereof is nearly expired; and that row of houses, yard and stable, Little Mill, presently possessed by Daniel M'Lauchlan, Alex. Currie, Ann Glen and others.

"Lot 8. That printfield at Little Mill with the houses thereto belonging lying on the north side of the high road as presently possessed by the said James Provan & Co.

"For further particulars applictaion may be made to James M'Kay in Old Kilpatrick, and Walter Aitken,

---

* This house was rebuilt in 1802, and about 40 yards of the burn arched in from the bridge over which the road comes back to James M'Ilwham's house, now called Distillery House.

Dalmuir, or to D. Hutcheson, writer, Glasgow, in whose hands the title deeds and articles of sale will be seen."

Practically, all the Mill lands were embraced in the foregoing catalogue, and we shall now see how they were disposed of.

Lot 4 was purchased by James Paterson, Auchentorlie, the author's great-grandfather, the said piece of ground being thereafter known as the "Folly" from the excessive price which was paid for it. On this ground now stands the dwelling houses on either side of the Public Hall, the Hall itself, Auchentorlie Terrace, and the Railway Restaurant. The old building adjacent to the restaurant was originally built by James Paterson, son and heir of the forementioned purchaser, as a joiner's workshop. This "foolish" purchase now returns to the grandson of the original investor a goodly annual sum in the way of feu duty.

Lot 5 was purchased by Captain James Scott, who shortly afterwards resold it to John Kerr, writer, retaining part of the orchard to the west of the burn and stretching down to the Clyde from the turnpike road, and on which Messrs. Scott & Sons' flourishing shipbuilding yard and Mr. Scott's dwelling house, which is called The Orchard, now stand.

Lot 6 was ultimately possessed by the late James Love, boatbuilder, Glasgow; while lots 7 and 8 were purchased by Walter Allan, whose descendants, the Misses Allan, Findlay Cottage, still retain part of the purchase.

Mr. Ronald Crawford, the first tenant in Frisky Hall, appears in Love's Glasgow Directories of 1787 and 1789, as "Crawford, Ronald, of Frisky, Esq.; lodgings, 2nd flat of Buchanan's back land, Trongate, by No. 120."

Frisky Hall was quite a feature in the scenery of the river, situated as it was on a most attractive spot with charming scenery around. Heron thus refers to it in his "Journey through Scotland," vol. i., folio 376, A.D. 1793. —"I particularly recollect the unusual aspect of one very showy (villa) close upon the eastern bank of the river. When I asked its name I learned it was Frisky Hall. It was illuminated and painted and dight up in that taste which mistakes finery for elegance." Dibdin, in his "Tour," folio 181, A.D. 1801, also mentions it and the "Temple" of Auchentorlie, situated, he remarks, on the summit of a precipice.

In 1834, Messrs. Mills & Wood established a ship-building yard on part of the ground which belonged to the bleachwork of old, west of Messrs. Scott & Sons' yard, and built steam vessels of a large class. In 1836 there were 31 journeymen employed at £1 1s. per week, 41 apprentices at 7s., 10 sawyers at £1 1s., 2 labourers at 10s., 4 smiths at from 15s. to £1 1s., and 6 joiners a 15s. to 18s. One of the steamers here built, the "Dumbarton Castle," plied on the river for many years. In a few years Mr. Wood and Mr. Mills relinquished the business, Mr. Wood restarting business in Dumbarton, where he built the "Tay" and the "Caledonia" steamers for the Royal Mail and Cunard S.S. Companies. Writing in 1838, Dr. Dibdin, in the second volume, folio 779, "Northern Tour," tells us he paid a visit to Mr. Kerr, residing at Frisky Hall, and says—"We had to traverse a plank, lopsidedly placed and slippery with saturated moisture, which was put across a ditch adown which galloped a mountain torrent all foam and fury. We dined at a neighbour's of the name of Mills, an enterprising and intelligent shipbuilder. On returning home, although we had scarcely 300 yards to walk, the blackness of the night seemed to threaten us with extinction. Ebony is not so black as was that night."

In 1850 the Balloch and Dumbarton Railway was opened and Frisky Hall was turned into a hotel. On the completion of the line through from Glasgow to Helensburgh, the hotel, then under the care of Mrs. Comrie, was vacated, and after waiting for some time for a tenant, the Railway Company had it fitted up for their workmen. Now, Messrs. Scott & Co.'s building yard is pressing hard on it, and the removal of the old building is only a question of time.

The distillery of Messrs. Hay, Fairman, & Co. was established about 80 years ago on the site of Messrs. Provand & Co.'s printfield, and has been carried on with varying success until the present day. The quality of the spirits produced is such that the demand exceeds the supply. The houses occupied by the revenue officers date back to the year 1772, while the oldest portion of the manager's house bears the date 1791. The foot-path from the village to the river is known as the Fisherman's road, and a right-of-way to the river-side exists at the east end of the railway station, and is occasionally used by the Distillery Company when importing peats.

The first post office for the district was situated at Little Mill, and was known officially as Dunglass post office. The village school, for a long period, was held at Little Mill in various houses, the last being where Mrs. Sinclair now keeps a grocer's shop. Previously it had been a smithy and rented by Sandy M'Gregor, who was, in the manner of the times, nicknamed St. Helena, from a habit he had of continually crooning over a song, one line of which ran thus—

> " Boney (Napoleon I.) has gone to a place he ne'er can delight in."

Sandy was without a striker, and his better half, when occasion required, could swing the fore-hammer to good purpose. In 1861 the Bowling Public School and Hall was erected by public subscription, and when the School Board became responsible for the education of the children the building was handed over to them. On the erection of Gavinburn School for the joint use of the villages of Kilpatrick and Bowling, the School Board, after considerable delay, and after attention had been drawn in the House of Commons to the circumstances, handed back the building to a committee of the inhabitants chosen at a public meeting this year (1894).

To the munificence of the late Andrew Buchanan, Esq., of Auchintorlie, the village owes the Buchanan Institute which he erected for the use of the inhabitants. The building, the style of architecture of which is Gothic, from designs by Mr. John Paton, C.E., Old Kilpatrick, was opened in December, 1884, and forms a fitting memorial which will keep the donor's memory fragrant for many years to come.

CHAPTER XIV.

LANDS OF AUCHENTORLIE, DUNNERBUCK, AND DUNGLASS.

AUCHENTORLIE estate, as now held by Mr. Fergusson Buchanan, is composed of a variety of lands. It consists of the barony of Auchentorlie proper, with the exception of the portion which is situated in the county of Renfrew, and includes the muir of Colquhoun, Dunerbuck, Silverbanks, Connalton, Dunglass, and part of the Little Mill acres, all of which belonged to the Colquhouns.

The lands of Auchentorlie formed a part of the barony of Erskine between 1330 and 1390, when Isabella Fleming of Dalnotar granted to Sir Robert Erskine, knight, a charter, which was confirmed by David II., of Auchentorlie and Dunerbuck with the fishings as held from the lands of Barrochan, on the south side of the Clyde.

In 1452 Robert de Lyle granted in feu to the monks of Paisley the third of the fishing of the Crukyshot in Clyde, a pertinent of the lands of Auchentorlie and Dunerbuck, together with a particle of land for building a house for the preservation of the fish and for a habitation for the monks' servants, and permission to take wood for hanging their nets upon from the wood of Auchentorlie and Dunerbuck. Annual payment for this was five merks. Lord Lyle, by insurrection, forfeited

ARMS OF FERGUSSON BUCHANAN OF AUCHENTORLIE.

Or, a lion rampant sable between two otters' heads erased in chief proper, and a cinquefoil in base of the second within a double tressure flory counterflory of the last, 1st and 4th quarters for Buchanan; azure, a buckle argent between three boars' heads couped within a bordure of the last, 2nd and 3rd quarters for Fergusson.

these lands, which were then gifted by the Crown to Archibald, Lord Campbell, eldest son of Colin, first Earl of Argyle. The charter is dated 8th July, 1489.

These lands afterwards became the property of John Maxwell of Dargavell, who obtained from Lord Lyle

a charter of the "five merk land of old extent of
Auchentorlie and Dunerbuck with the mill thereof,"
and was infeft therein on 17th December, 1541.
Robert Master of Boyd, who died soon afterwards, had
a charter of the lands of Auchentorlie, dated 14th
October, 1550.*

It † reads as follows :—"Apud Jedburgh, 14th October,
1550.—Regina, etc.,‡ tanquam senescalla Scotie concessit
Roberto Magistro de Boyde heredibus ejus et assignatis
—10 libratas terrarum antiqui extentus de Auchintuerlie,
Dunnerbuke et Spittale, cum earum molendino, piscaria
et lie cowbilldrauchtis nuncupatis Crukitschottis (et
Spittellschottis) super aqua de Clyde, vic Dunbertane :—
quas Joh. dom. Lile, cum consensu Johannis Lyndesay
de Covingtoun, resignavit."

Not long afterwards, as will be seen from the copy of
the charter § which follows, these lands were held by
Joan Boyd, wife of Patrick Hamilton of Bogside.

"Apud Striveling, 6th April, 1554.—Regina, etc., confirmavit cartam Roberti Magistri de Boyde—qua pro
summa pecunie sibi persoluta vendidit Joanne Boyd
spouse Patricii Hammiltoun de Bogsyde in vitali redditu

---

* Irving's Hist. of Dumbartonshire, fol. 106.
† Registrum Mag. Sigillum, fol. 121.
‡ In this Charter the Regent is styled Earl of Arran only.
§ Registrum Mag. Sigillum, fol. 209.

—8 marcat terrarum antiqui extentus de Akintweirlie et Dunnerbuck, in quibus dicta Joanna prius infeodata erat, in comitatu de Levenax, vic Dunbartane. Reddend regine unum den, argenti nomine albe firme. Test. Archd. Boill, Alex. Boyd in Craig, Alex. Cunyngham, et Geo. Boyd, notario publico. Apud Kilmarnock, 11 Oct., 1550."

On 29th December, 1559, John Boyd of Marston granted to Margaret Colquhoun, Lady Boyd, a liferent charter of the £10 lands of old extent of Dunerbuck and Auchentorlie with the mill. This charter was sealed at Dunglass.

Towards the end of the 16th century we find Robert Boyd of Badinhaith selling part of these lands to Robert Scott. The charter reads as follows:—

"30th October, 1591. Rex confirmavit cartam Roberto Boyde of Badinhaith . . . vendidit . . . Robert Scott et Eliz. ejus spouse hereditarie,—cum red. 100 merks de suis 8 mercat terrarum de Dunnerbok et Auchintourlie antiqui ext. in parochia de Kirkpatrick, vic Dumbartane. Reddend unum den. albe firme—cum precepto sasine directo Joanni Kneland Juniori de Foscan. Apud Glasgow, 13 Oct., 1589."

Under date of 20th February, 1602, we find the following charter in the Registrum Magnum Sigillum:—
"20th Feb., 1602.—John Colquhoun filio primogenito

Alex. Colquhoun of Lus. 10 librat terrarum antiqui extentus de Dunnerbuck et Auchentourlie cum tenentibus, etc., cum molendino de Auchentourlie et piscatione super aquam de Clyde vocata Cruikitschot et Spittillschot—que fuerunt quondam Robt. dom de Boyde et ejus predecessorum, etc., etc."

By a contract made at Dunnerbuck and Dunglass on January 19th, 1605, between Thomas Lord Boyd and Alexander Colquhoun of Luss, the latter became bound to deliver to Lord Boyd the recognition which he had obtained of the lands of Dunerbuck and Auchentorlie, Spittal Mill, &c., and Lord Boyd bound himself to pay to Luss for the same the sum of £2000 Scots.

The exact period of the acquisition of the barony of Auchentorlie by the Colquhoun family has not been ascertained, but it was the property of Sir John Colquhoun of Luss in the year 1652.

The lands of Auchentorlie and Dunerbuck were disposed of by Sir James Colquhoun of Luss to his son Humphrey and Margaret Houston, 1684. Sir Humphrey feued Auchentorlie to John Colquhoun previous to 29th April, 1693, on which date he is designated John Colquhoun of Auchentorlie. Above Dunglass John Colquhoun built a small convenient residence.

In 1695 Sir Humphrey sold to John Colquhoun of Auchentorlie and his heirs the lands of Auchentorlie,

Dunerbuck, and Connalton, with the salmon fishing in the water of Clyde belonging thereto, the mill of Auchentorlie, and the whole wood upon these lands, and that part of Connalton grass above the Liggate or highway possessed by the tenants of Dunglass, with a proportion of the churchroom and churchyard of Kilpatrick. The price of the lands was for Auchentorlie and Dunnerbuck £7020 13s. 4d., and for Connalton £5587 10s. It may be interesting to note here that the following parties were crofters in Connalton in the year 1588:—John Finlay, Patrick Finlay, his father; James Donald, Robert Lang, Patrick Colquhoun, John Lang.

The above-mentioned John Colquhoun of Auchentorlie was the son of Matthew Colquhoun sometime in Erskine. He married, first, Agnes Colquhoun who was of the family of Colquhouns in Milton of Colquhoun, and second, Agnes, eldest daughter of Andrew Colquhoun of Garscadden, and died on 14th December, 1697, within a year and a day of his second marriage. He was buried in Kilpatrick churchyard where his tomb was to be seen until a few years ago. It bore the Colquhoun arms, and the inscription was in Latin.

Dunerbuck lands were acquired by the Edmonstone family from the Colquhouns, and John Scott, tenant in Overtoun, was infeft in them on 24th August, 1751, being succeeded by his son John, who entered

into possession 24th April, 1775. John had three
sons—William, James, and Walter. William became
proprietor of Dunerbuck, and James and Walter had a
feu disposition of the east and west cottaries called the
Dyke. In 1808 William Scott made a disposition of the
lands of Dunerbuck in favour of his three sisters—Marion,
Janet, and Mary Scott—their respective husbands being
John M'Farlane, William Lindsay, and Matthew Clark,
and by them they were sold to Auchentorlie, who also
purchased some time later the superiority from Duntreath.

Connalton was situated very near where the present
Auchentorlie house stands, but rather more on the
brow of the hill overlooking Dunglass. On the hill
near Greenland farm a few huts called Riggangower
formerly stood, but no trace of them now remains.
The name, however, is still shown on the ordnance
survey map. It is said that the houses were removed
when Greenland farm was laid out. The following
fragment of a ballad dealing with the subject still
lingers in the district :—

> The lassies a' frae far and near,
>   Cam' wi' their lint and tow ;
> And many a happy day was spent
>   In auld Riggangower.
>
> Auld Riggan he sat by the fire,
>   Biggin' on the kowes ;
> And nuts and slaes grew on the braes
>   O' auld Riggangower.

Robt. Balderston.

OLD POST OFFICE AND SCHOOL, LITTLE MILL.

> But the moudiewort wild elf cam' up,
>   An' yirded in the knowe ;
> And girt the biggins a' fa' doun,
>   That were in Riggangower.

In 1709 these lands were sold by Elizabeth Colquhoun to Mungo Buchanan, writer to the Signet, Edinburgh, who, in 1737, sold Auchentorlie to Andrew Buchanan of Drumpellier, Provost of Glasgow. Andrew Buchanan subsequently sold the lands to his brother Archibald, who, on 5th December, 1754, as the title deeds inform us, sold to John Donald, tenant in Cochnoch, the just and equal half of all and whole these parts of the lands of Auchentorlie presently possessed by William Donald and John Paterson, the three acres of land of the croft foot of Auchentorlie as possessed by Archibald Glen, and the just and equal half of all and whole that poffle of land at the Little Mill of Auchentorlie as same is possessed by William Glen ; the feu duty being 50 merks. The witnesses to the transfer and instrument of sasine are George Buchanan of Auchentoshan and John and Peter Paterson of Auchentorlie. In 1768 John Donald sold to John Paterson the east half of these lands, the west portion being acquired by George Thomson, banker in Glasgow, in 1783, from John Paul, with special advice and consent of Jean Knox, his mother, " widow of John Paul, farmer in Carleith, and of William Donald, eldest son procreat betwixt John Donald, in Upper Gavinburn, and the deceased Jean Paul, his wife, my sister." In 1786 Thomson sold these lands forming the west half of Auchentorlie to George Buchanan, son of Archibald Buchanan of Silverbanks, the boundaries between West and East Auchentorlie being settled on by both proprietors on 1st November, 1786. In 1842 John Paterson sold the east portion of the Auchentorlie lands to Andrew Buchanan, all as purchased in 1768, with the exception of a small plot feued on 31st August, 1824, to Archibald Paterson, on which Rosehill House now stands, the property of his daughter Janet, who married James Gilfillan, 1875.

Andrew Buchanan, before-mentioned, Provost of Glasgow, sold the lands of Connalton and Silverbanks to his brother Archibald. The history of the Buchanans is bound up in that of Glasgow for practically 200 years. Towards the end of the 17th century George Buchanan, second son of Andrew Buchanan of Gartacharan, came to Glasgow to push his fortune, and prospered so as a maltster that in the years 1691, 1692, and 1694 he was deacon-convener and visitor to the trade. His sons were (1) George Buchanan of Moss and Auchentoshan, (2) Andrew Buchanan of Drumpellier, (3) Archibald Buchanan of Silverbanks and Auchentorlie and (4) Neil Buchanan of Hillington.

Archibald Buchanan, who was made a burgess of Rutherglen, 22nd July, 1740, and of Paisley, 23rd May, 1758, was succeeded in the Silverbanks and other lands, including those of Hillington, by his sons Peter and George, neither of whom left issue. George left the Auchentorlie estate and others to his nephew Archibald, eldest son of his brother Andrew Buchanan of Ardinconnal, Row, who was born, 12th July, 1745, and married, 3rd July, 1769, Jane, eldest daughter of James Dennistoun of Colgrain and Dennistoun of that ilk, and had issue two sons—Archibald, who succeeded his uncle George in Auchentorlie, and James of Ardinconnal. Archibald Buchanan married on 3rd June, 1816, Mary, second daughter of Richard Dennistoun of Kelvingrove, and died, 16th December, 1832, leaving issue six daughters and two sons. (1) Andrew, born, 14th March, 1817, who succeeded to the estate, and in 1851 erected the present mansion; during his lifetime the estate was extensively planted and improved. He married, November, 1845, Mary, youngest daughter of the late Sir James Fergusson of Kilkerran, Bart., and died, 20th February, 1886, leaving no issue. The estate devolved upon his brother, (2) Captain Richard Dennistoun Buchanan, born, 22nd September, 1830, late of the 72nd Highlanders, who died unmarried, 10th February, 1890. He was greatly esteemed and beloved by all, and his unlooked-for demise spread sorrow over the entire community. He was succeeded in 1890 by his nephew George James Fergusson, only son of George Hermand Fergusson, Esq., who died, 1870, by Georgina Grace Buchanan, daughter of Archibald Buchanan of Auchentorlie; born, 1862, married, 8th December, 1886, Grace, daughter of Claud Hamilton Hamilton, Esq., of Cochno, Barnes, and Dunmore Park, Stirlingshire, and has issue two daughters, Noel Grace and Avril Nora.

The old mansion, superseded by the present edifice, was called Silverbanks, and was built early last century. Archibald Edmonstone, who was created a baronet of the United Kingdom, May 3, 1774, was born there, October 10th, 1717. He was the eldest son of Archibald Edmonstone of Duntreath, who held considerable property in the parish.

The antiquities found in this district are few so far as recorded; but as the present proprietor, G. J. Fergusson Buchanan, Esq., has a leaning towards archæology, and being of an observing mind, important discoveries may yet be made in what has hitherto been a district considered bare of antiquarian remains.

In 1889 or 1890, as already mentioned, two stones with cup markings were found built into a wall to the north-west of the old Auchintorlie farm house.

During the winter season of 1890-91 a basket-hilted

Highland broadsword of the usual type was found. The following description of it is from the pen of D. Murray, LL.D., Cardross, who exhibited the sword at the February meeting, 1891, of the Archæological Society of Glasgow :—"The blade is flat, without median ridge, double-edged, 35¼ inches in length and 1⅜ inches in breadth at the joint. The taper is very slight, being only ⅜ of an inch in 33 inches. The hilt is open steel work, terminating in an acorn shaped pommel. The grip is 4½ inches in length, and is still surrounded with wood, which had been covered with leather, of which a fragment remains, and the wood shows that a strong wire had been twisted spirally round it. The sword, when found, lay flat in the burn, a stone covering the nine inches next the hilt. The remainder was bare. Probably it had all been covered with sand or gravel, which being washed away brought the blade to view. The part which the stone covered is well preserved. The remainder of the same and the under side are puckered and pimpled by rust. The protecting stone has preserved the inscription 'Andr(e)a' running along the blade, with four punched heads ; one head preceding the AN, the DR, and EA, and one following the last two letters. The heads are well cut and stand at right angles to the letters. The heads and letters occupy a flat space five inches in length, with two parallel grooves or channels on each side. There are corresponding grooves on the other side, and four heads similar to those on the other side, but no lettering is visible. It is a reasonable conjecture, however, that the letters of the word 'Ferara' or 'Farara' alternated with the heads. The heads are surmounted by thick broad-brimmed hats of a Spanish or Moorish type. The edges of the blade are much hacked, but it still retains its temper and can be easily bent.

"Claverhouse's sword, lent to the Glasgow International Exhibition of 1888 by the Duke of Montrose, has the word 'Andrea' on the one side 'Farara' on the other, with a series (said to be seven) of crowned heads on each side (see 'Scottish National Memorials,' pp. 118, 261). Its length is 38⅛ inches, breadth at the junction 1⅜ inches, and grip 3½ inches in length. The two weapons therefore very closely correspond in general appearance and are presumably by the same maker. The style of the heads on the present sword gives some support to the suggestion that Ferrara blades were originally of Spanish manufacture, and took their names from Feraria in the province of Corunna. Ferreira, it will be remembered, is a common Portuguese surname."

At Dunglass some years ago a rapier of the time of the Commonwealth was found in excellent preservation. In the burn, not far from where the Ferrara sword above described was found, Mr. G. J. Fergusson picked up the broken rapier shown in the illustration. It has Solingen marked on the portion of blade left.

FERRARA SWORD AND RAPIERS.

On the crest of Ardconnal or Sheep Hill the remains of an ancient fort are clearly visible, and a small portion has the appearance of being vitrified.

DUNGLASS.

This stronghold of the barony of Colquhoun, according to the "Book of Colquhoun," claims a high antiquity. The year 1380 is said to be the date of its erection, but the authority on which this affirmation rests is uncertain. It was, however, one of the residences of Sir John Colquhoun, Chamberlain of Scotland, 1439 to 1478, during whose occupancy the brutal murder referred to in page 130 was committed.

After Sir John's death it was possessed by Elizabeth Dunbar, Countess of Moray, his widow, in liferent. In

1484, in a litigation with her stepson, Humphrey Colquhoun, regarding it, she was ordained by the Lords of Council to uphold the place and orchard of Dunglass in good repair.

In 1489 the royal army occupied the castle while besieging that of Dumbarton, which was held against James IV. by the sons of Lord Darnley. In this connection the following extracts from the accounts of the Lord High Treasurer are of great interest:—

"On the 26th June the Parliament assembled at Edinburgh and sat till the 4th July. On the second day of its sitting decree of forfeiture was passed against Lord Lyle, the Earl of Lennox, and his son Matthew Stewart, with their abettors, and it was further determined that for the recovery of the houses and castles held by the rebels in the west, the king should pass in person to Crookston and Duchal to be there on the 19th July, and with him all the barons, gentlemen, and freeholders south of the Forth who should be summoned thereto. Also, that on the day of the king's arrival at Glasgow, the chancellor should proceed to besiege Dumbarton castle with the men of Argyll, Lennox, Menteith, and Strathearn from Tay west; these to be succeeded after twenty days' service by the lords, barons, and men of Angus, Fife, Kinross, Clackmannan, Perthshire from Tay east, Stormonth, Atholl, and Rannoch, to be followed after a similar interval by the Earls of Huntly, Marischal, and Errol, and Lord Forbes, with the men of the Mearns and the country north of the Mounth."

Messengers were sent on the 10th July into Lothian, Tweeddale, and the south, "to warn the country to the siege of Dumbarton," and on the same day the gunners "cartit Mons," the great bombard from the castle of Edinburgh, on its way westward. The transport of heavy artillery over the best roads which then existed was a formidable task. Men were sent before that 'rest the gayt,' *i.e.*, cut the way, and the sheriffs of the district through which they passed were ordered to provide oxen to draw the guns.

"After the reduction of Duchal and Crookston the siege of Dumbarton made little progress though relays of the feudal army had succeeded each other. Fresh levies were therefore summoned from the west and south to assemble at Glasgow moor, and on the 18th of October the king proceeded to press the siege in person. The besieging force having been driven from the shelter of the town, had fallen back upon Dunglass castle, about 3 miles from Dumbarton castle, which, repaired and strengthened, was made the base of operations. Here the chief officers of state were in camp, each having a certain number of men, for whom wages were received from the Treasurer, and hither materials for the siege were quickly collected, the great gun Duchal being brought from Arkil near Paisley, and boats, conveyed overland, from Daldres (Grangemouth) and Blackness.

" Messengers were in the meantime gathering in the contributions granted by the ' kyrkmen ' for the wages of Dunglass, and summoning fresh levies. The castle of Dumbarton surrendered early in December, and the same year, 1489, the king kept Yule at Edinburgh."

Entries in the Treasurer's books connected with Dunglass are as follows :—

" 1489. Oct. 22. Item in Glesco to the King xxiij. Item till a caryage man to pass to Edenburght for powder to Dunglasse xij s.

" Do. 31. Item to thre boytis that brocht the gun called Duchal frae Archkil to Dunglas vj. Item to the master of household and the lords witht him at Dunglas the first xj. days j^cxiij. Item to werkmen as maid up the walls of Dunglas xj.

" Nov. 20. Item to Ormond Herald to passe in Fyf and Anguse to the Kyrkmen for the wages of Dunglas xxj. Item to Schaw the currour to passe one the suthsyde the water for the samyn.

" Do. 24. Item giffin the chancellor (Earl of Argyl) the chamerlane (Alex. Home of Home) and Lord Drummond for their wages in Dunglas xxiij. dais j^cxxx lb."

The old castle continued to be occupied as a place of residence by the Colquhoun family in the following century, as appears from feudal charters granted by them to their vassals, from the castle of Dunglass, in the year 1511 and subsequently. In the same century the manor of Dunglass is mentioned in the gift by King James the Fifth, of 30th June, 1541. September 16th, 1568, Lord Sempil was "charged to intromit with Dunglas and to be kept in His Highness' name (The Regent)." In 1591 John Colquhoun, parson in Kilpatrick, Walter Colquhoun of Barnhill, and Walter Colquhoun and James and Adam Colquhoun in Milton, were included in a bond against molestation from the Clan M'Farlane. In the beginning of the next century it is also frequently mentioned as a residence of the Colquhouns. When King James the Sixth, moved by the formidable incursions of the M'Gregors into the lands of Luss, dispensed with the provisions of an act of parliament forbidding the carrying of arms, and on 1st September, 1602, granted license to Alexander Colquhoun of Luss and his tenants and dependants to carry arms for their defence in any part above the water of Leven, he extended the same liberty to the said Laird's place of Dunglass and lands of Colquhoun. In the Privy Council Records for the years 1593-1608 (page 482) a confirmation to John Colquhoun, son of Alexander

Colquhoun, appears. It reads as follows:—" 1st Feb., 1602. Confirmation to John Colquhoun, son of Alex. Colquhoun of Luss. Terras et barenoriam de Colquhoun cum manrie loco de Dunglas, molendinis, etc.; terras de Gartscube cum manerie loco, molendinis, piscatioribus tenentibus, etc., vic Dumbartone."

After the memorable conflict of Glenfruin in 1603, the depositions of various persons were taken in the presence of Alexander Colquhoun and a Notary Public at Dunglass. The castle of Dunglass, though less important for military purposes than the castle of Dumbarton, which from its strong situation by nature afforded great advantage both for attack and defence, was yet, from its position as commanding the passage of Clyde, regarded as of no small military importance, and in times of civil commotion each of the conflicting parties was eager to possess it.

The following entry appears in the Memorabilia of the City of Glasgow Council records (fol. 106):—"
16th 1640. The said day ordains Johne Kirkwood to goe out with the companie who are direct for ane recrew to Capt. Porterfield and to convoy to Dunglass to the armie."

The Covenanters, in their struggles with Charles First, having gained possession of the castles of Dumbarton and Dunglass, garrisoned and provisioned them in order to strengthen themselves against Montrose, who, with unremitting efforts, was endeavouring to collect the northern clans around the royal standard. In 1646, in the month of June, General Leslie, on behalf of the Lords of the Covenant, garrisoned the castle with an ensign, a sergeant, and thirty privates.

The surrender of Dumbarton * and Rossdhu castles to Oliver Cromwell, in 1652 and 1653 respectively—the latter belonging to the Colquhoun family, who stoutly fought against the famous Ironsides—was the last occurrence of any military importance on the Clyde, and judging from the measure of retribution dealt out on similar occasions, we may safely infer that Dunglass castle owes its ruinous state to Oliver's soldiers. In this we are supported by the reference to Oliver Cromwell in Maitland's "History of Scotland," published the following century; and possibly it was this probable destruction of the building that led Pennant to connect it in error with the destruction of the castle of the same name in Haddingtonshire, which was blown up in 1640 by the treachery of a page, the Earl of Haddington and others losing their lives by the explosion.

---

* "Upon the fyft day of Januar being Handsell Monday 1652 the Castell of Dumbartane was cowartlie renderit sa now the Englisches has all the thrie castellis strengthis of this nation in thair power that ar most considerable."— "Nicoll's Diary," page 79, as quoted. "Letters from Roundhead Officers." "Bannatyne Club Publications."

In the year 1703, 27th June, Dunglass witnessed the gathering of the military tenantry of Argyle, summoned there according to the common form used on such occasions, in order to accompany the remains of Archibald, first Duke of Argyle, and those of his father and grandfather, to the family place of interment at Kilmun. A suitable entertainment was provided for the numerous company, and after the remains of the Marquis and Earl were shown, their heads being properly disposed in the coffins, they were put on board of a principal barge, decorated with suitable devices, and with vassals marshalled under their various chiefs, bagpipes playing, and Dumbarton castle saluting with minute guns, the procession sailed down the Clyde.*

When the castle of Dunglass fell into a ruinous state it sustained great injury, not only from being entirely neglected, but from wanton destruction. In the year 1735, when the taste for preserving ancient ruins had hardly any existence, the Commissioners of Supply for the County of Dumbarton recommended some of the freestone of the old ruinous house of Dunglass to be used in repairing the quay there at the expense of the county. This Gothic barbarity continued to be ruthlessly perpetrated under various pretexts while the castle

---

* An Account of the Depredations committed on the Clan Campbell and their followers during the years 1685 and 1686, page 123.   Edinburgh, 1816.

and lands continued the property of the Edmonstones
of Duntreath, who acquired them in 1732 ; but in 1812,
Mr. Andrew Buchanan of Silverbanks acquired by a feu-
disposition from Sir Charles Edmonstone the farm and
lands of Dunglass, Littlemill, castle and shore thereof,
for a payment of a feu duty of £5 sterling yearly,
and at once put a stop to the destruction of the
castle, and partially restored what remained of it. The
only portions of the old castle now remaining are the
south-west wall next the Clyde, and the north-east wall
with the doorway.   On the south-east side of the west
wall was a battery full of arrow holes, which commanded
the river.   This battery fell into the Clyde on the night
of the 23rd March, 1823, during a terrific gale.   The
conical dovecote to the east of the battery is still
entire, and it, along with the building on the west,
forming the lower portion of the tower, evidently belongs
to the 16th century.   The form of a shield rudely
carved on the northern turret seems to belong to that
period.   The initials V.C may be those of Sir H.
Colquhoun who was killed at the battle of Banachra.
It is said the original stronghold of the Colquhouns
stood near Middleton farm, Milton of Colquhoun, an
old building standing on the eastern slope of Dumbuck
hill being still known as Colquhoun house, and that
its stones were employed to build the castle of Dun-

glass. The site of Dunglass being so commanding
has led many writers to think that the Romans
would make it one of their most important fortresses
to protect their shipping in Bowling Bay in the
immediate neighbourhood. Doctor Jamieson seems
inclined to honour Dunglass with being the Alcluith
of the ancient Britons. He writes, " With abundant
propriety might Dunglass be denominated Petra Cloithe,
as being a rocky height on the margin of the flood,
and although the designation may seem still more
applicable to Dumbarton because of the striking appearance, it may be questioned whether this is of sufficient
importance to overbalance other objections."

In Sliezer's "Theatrum Scotiæ" (1690), the illustration of Dumbarton Rock is from Kilpatrick, and
shows Dunglass castle to have a large square tower with
smaller buildings attached. No view of Dunglass, previous
to its partial destruction, is known to exist. In the introduction to the 1874 edition of this antique work, Dr.
Jamieson, already quoted, writes (folio 20), "Mr. Buchanan
of Auchentorlie says there are the remains of lines similar
to the Roman wall running in a north-west direction from
Dunglass castle to the top of the hill, near the line of the
Temple in the wood. At the top there are vestiges of
building, and in the middle of the wood a mound known
by the name of Trennass castle."

Robt. Balderston.

DUNGLASS CASTLE.

In 1760, Bishop Pocoke, writing of Dunglass, which he visited during his tour in Scotland, says, after referring to Kilpatrick, "A mile further is Dunglass castle, on a rock, three sides of which are covered by the water of the river. There are some fine hewn stones in it. This old castle, which was small, is in ruins."

During the summer of 1888, when considerable repairs were being executed on Dunglass cottage, the incoming tenant, Mr. Donald M'Intosh, found a stone forming the lintel of a window, bearing the initials "W. C." and "M. H." with the Colquhoun arms between; the year 1620 is also cut, and the initials "S. D." stand above all, with a considerable space between the letters.

WINDOW LINTEL.

Irish limestone conveyed to Dunglass in sloops was in the early part of this century calcined at Dunglass, but the kilns were demolished when the demand ceased on account of the Garscadden lime being worked and supplied at cheaper prices.

The derivation of Dunglass is variously given, two of

which are "the grey rock" and "the green rock." In the parish of Strathblane there is a basaltic rock 400 feet high, which, with the castle in Haddingtonshire already mentioned, are the only places with the same nomenclature known of in the Lowlands.

Dunglass castle is classed in Ross and M'Gibbon's work on the Castles of Scotland as belonging to the 3rd period of Scottish architecture, A.D. 1400 to 1542. There used to be an inn at Dunglass which, as already mentioned, was frequented by the storm and tide stayed fly-boats.* In connection with this ancient inn, which was in existence as early as the end of the 16th century, the following advertisement from the *Glasgow Mercury* of 19th July, 1781, is of interest :—

" Robt. Miller, vintner at Dunglass, continues to keep the inn there, lately his father's, and has laid in a good assortment of liquors, &c. The situation is remarkably pleasant, having a most extensive prospect up and down the river Clyde, and travellers can be well accommodated. The stage coach betwixt Glasgow and Dumbarton goes daily ; and, on Saturdays, can set down company at Dunglass from Glasgow at ten forenoon, and take them up at six in the evening, and there are daily opportunities by water. Stables well supplied with corn and hay. On

---

* See page 16.

the shortest notice a boat and net may be had for pleasure on the river."

In the same newspaper for 23rd March, 1780, the following advertisement appears :—

" To be sold by public roup on Saturday, 8th April next, in the house of John Millar, vintner at Dunglass, at 12 midday, a new boat, burden 10 to 15 tons, as she now lyes below Silverbank. She will answer either for a pleasure or packet, for plying on the river, &c. For particulars enquire at John Murray, wright, Silverbank."

A striking feature in the scenery of the river is the obelisk, which stands in the castle gardens, dedicated to the memory of Henry Bell, the father of steam navigation. This monument was erected by public subscription, and was the first public tribute to the memory of this great benefactor. Dunglass cottage was long the residence of Mr. George Mills, who died at Glasgow, 1881, the versatile author of the " Beggars' Benison," 2 vols., 1866, and " Craigclutha," 1 vol., N.D. He had been merchant, shipagent, shipbuilder, and shipowner in his day. His father, William, was one of the earliest promoters of steam navigation on the high seas, and died in 1857; he was Provost of Glasgow 1834 to 1837.

CHAPTER XV.

LANDS OF COLQUHOUN.

THE first notice we have of the lands of Colquhoun is during the reign of Alexander II., 1214-1249, when Maldowen or Malcolm, third Earl of Lennox, who granted the church and lands of Kilpatrick to the Abbey of Paisley, granted a charter of the lands of Colquhoun to Humphrey de Kilpatrick, to be held for the third part of the services of one knight. The charter, which, after the manner of the times, is written in Latin, may be translated as follows:—"To all his friends and men present and to come, Maldowen, Earl of Lennox, greeting. Let all men present and to come know that I have given, granted, and, by this present charter, have confirmed, to Umphredus de Kilpatrick the whole land of Colquhoun by its right division, with all its just pertinents, to be held by him and his heirs of me, and my heirs in feu and heritage, freely, quietly, fully, and honourably in wood and plain, in meadows and pastures, in pools and mills, in fishings, and in all other easements belonging to the foresaid lands, he and his heirs rendering therefrom to me and my heirs the third part of the service of one knight for every service and exaction ; before these witnesses—Sir Walter, Steward of our Lord the King ; Malcolm, my son ; Gillespie Galbraith, Hamelyn, Malcolm, Duncan, my brothers ; Malcolm Reg. ; Doven, my chamberlain ; Fergus Makcomyng, and many others."

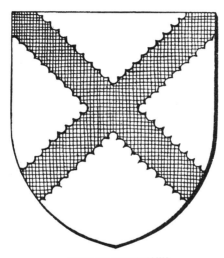

ARMS OF COLQUHOUN.

Argent or saltire engrailed sable.

Sir William Fraser in his " Book of Colquhoun," from which much of the matter contained in this chapter is derived, discusses the probability of Humphrey de Kilpatrick being descended from the family of that name belonging to Dumfries, but he is unable to trace any connection.

In the year 1250 Humphrey of Kilpatrick was witness to a charter by Maldowen, of some pasture lands in the Lennox, to the monks of Paisley. Humphrey first of Colquhoun had a son Ingelram de Colquhoun, who witnessed a charter of Malcolm fourth Earl of Lennox, in favour of Malcolm son and heir of Sir John de Lus, of the lands of Lus, in 1280. His son, Humphrey, is witness in a charter of Malcolm, fifth Earl of Lennox, in favour of Sir John de Lus, which was confirmed by Robert I. in 1316. Sir Robert Colquhoun, son of Humphrey, married, in the reign of David Bruce, the daughter and sole heiress of Humphrey of Lus, and was thereafter, in a charter dated 1368, designated "dominus de Colquhoun et Lus." As usual there has been a good deal of controversy as to the origin and meaning of the name Colquhoun. Mr. Tytler, in his History of Scotland, in the appendix to the second volume, gives an extract from the "Compotum Constabularii de Cardross," vol. I., in the accounts of the Great Chamberlain of Scotland, under date 30th July, 1329. It reads as follows :—
"Item, In construccione cujusdam domus ad opus Culquhanorum Domini Regis, ibidem, 10 soldi." It has been conjectured that this obscure word, Colquhanorum, has to do with the chase, and when we remember that several of the portions of the Colquhoun lands derive their names from the game which formerly abounded in

the district the conjecture is almost verified. We have Dumbuck, the hill of the deer; Glenarbuck, the glen of the deer; and Dunerbuck, similar in meaning to Dumbuck. The old castle or mansion house of the Colquhouns stood on the site of the present farm house of Middleton. This farm was tenanted for centuries by a family called Govan, the last representative of which, who died several years ago, gave a distinct description of the ruins of the old castle. A part of the wall was standing about seventy years ago on the north-east side of the present farm house. It was then as high as a man, while standing on the ground, could reach with his hand. That part of the wall was taken down by the late tenant, Mr. Ferguson. The walls exceeded a yard in thickness, and were so solidly built that, when such portions of them as remained were from time to time removed, the stones were more easily broken than the lime with which they were cemented together. The foundations are represented as having extended over a large area of ground, and part of them were discovered in 1868 in course of excavations being made in connection with agricultural improvements. The portion referred to extends to about 70 feet in length.

To the north-west of the old castle, and below the Muir of Colquhoun, is a knoll or mound called Chapel Knowe. In the centre of this knoll there is the appearance of the foundations of a small building, and the state of the surrounding ground indicates that in early times it had been used as a place of sepulture. A tradition is preserved among the old people in the district that on this knoll a chapel formerly stood, and it is said that part of the walls about 100 years ago remained. Within this century tombstones have been excavated from the ground on the Chapel Knowe. On the south-west side of the Chapel Knowe, and only a few hundred yards from it, is the farm of Chapelton, a name obviously derived from its vicinity to the chapel. From its standing on elevated land it was formerly called High Chapelton, and the lower lands at Milton were called Low Chapelton. High Chapelton is now called Mattockhill.

The lands of Colquhoun extended nearly to the foot of Dumbarton Rock, embracing the hill of Dumbuck, with the adjacent eminences Dunbowie and Dunbar, the lands of Barnhill and Overtoun and Garshake also formed part of the Barony. Wallace is said to have watched the English garrison in Dumbarton Castle from a cave in Dumbuck Hill, while George Buchanan details very particularly, in his History of Scotland, how the Bruce, while going through the wood of Colquhoun on his way to Dumbarton Castle, at the invitation of the Governor, Sir John Monteith, the betrayer of Wallace, was met by a carpenter of the name of Rolland, from the town of Dumbarton, who informed him of an ambush which was laid in the Castle to seize and carry him to England. This timely warning was paid heed to and Bruce saved from an ignominious fate.

The Colquhoun motto, " Si je puis "—If I can—is said to have had its origin in a hunting incident in the vicinity of Dumbarton Castle.

In the year 1533 the lands of Colquhoun were a lordship. In that year a considerable part of the lordship of Colquhoun—namely, the lands of Chapelton, with the mill and mill lands thereof, extending to £10 lands of old extent; the lands of Middleton, extending to 6 merks land of old extent; the lands of Milton, extending to 8 merks of land of old extent; and also a half part of the Mains of Colquhoun, extending to 8 merks, with a half merk land of old extent—were sold by Sir John Colquhoun, 11th of Colquhoun and 13th of Lus, to Laurence Crawford of Kilbirnie, who was infefted in them on the 26th September of that year.

The Colquhouns appear now and again in the burgh records of Dumbarton. The following is an extract dealing with one of the Milton of Colquhoun feuars :—

" Aucht of August, 1631. — Forasmeikle as Patrick Colquhoun in Miltoun of Colquhoun, of set purpose, maliciouslie, on Monday the 1st August inst., cum behind James Fallisdaill's bak, having sword and quhyngr about him and ae staff in his hand, and thair, unbeknawn to the said James, straik him on his heid wi ae staff, to the effusion of his bluid, and that in the horss mercat in the tyme of the fair. Thairfor, seeing it is notour to the provost, baillies, and counsall that thair was na p'icular quarel betwix them, but only that the said Patrick, out of revenge, did the same (he, on a former occasion, requiring to be forcibly put in ward by Fallisdail) : find the action and the wrang dun to them and the burgh, and cocluids that redress be sought by law at the touns chargis."

" 17th Sept., 1632.—Patrick Colquhoun being deadlie sick, and at the poynt of death, craves pardoun for the wrang done by him to the toun."

In 1643 John Colquhoun of Milton was one of the Commissioners for the shire.

By a feu contract dated 31st May, 1672, Sir John Colquhoun of Luss feued off to Robert Colquhoun, in Milton of Colquhoun, one quarter of the lands of the Milton of Colquhoun, and on 13th November, 1695, Sir Humphrey Colquhoun of Luss sold to John Colquhoun of Middleton of Colquhoun the lands of Chapleton, Chapelcroft, Middleton, and Meikle and Little Overtoun. In the early part of the eighteenth century Edmonston of Duntreath possessed the superiority of the lands and

Barony of Colquhoun. On 4th April, 1750, a Precept of Clare Constat was granted by Archibald Edmonston in favour of John Colquhoun, son of John Colquhoun, portioner in Miltoun of Colquhoun, in the one quarter of the lands of Milton of Colquhoun and one quarter of those of Carcaston, now called Dumbuck. The deed is witnessed William Govane in Middleton and Walter Williamson in Mains of Colquhoun.

About this time John Colquhoun, with consent of Elizabeth Williamson, his spouse, sold to Archibald Buchanan of Glasgow, three-fourths part, *pro indiviso*, of the said quarter of Milton and Carcaston lands, and his brother german, Walter Colquhoun, likewise conveyed to Mr. Buchanan his one-fourth part of these lands, with exception of the brewhouse and laigh cellar, to be retained by him in liferent, which had been conveyed to him, 1734, by the said John Colquhoun.

By a feu contract dated at Dunglass, 26th August, 1736, Archibald Edmonstone of Duntreath sold to Andrew Buchanan of Hillington the lands of High and Low Chapelton of Colquhoun with the lands of Hillhead, and the one part of the moor of Colquhoun nearest to the lands, together with the wood of Craigannoch, with the liberty of fowling, hawking, or hunting within the bounds of said lands. The grant reserved the privilege of fowling, hawking, or hunting upon any part of the lands either of moor or dale, and also the privilege of salmon fishing on the Clyde which was not sold.

As showing the obligations of the Colquhoun vassals, the following is taken from a feu charter between Sir Humphrey Colquhoun, Knight and Baronet, and James Colquhoun, executed at Rossdoe on 13th May, 1706, of the Miln of Colquhoun, the Miln lands and pasturage of the Glen of Colquhoun, viz. :—" And also the said James Colquhoun and his foresaids being always obliged to ride with the said Sir Humphrey Colquhoun and foresaids in honest and decent equipage, according to his quality and ability, four journey ilk year, ilk journey not exceeding twenty miles from his own house, upon their own charges and expenses, health of body permitting, and they being always warned to the said ridings, and also the said James Colquhoun and his foresaids compearing to all and sundry the said Sir Humphrey Colquhoun, his courts of the barony of Colquhoun, and thereat to be answerable for all actions of blood, wrong, riots, civil debts, and other actions that shall happen to occur, being always first lawfully warned thereto." * Captain James Colquhoun, Auchentorlie, being one of the witnesses to the feu charter.

---

* Macleod's Clyde District of Dumbartonshire.

There was a mill for grinding victual on this estate which has been incorporated within these last few years with the paper mill.

The dues and multures chargeable at the mill of Colquhoun were—" $\frac{1}{4}$ part peck shellings, $\frac{1}{4}$ part peck meal out of each boll oat shellings, and ane meal peck of sifted meal out of ilk rough boll of bean, pease, or rye it shall happen them to grind.

In 1807 Andrew Millar of Dalnair bought from Charles Edmonstone the superiority of the lands of Connalton, Chapelton, Meikle and Little Overtoun, and one-fourth of Milton of Colquhoun. In 1823 his brother Andrew sold the superiority of these lands to John Cross Buchanan of Auchentoshan, from whom they passed to Auchentorlie.

In 1777 the Muir of Colquhoun was divided amongst the proprietors of the Colquhoun Barony—Edmonstone of Duntreath; James Buchanan of Drumpellier; Peter Buchanan of Silverbanks; Gabriel Lang, merchant, Greenock, Meikle Overtoun; and William Brock, Little Overtoun.

The boundaries agreed on were: Lands of Connelton— from Connelton yett up to Wester Kelloch, Glenburn, to the Clattering ford; from thence to the march of Dumbarton Muir, near the Toddholes; thence to the Black burn and down said burn to Loch Humphrey;

from thence along Provost Buchanan's Dyke, down the Easter Kelloch glen to the west neuk of Papert Hill; and from thence to Connelton yett.

Lands of Chappelton—On a line to Dumbarton Muir Toddholes and Blacklinn spout; and thence to Rashielea; thence to a pit-stones on the north end of the Holly craig.

James Buchanan was found to have a just right and title of that part of the Muir of Colquhoun enclosed, occupied, and possessed by him and his predecessors without interruption, and commonly called the Provost's park.

Lands of Middleton—By a line from north end of Holly craig to the southmost end of the Black stable; from there to Rashielea; and thence to the pit-stones near the head of Tom's Moss; thence to Balloch brae, and along the brink of the Lang craig to Holly craig.

Little Overtoun—Balloch brae to brink of Lang craig, Meikle Overtoun; from the pit-stones at Carsballoch, along the brink of the Lang craig opposite to Craigneckhead dyke; thence to Garshake burn; thence to Blacklinn spout; and from there to Rashielea and Carsballoch.

Towards the end of last century a manufactory for bleaching and calico printing was established in Milton of Colquhoun, and it is a fact worthy of notice that the first factory for weaving cloth by power other than by hand was erected here and continued in operation many years. In 1792 Macdowall & Co., who came of an old Renfrewshire family, owned the works, and they were then so extensive that we find many references to the size and importance of the business in the diaries of English travellers * who were passing too and from the Highlands by the Dumbarton road. In 1817 Mr. Patrick Mitchell purchased the works and improved on the methods of working them. On his death, in 1848, his nephews and successors, Messrs. Muter & Millar, created further improvements by introducing machinery, and carried on the business until 1864 when Mr. Millar retired, having been bought out, and thereafter Mr. Muter relinquished the trade. After lying idle for some time, the buildings were remodelled and made suitable for a paper manufacturing business, which was carried on by various firms without much success until 1893, when they were shut up.

BARNHILL.

To the north - west of Dumbuck is the estate of Barnhill, which since the 16th century has been in the

---

* Lettice's Tour in Scotland, 1792.   Stoddart's Local Scenery and Manners in Scotland, 1799-1800.

possession of the Colquhouns and their descendants; but the probability is, judging from its modern appellation, that it formed part of the lands of Colquhoun as originally granted during the reign of Alexander II., receiving the name of Barnhill on its being handed over to a cadet of the family.

In 1543 John Colquhoun of Luss granted a feu charter of the wester half of Barnhill to John Colquhoun in Milton of Colquhoun and to Janet Lang, his wife. Walter, their son, succeeded, and was infeft in 1555. He was twice married, first to Janet Wright, and second to Isobel Douglas. He and his son John were slain at Glenfruin along with others of his clan.

On 20th January, 1604, Allaster M'Gregor of Glenstrae, and several others, stood trial, and were condemned to be hung, for the part taken by them in the conflict of Glenfruin. They were charged for having " Slauchteris, schamefullie, crewallie, and barbaruslie murderit and slew Walter Colquhoun of Barnhill; John Colquhoun, younger, thereof; John Colquhoun, Dalmure; and dyvers vtheris persons, etc., etc."

Walter Colquhoun, son of the above-mentioned, was infefted in the lands of Barnhill, with Margaret Logan, his future spouse, on 25th January, 1610. Several years after this, we learn from the Register of the Privy Council that a complaint was lodged by Alexander

DUMBOWIE HILL FORT.

Colquhoun of Luss . . . and by Patrick Colquhoun of Auchintullie (Auchentorlie?), and Walter Colquhoun, now of Barnhill, "as oy to umquhill Waltir Colquhoun of Barnhill, his guidsir, and as sone to umquhill Johnne Colquhoun of Barnhill, his father, with the remanent kin and freindis of the saidis umquhill John Colquhoun, feur, of Auchintullie (Auchentorlie?), umquhill Walter Colquhoun of Barnehill, and umquhill Johnne Colquhoun, his sone," etc., etc., against the Earl of Argyll, as responsible for a number of the Macgregors, and their associates, who had committed slaughters and depredations on pursuers, "all herreit (harried) and put to beggerie be the Clan Gregour, to the number of fyve hundreth men, wemen, and childrene"; the Earl was assoilzied.

In the Burgh Records of Dumbarton we find the following notice:—"1630. June 19th. Decimo nono June. Anent the actioun perseuit be James Tailyeir againe Walter Colquhoun of Barnhill for twentie shillings for lintseid, and againe David Scot, Cowpar, for 13s. 4d. for the same, thay alleg^t the seid was not sufficient nor evir grew, and as they lost thair crop for the haill yeir, the persewir ought to satisfy them for skaith sustenit. Defenders absoluit." *

"Quarto May, 1631.—Walter Colquhoun of Barnhill decerned in the unlaw of 10 pounds for extending beyond his mairch." †

---

* † Irving's History of Dumbartonshire, fol. 495 and 498.

Walter, who was one of the Commissioners for the shire in 1643, by a second marriage with Jean Colquhoun, had issue, a son, James of Barnhill, who married and had three sons—James, Humphrey, and Alexander. The wester half of the lands of Barnhill were in possession of the family till 1696, and were added to by the fore-mentioned James acquiring the easter half in behoof of his brothers. He married, and, having no prospect of a family, conveyed the property, between the years 1734 and 1739, in favour of his brother Humphrey, a bailie of Dumbarton, who married twice, and had one son, Walter, his heir, and two daughters; Margaret married to Neil Campbell, Sheriff-Substitute of Dumbartonshire, and had three sons and three daughters—Alexander, of Barnhill, Sheriff-Substitute of Renfrewshire; Humphrey Walter, of Crosslet, late Sheriff-Substitute of Dumbartonshire; and Ilay, who died at age of 19. Sheriff Neil Campbell's daughters were— Susan, unmarried; Grace Williamson, married Alexander Smith; and Elizabeth, married Robert Mackenzie of Caldarvan, had four sons, only two survived—R. D. Mackenzie and Walter. Janet married Rev. James Oliphant, minister of Dumbarton. Walter Colquhoun was infeft in Barnhill in 1798 on a precept of clare constat from Archibald Edmonstone of Duntreath; he died unmarried in 1827. He was succeeded by his nephew, Alexander Campbell, who married Fanny, daughter of

Robert Orr, and had two sons—(1) Neil Colquhoun Campbell, born October 17, 1813 ; (2) Robert Orr Campbell, born 1815 ; and six daughters—(1) Janet, (2) Margaret, wife of the late Rev. James Begg, D.D., Free Church, Newington, with issue (surviving) two sons and a daughter ; (3) Fanny, married to the late James White, Esq., of Overtoun, with issue, one son, John Campbell White of Overtoun, now first Lord Overtoun, and six daughters ; (4) Susan, married to R. D. Mackenzie, Esq., of Caldarvan, with issue, one son and five daughters; (5) Elizabeth, married to Walter M'Kenzie, Esq., of Edenbarnet, with issue (surviving), two sons and two daughters ; (6) Alexander Grace, married to Andrew Jameson, Esq., with issue (surviving) one son. On 2nd October, 1862, Sheriff Alexander Campbell of Barnhill died, aged 86, and his eldest son, Neil Colquhoun Campbell, Sheriff of Ayrshire, succeeded to the family property. He married Mary Paterson, daughter of William Orr Paterson, Esq., of Montgomerie, Ayrshire, surviving issue a daughter, Annie Colquhoun Campbell. Sheriff Neil Colquhoun Campbell died 3rd April, 1883, and his daughter has succeeded to the family estates.

LANDS OF OVERTOUN OF COLQUHOUN.

I.—LITTLE OVERTOUN.

In 1657 the lands of Overtoun are mentioned in the County Valuation Roll as belonging to the Laird of Luss.

In 1736 Little Overtoun was bought at public roup from Archibald Edmonston of Duntreath by James Brock in Upper Dalnotter, the deed of sale being dated at Edenbarnet 28th August. The boundaries between Little and Meikle Overtoun, which hitherto had been undefined, were at this period settled by four honest men. The rent of Little Overtoun at this time is stated to be £80 15s. 8d. Scots and 3 bolls of meal and 4 bolls of bear. In 1763 William Brock, son and heir of the deceased James Brock, was infeft in the lands, and in 1779 he granted a disposition of the lands (subject to a right to redeem them within 15 years) to his uncle William Govan.

In 1780 William Govan sold the lands to James Donald, Dalnotter, who, the same year, parted with them to George Lang, merchant, Dumbarton. In 1802 George Lang disposed of the lands to James Lang, merchant, Dumbarton, who in turn in 1828 conveyed them to Archibald Buchanan of Hillington.

II.—MEIKLE OVERTOUN.

As with Little Overtoun, the lands of Meikle Overtoun with part of the Muir of Colquhoun were bought in 1736 from Archibald Edmonston of Duntreath. James Duncanson in Garshake was the purchaser, but in 1761 he sold them to Gabriel Lang, merchant in Greenock, in whose family they remained until they were sold in

1860 to James White, Esq., by G. Hamilton Lang. James White of Overtoun, second son of John White of Shawfield, Rutherglen, was born in 1812. In the early part of his business career he was a member of the firm of Couper & White, lawyers, until 1851, when he joined his father and elder brother, John, in the Shawfield Chemical Works. A successful man of business, and one of the foremost men of the time in Glasgow, Mr. White was in a position to erect a magnificent mansion, in the baronial· style, on the Overtoun lands, and to effect vast improvements on the estate. As already mentioned, he married, 7th September, 1836, Fanny, daughter of Sheriff Campbell of Barnhill, and had issue six daughters and one son—(1) John Campbell; (2) Fanny Campbell; (3) Jessie; (4) Susan Campbell; (5) Jane Campbell, deceased; (6) Margaret Campbell, deceased; (7) Elizabeth Campbell, deceased. On his decease, 8th March, 1884, a statue was erected by his friends and admirers at the entrance to the Necropolis of Glasgow. Mrs. White died, 18th January, 1891.

John Campbell White, born at Hayfield in November, 1843, was educated at the Garnethill Training School and at Glasgow University, where he graduated as M.A. in 1864. On 18th September, 1867, he married Grace Eliza, eldest daughter of J. H. Maclure, Esq., writer, Glasgow. They resided at Crosslet House, near Dumbarton, until the lamented decease of his father and mother, when they removed to Overtoun. On 23rd June, 1893, Mr. Campbell White was created a Peer of the Realm by Mr. Gladstone and assumed the title of Baron Overtoun of Overtoun. In politics a Liberal, Lord Overtoun holds office as President of the Dumbartonshire Liberal Association, in which position he has rendered eminent service to the party.

It is as a philanthropist, and as the foremost leader in all that tends to the social and religious welfare of the people, that Lord Overtoun is best known.

Lord Overtoun's arms are given on the dedication page by the collotype process. Or, an eagle displayed between three quatrefoils, two and one azure, on a chief engrailed of the last, a besant between two garbs or. Crest—an arm embossed proper, a hand grasping two branches of laurel in orle vert fruited or. Motto (over the crest)—"Virtute." Supporters—on either side an eagle, wings elevated azure, each charged on the breast with a quatrefoil and standing on a garb bendwise or.

DUMBUCK.

In 1815 Sir Charles Edmonston sold to General Thomas Geils, Madras Artillery, of Ardmore, the lands of Middleton of Colquhoun, with the park and Mains of Middleton as possessed by William and Robert Govan and Peter Scott; the lands of Milton of Colquhoun and Carcaston, now called Dumbuck, and the lands of Easter, Upper, and Lower Colquhoun.

Ten years later General Geils' trustees sold the Middleton lands to Archibald Buchanan of Hillington, retaining the others which now form the estate of Dumbuck.

There is a cave on the west side of Dumbuck Hill called Thomas of Ercildoun, or Thomas the Rhymer's cave, and tradition has it that William Wallace, with his companions, occupied a hollow on the front of the the hill on several occasions.

ÇOPED TOMBSTONE, OLD KILPATRICK CHURCHYARD (see page 103).

CHAPTER XVI.

LANDS OF DALNOTTER,* AUCHENTOSHAN, DALMUIR, AND DUNTOCHER.

DALNOTTER.

DURING the reign of Alexander II., 1249-1285, the lands of Dalnotter were held by Hugh Flandrensis or Fleming, who inherited them from his father, whom it is conjectured was Malcolm Fleming who witnessed the deed of gift of the church of Largs to the Abbey of Paisley by Walter the High Stewart, who died in 1246. Malcolm is styled vicecomes or sheriff, which shows that thus early he had been appointed to the high office of sheriff of the Lennox, an honour more ancient than the earldom of Lennox itself.

In 1288 Duncan, Earl of Fife, held this office, and William Fleming, presumably of Dalnotter, was constabularis or collector of dues.

Originally from Flanders,† the Flemings, who were the

---

* Often Dalnottar.   † Hunter's History of Fleming, fol. 464.

greatest trading people of their day, passed into England, and having there taken part in the civil wars between Stephen and Henry II., they were banished by the latter and took refuge in Scotland, and entered into the service of David I., who, from his munificence in endowing ecclesiastical foundation with grants from Crown lands, was styled by James VI. as "ane sair sanct for the Croun."

Towards the end of the 13th century the family of the Flemings of Dalnotter seems to have merged into that of Biggar in Lanarkshire, a Fleming having married a daughter of Sir Nicolas de Biggar, and, receiving with her the lands of Biggar, became the progenitor of the family of Fleming who possessed Biggar estate for some centuries.

Robert Fleming, who is supposed to be son of Malcolm, sheriff of Lennox, supported the Bruce in his endeavours to free Scotland from the power of Edward. According to Hollinshed, whose histories were published in 1577, Fleming, when Bruce enquired if Comyn was dead— whom he had just stabbed in the church of Greyfriars, Dumfries—lifted up the bloody head and exclaimed, "let the deed shaw," an expression which was adopted as the motto on the crest of the Lords of Biggar. Robert died previous to 1314. His son Malcolm was a warm supporter of Robert Bruce, and no doubt was

present with his retainers at Bannockburn. In consideration of his services his Dalnotter possessions
were augmented by the grant of several estates in the
Lennox, among others the Barony of Kirkintilloch and
other lands.   Bruce also appointed him to the office
of Sheriff of the Lennox and Governor of Dumbarton
castle.   King Robert spent the declining years of his
reign at Cardross, in our neighbourhood, where he had
built a hunting lodge for himself, receiving the attentions
of the lords and barons who had fought with him for
the independence of Scotland.

Malcolm Fleming was succeeded by his son Malcolm,
who remained steadfast to David II., the youthful son of
Bruce, and succeeded his father as keeper of Dumbarton
Castle.   This Malcolm fought at Halidon Hill in 1333
and was fortunate enough to escape, and fled to his
strong Castle of Dumbarton.   On the 9th November,
1341, Malcolm, for his services to the Crown, was
raised to the dignity of Earl of Wigtown.   He died
about the year 1362, and was succeeded by his grandson
Thomas, second Earl of Wigtown.   On account of a
quarrel with the native population Thomas disposed
of his lands, privileges, and titles to Wigtownshire to
Archibald Douglas; the deed conveying these lands is
dated 8th February, 1371.   Thomas, on demitting the
title, took up his abode at Fulwood, on the banks of

the Gryffe, in Renfrewshire. The successor of Thomas Fleming was Sir Malcolm Fleming of Biggar, who was appointed by David II. sheriff of the Lennox in 1364.

Sir Malcolm left two sons, David and Patrick. Patrick, in April, 1369, exchanged his lands of Dalnotter and Garscadden for the lands of Bord, etc., near Croy, belonging to Sir Robert Erskine, whose ancestors from time immemorial were proprietors of Erskine estate.

As mentioned in page 202, Isabella Fleming of Dalnotter granted to Sir Robert Erskine a charter of the land of Auchintorlie and Dunnerbuck. Some years later (1372), as we learn from the burgh records of Dumbarton, Patrick de Greym, son and heir of Sir David de Greym, "dominus de Dundaff," engaged to support a chaplain at the altar of the Holy Cross in the parish church of Dumbarton for the soul of Isabella Fleming, "quoad omnia de Dalnotter," and for the souls of his parents, of himself, and of all the faithful dead, and for which pious purpose he disposed of the lands of "Kyllemonethdam et Kyllerman" in the Earldom of Lennox, which had been conveyed to him by the foresaid Isabella with a penalty of 20 lib. in case of failure.

Dalnotter remained, as part of the Erskine estate, in possession of the same family till 1638, when it was sold to Sir John Hamilton of Orbiston, whose grandson

William Hamilton sold it in 1703 to Walter, Lord Blantyre. During the latter part of last century Lower Dalnotter was in the possession of the Campbells of Succoth, who sold it again to the present Lord Blantyre's father.

The mansion of Dalnotter was built by the present Lord Blantyre on the site of the old house. Monipenny, writing in the 17th century, describes Dalnotter as one of the strong places in the Lennox.

The estate is bounded on the west by the Lusset burn, on the south by the river, and on the east by the Mount Blow and Auchentoshan lands, and on the north by Kilpatrick Moor. North Dalnotter farm, presently tenanted by Mr. John Bowman, who has succeeded his late father James, was called at one time by the country people Toddal or Tittal Bog.* In this farm is included the old steading of Gowkstane, the ruins of which are to be seen on the hillside east from the abandoned steading of Burnbrae. At the burnside, where the Duntocher Road passes through the estate, there stood a few houses called Sandyford, and it was here, in 1793, when the road was being improved and a bridge built, that a sculptured stone was found which hitherto had been used as a footbridge over the burn.

* See page 158.

It was removed to Mount Blow House garden, where it stood until the purchase of the property by the Corporation of Glasgow, when, for its safety, it was lodged in the Kelvingrove Museum. As late as 1757 there were two such stones forming a footbridge at Sandyford, Maitland * having carefully measured them when investigating the line of the Roman Wall. Where the other stone has gone to, a strict search at this late date has failed to discover.

Towards Duntocher stood the Dalnotter Ironworks, where wrought-iron goods of all sorts were manufactured on an extensive scale. In 1811 four water-wheels were employed, and 400 hands found occupation at an average wage of 2s. 8d. per day, which was then considered a capital wage. About 2500 tons of coal were annually consumed, the cost of which was reckoned at 11s. 10d. per ton.†

In 1681 the lands of Dalnotter and Garscadden, with the mills and fishings in Clyde, were created a Barony in favour of William Hamilton of Orbiston.

AUCHENTOSHAN.

As already mentioned, this estate was included in the lands of the Abbey of Paisley. As early as 1516 we

---

* See page 35.   † Old Statistical Account.

learn from the Abbey Rental Roll that there were tenants of the name of Johnstone of Affleck or Auchinleck, who retained part of the lands until 1767, when they sold them to George Buchanan. In 1551 Robert Hamilton appears as tenant, and also James Johnstone, with several others.

James, first Earl of Abercorn, feued, in 1612, half of the estate to Matthew Hamilton, son of Andrew Hamilton of Cochno, he having been tenant for some years previously. As early as 6th September, 1602, Matthew Hamilton of Auchentoshan summoned Alexander Colquhoun of Luss before the Privy Council to answer a complaint regarding two mares, worth £40 Scots each, which John Buchanan *alias* M'Wattie (for whom Colquhoun had become cautioner) had witheld, the said mares having been sent to the "gersing." Neither Colquhoun nor M'Wattie appeared before the Council, and were duly "put to the horn." On the 29th September, however, John Logan of Drumchapel appeared for the delinquents before the King and Council, and gave bond for 300 merks that they would appear on the 16th November following. The deed registered by Mr. Humpra Blinschele, advocate, is subscribed at Dunglass, 27th September, 1602, before Matthew Colquhoun, burgess in Glasgow; Alexander Colquhoun, son of Alexander Colquhoun, in Hill (Hole?); John Colquhoun, parson in Kilpatrick; and Mungo Darleith, servitor to the Laird of Luss.

Matthew's son, William Hamilton of Auchentoshan, married Jean, daughter of John Stirling of Law, and was succeeded by his daughter, Jean. William Hamilton's tombstone still lies in the Auchentoshan enclosure in Kilpatrick churchyard with the date 1666.* In 1657 William Johnstone's portion of Auchentoshan was valued at £30 and William Hamilton's at £80 Scots yearly. Jean Hamilton married Walter Buchanan of Moss, grandson of John Buchanan, who, in 1625, had a disposition of the lands of Moss from "his loving cousin and friend," Walter Buchanan of Drumikill. They were

TABLET ON AUCHENTOSHAN HOUSE.

paternally descended from Walter, who, before 1394, was the 13th Laird of Buchanan. Their son, Walter Buchanan of Moss and Auchentoshan, married, in 1696, Rebecca (with a tocher of 3000 merks), second daughter

---

* See page 105.

of Gabriel Hamilton of Westburn by his wife Margaret, daughter of Sir Robert Cunningham of Gilbertfield. On the 6th March, 1745, George Buchanan of Moss and Auchentoshan, and Mary, his wife, daughter of George Buchanan, bailie of Glasgow, and son of Andrew Buchanan of Gartacharan, a cadet of Leny, and ancestor of Drumpelier, Auchentorlie, and Craigends, had from Archibald Buchanan of Drumikill a charter of confirmation of the lands of Moss, dated at the mansion house of Auchentoshan, in presence of the following witnesses— James Hamilton of Barns, James Hamilton of Hutcheson, Hugh Spreull Crawford of Coudonhill, Aula M'Aulay of Ardencaple, James Anderson of Stobcross, John Spreull of Milton, and John Stirling of Law.

In 1793 Anne Buchanan, daughter and heiress of Neil Buchanan of Moss and Auchentoshan, married William Cross, West India merchant, Glasgow,* and was succeeded by their eldest son, John Cross Buchanan, who married Jean, daughter of Andrew Wardrop, younger of Torbanehill. He died July, 1839, a premature grave closing over him at the age of 36. In 1833, Mr. Cross Buchanan published a volume of poems entitled "Edith"

---

* An interesting footnote, in Vol. I., page 544, of Gordon's "Glasgow Facies" gives particulars of the Cross family back to the year 1663. Sheriff Cross, one of the members of the family, an eminent agriculturist, is said to have been the first who introduced the cultivation of turnips in the fields in the neighbourhood of Glasgow in 1756.

of more than average merit; two songs, written by him, are to be found in "Whistle Binkie."* In 1827, he built a new front, and made other alterations on the old mansion-house of Auchentoshan. John Cross Buchanan left four

ARMS OF CROSS BUCHANAN.

Quarters 1st and 4th for Buchanan—Or, a lion rampant sable, holding in the dexter forepaw a cinquefoil ermine, within a double tressure fleury and counterfleury of the second. 2nd and 3rd quarters for Cross—argent, a raven, wings endorsed proper, between four cross crosslets fitchée gu.

sons and three daughters—(1) William Cross Buchanan, C.E., engineer-in-chief of the Mexican Railway, which great work, of eight years' duration, was completed under his superintendence in 1873. Married Mary King, in Valparaiso, and died in 1891 leaving issue, one son,

---

John Peter, and five daughters, the eldest of whom, Edith, seems to have inherited the poetical genius of her grandfather. (2) Anna Boleyn; married Thomas Craig Christie, Esq., of Bedlay, Lanarkshire, and has issue, two sons and four daughters. (3) John, eleven years H.B.M. Vice-Consul, and for many years an important merchant in Mexico. (4) Marian Amy Ann, unmarried, resident in Helensburgh. (5) Hector, married, tea planter, Ceylon. (6) Walter, married, tea planter, Ceylon. (7) Susan, unmarried, resident in Edinburgh. In 1810 and 1827, Mr. William Dunn of Duntocher acquired fully 8 acres of that land, with the burn; and on Mr. Cross Buchanan's decease his trustees sold Auchentoshan to William Dunn for the sum of £21,000. On the death of William Dunn, he was succeeded by his only surviving brother, Alexander, who died in 1860, and in 1873 his trustees sold Auchentoshan, for £27,000, to James, eldest son (by Sarah, daughter of the late George Park, Esq., of Waterside) of Robert Black of Kelvinhaugh, who died 1879; he was grandson of Mrs. Park, only sister of William and Alexander Dunn.

James Black died 1889, unmarried, and was succeeded by his brother, William Dunn Black, born 1843, who married, 1874, Augusta Charlotte, second daughter of Rev. James Bush, rector of Ousby, Cumberland, and has issue, three sons.

In the year 1890, when the foundation for an extension of Auchentoshan House was being dug, a small jug of red earthenware with a yellow glazed exterior, with about 60 silver coins of the reigns of Alexander III. and Edward I. was found, the coins being in an excellent state of preservation.

ENGLISH SILVER PENNIES. EDWARD I., 1272-1307

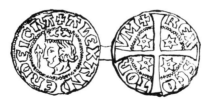

SCOTTISH SILVER PENNY. ALEXANDER III., 1249-1285.
COINS FOUND AT AUCHENTOSHAN.

The lands of Mount Blow, about 24 acres in extent, were feued from Auchentoshan by Robert Donald, Provost of Glasgow, in 1767, who erected the present mansion-house. They were acquired, in 1822, from Bowie's trustees by William Dunn, and, in 1877, the greater portion was sold by Mr. Alexander Dunn Pattison to the Glasgow City Corporation. A distillery erected in the year 1830 stands on Auchentoshan estate, the site having been formerly used as a lint-hole for steeping flax.

DALMUIR.

Sometime about the year 1250 Malcolm, Earl of Lennox, granted to Walter Spreull, who seems to have been his factor or land steward ("senescalli comitis de Lennox") after the resignation of Roger, son and heir of Richard de Dundever, the lands of Dalmore, or, as they are now called, Dalmuir—the grantee performing the foreign service of the king as much as pertained to a quarter of a plough in the Lennox The said Walter Spreull in the year 1296 signified his allegiance to Edward I. by signing the "Ragman" Roll at Berwick on Tweed. The Spreulls were also possessed of the lands of Cowdon and Dalchurn. Not much is known of them in connection with the Dalmuir lands until the year 1509, when we find John Sprewle, laird of Coldoun, mortgaging 2½ merks worth of land of the £5 lands of old extent of Dalmure, lying next the water of Clyde, to Sir Dionysius Auchinleck, chaplain in the church of the preaching friars, Glasgow. The debt was discharged on 10th November, 1512.

Sometime before this Dalmuir was the scene of a spulzie characteristic of the distracted and troubled state of the county. The matter is thus referred to in the Lennox Charters, vol. ii., folio 142 :—" Deliverance by Robert, Lord Lyle, Sir John de Ross of Halkhead, and others, upon the compromise entered into by John, Earl of Lennox, and Sir John Sempill, 16th March, 1491." They agreed to become friends, and " as for the corn and hay taen out of Dalmuir to the instis costis, we consall and ordayns the said Master Matthew (son of the Earl of Lennox) to geff to the Laird of Coldoun fourty bollis of attis (oats) betwixt and the next Martymes ; and for the hay to geff at is was pryst be sworn men in tyme, xx^s."

On 3rd December, 1553, Lord Semple received a grant from the Privy Council of "al and hail the ten pound land of Dalmuir."

The Dalmuir lands were long held by the Spreulls, the latest writ amongst the Smollett papers, dated 17th January, 1621, being an instrument of sasine in favour of James Spreull of Coldoun of the lands of Dalchurn and Dalmuir.

As we have already mentioned * the Spreulls were

* See page 88.

tenants under the Abbey—Edenbarnet and Duntocher lands being partly held by them. Passing from the Spreulls about the year 1728, the Dalmuir lands were possessed by various proprietors until the late William Dunn of Duntocher purchased them from the heirs of Alan Dreghorn of Ruchill, and in 1828 from the heirs of Mrs. Hamilton Dundas. About the year 1765 paper works were erected by Edward Collins, who came from England, and were carried on by him for a long time. In 1793 he employed some 84 persons, not only in papermaking, but also in bleaching cloth, which he advertised as being done after the Irish manner.

At the end of last century Lord Dundas, under the superintendence of the Earl of Dundonald, who was in his knowledge of chemistry far ahead of his time, erected works for the manufacture of soda on a large scale from soapmakers' leys which were formerly run off as waste. Latterly Messrs. Charles Todd & Co. were the proprietors of these works, and afterwards Messrs. C. Tennant & Co., who removed the business to St. Rollox, Glasgow. In 1845 there were 80 to 100 persons employed by Messrs. Todd.

In 1859 part of the land on which these works stood was feued to the Clyde Trustees, who erected thereon workshops and slip for the repair of the dredging plant used in connection with the river.

Dalmuir House, erected by Richard Collins on a feu from the Boquhanran lands about 1818, was sold by Edward Collins, his son, to Mr. William Dunn. The house and some 70 to 80 acres are held by the trustees for Mr. A. Dunn Pattison.

LANDS OF BOQUHANRAN.

The £8 lands of Boquhanran and Auchengree, forming part of the Abbey possessions, were feued * to William Edmeston, a cadet of the family of Duntreath, and on the occasion of the marriage of Sir James Edmonstone of Duntreath to Margaret, second daughter of Sir John Colquhoun of Luss, they were by a Crown charter conveyed to that lady who was duly infeft on 12th and 13th February, 1585.

Of the chapel † that stood on these lands nothing remains unless, perchance, ‡ an old corbelled stone which now surmounts one of the outhouses of the farm of North East Boquhanran. Of the Aitkens who held the chapel land under the Abbey none now remain; but until very recently § there were representatives of that family residing in the neighbourhood. William Dunn acquired Boquhanran from Sir Charles Edmonston of

---

Duntreath, who died in 1821. Auchengree was sold in 1815 to George Wilson. On Mr. Alexander Dunn's decease Boquhanran became the property of the heirs-at-law, William Park, John Macindoe and his twin brother George Park Macindoe.

DUNTOCHER.

The lands of Duntiglennan, Duntocher, Faifley, Auchinleck, and Braidfield, are all named in the Abbey Rental Book already referred to,* and after the Reformation passed into the possession of various parties. Granted heritably with the other Abbey lands to Lord Claud Hamilton, commendator of Paisley, they were sold to Sir William Hamilton of Orbiston in 1638, who, on 13th February, 1643, had a charter from the Crown erecting into a free Baronie and Regality, among other lands, those of " Duntiglennan, Bowwarthill, Easter and Wester Cochnochs, Duntocher, with the Corne Milnes and Walk Milnes thereof, Milnlands, Multures, and Milne dewties and pertinents of the samen. The lands of Milnetoun, Milnecroft, Edinbarnet, Craigbargeoch, Auchinleck, Ffairclay, Braidfield, Balquharren, Auchengrie, Chappelland, Easter and Wester Culbowies. The lands of Barnes and meadows thereof, with the

---

* Page 80.

fishings of Cruikedshott and Linbranie, and with the mures of Kilpatrick, Cochnoch, Auchengrie, and Edinbarnet ; with all and sundrie castles, towers, fortalices, manor places, houses, biggins, yairds, orchyairds, dowes, dowcats, coalls, coallheughis, etc., etc."

In 1703 the Duntreath family acquired most of these lands or the superiorities. In 1541 James Douglas and Thomas Spreull appear in the rental roll as tenants in Drumtoquhyr, and they appear to have retained possession of their holdings notwithstanding the vicissitudes of the times, the farms in question retaining the names of Milton-Douglas and Milton-Spreull until their acquisition by Mr. William Dunn or his heirs. In the County Valuation Roll, 1657, Milton-Douglas is valued at £85 and Milton-Spreull at £97 10s. Scots. Mr. William Dunn acquired one half of the lands from Sir Charles Edmonstone, and a portion of the same lands called Cowbreggan in 1815 from James Smith of Faifley ; the portion held by James Logan was sold by him in 1824 to Mr. Dunn.

In 1815 John Paterson sold half of the lands of Milton of Duntocher to William Dunn, who in 1823 acquired that part of Easter Milton called Gowdenhill from William Taylor and curators.

Duntiglennan was held by the Spreulls in 1728, and in 1824 was purchased by William Dunn from David Kay. Later on William Dunn conveyed it to Lord

Blantyre, in exchange for water rights at Loch Humphrey, those of Auchentorlie being also purchased at same time. Faifley—variously spelled Ferclay, Ferchlay, Farchlay, Ffarchlay, Ffarklay—a twenty shilling land of old extent, was long possessed by the Smiths under feu from Cochno. The bulk of the land is still held by that family. From 1809 to 1827 William Dunn acquired small portions from the Smiths and another proprietor of the name of Clark. The ample water supply of this district was early taken advantage of, the Waulk Mill at Faifley being mentioned in Orbiston charter of 1643. Auchinleck, long held by the Johnstones, who were Abbey tenants, now belongs to Mr. Fergusson Buchanan of Auchentorlie, Archibald Buchanan having purchased it in 1757. A small portion was purchased from Auchentorlie by Mr. Dunn in 1827.

Braidfield.—These £4 lands of old extent, including Watchhills and Cleddans, were conveyed to Gavin Cleland of Gartscherie, 18th November, 1565, by John Hamilton, Abbot of Paisley, "pro magnus pecuniarum summus persolutis et aliis gratitudinibus." Like the adjoining lands they came into possession of the Duntreath family, and were acquired from Sir Charles Edmonstone by William Dunn.

In 1786 the manufacture of coarse woollens on a large scale was established at Duntocher, and is said to have been the first of the kind in Scotland. A large building was erected, with sufficient machinery for preparing and finishing 1000 yards cloth, containing 1200 lbs., daily. This factory proved a ready market for West Highland wool while it continued working. In the Old Statistical Account, vol. 3, we are informed that the greatest part of the wool produced annually in the parish of Lochgoilhead and Kilmorich, in quantity about 3000 stones, was sold to this factory and conveyed to Duntocher at the expense of the purchasers. After being carried on with enterprise for a few years it was abandoned, and about the year 1808 was purchased by Mr. William Dunn, the village being then almost deserted.

In 1813 Mr. Dunn acquired the Dalnotter Ironworks, which were then closed, from Richard and Robert Dennistoun, and on their site built the Milton Mill, now ruinous, he having acquired in 1811 the Faifley Spinning Mill from the Faifley Spinning Company.

The Duntocher and Faifley Mills were first greatly enlarged; and the Hardgate Mill, afterwards started in 1831 and re-erected in 1851 after being destroyed by fire. Thus four establishments were exclusively employed in spinning and weaving cotton. At first the machinery was driven by water-power, there being six water wheels of various dimensions employed, but in 1835 powerful steam engines were in operation, and

1417 workers employed.   Mr. William Dunn was in
many ways a remarkable man.   He was a native of
Kirkintilloch and bred to the trade of a blacksmith
there.   In early youth he came to Glasgow and soon
distinguished himself by his ingenuity and shrewdness.
He engaged in the manufacture of cotton spinning
machinery and was very successful.

Mr. Dunn gradually acquired from different proprietors
the lands round about Duntocher village and these comprised his estate of Duntocher, which embraced in all
upwards of 2000 acres.   The charge for stipend on
Mr. Dunn's estate, as apportioned in 1833, amounted
to 34 bolls, 3 firlots, 1 peck, and $2\frac{27}{60}$ lippies meal; 15
bolls, 3 firlots, 2 pecks, and $\frac{15}{60}$ lippies bear; and
£26 3s. Scots money.   On his death at Mount Blow,
13th March, 1849, he was succeded by his brother
Alexander, who died 15th June, 1860.

After a long and intricate litigation raised in the
Court of Session, and finally carried to the House of
Lords, by the male heirs, the property of the Dunns
was divided on the basis of William Dunn's original
settlement as there established, with certain modifications.
In 1873 the trustees exposed the cotton mills and village
of Duntocher for sale.   They were purchased by the
late Robert Black of Kelvinhaugh, whose trustees now
administer the property.

CRAIGS AND DUNTOCHER UNITED PRESBYTERIAN CHURCH.

Of the churches in Duntocher, the earliest founded was that formed in April, 1777, in connection with the Associate (Burgher) Presbytery of Glasgow. It had its origin in the appointment of an unpopular assistant to the parish minster of Old Kilpatrick in 1776. At first the congregation had very great difficulty in getting a site on which to build a church, or even a place in which to meet for worship for two or three years, and services were held monthly in the open air. At last, towards the end of 1780, a site was obtained on what was then called the Craigs of Kilpatrick, from which the church came to be called the congregation of Kilpatrick Craigs. A meeting house was built on it and opened in August, 1781. In the building of the church tradition reports that great opposition was encountered, and that the miners of Snab and Langfaulds quarried the Craigs within the feu for stones, while their wives carried the lime from the neighbouring parish on their backs in creels. The first minister, Rev. Mr. Archibald Wood, was settled in August, 1787, but died six months later, and was buried in the church in front of the pulpit. After an interval of two years, or fourteen years from its formation, the second minister, the Rev. William Watson, from Largs, was ordained.

In 1799 Mr. Watson adhered to that party in the Associate Synod which disapproved of the new preamble to the formula for ordination and which withdrew and formed the Original Associate, or "Auld Licht Burgher," Synod. A large portion of the congregation, however,

TOKENS—KILPATRICK CRAIGS, "AULD LICHT," CHURCH, 1789.

held different views and left him and formed a New Licht congregation. It was nick-named the "Meal Kirk" because it met for a time in the meal loft of the mill. It next met in the Sandyflats. In 1822 the congregation removed to a new church in Duntocher on a site granted by Mr. William Dunn. The division into two congregations gave rise to great bitterness, and eventually to law proceedings which were not closed until thirty years after, when, in 1829, the "Auld Licht" paid the "New Licht" party £200 in full of all claims. During this dispute Mr. Watson was translated to East Campbell Street, Glasgow, and the Rev. James Gardner was ordained on 23rd November, 1802, in the Craigs. Ten years later the Auld Licht Synod divided on the question of joining the Established Church. Kilpatrick Craigs then returned to its old connection with the United Secession Church. In 1847 the United Secession Church united with the Relief and became the United Presbyterian Church. Mr. Gardner retired from the ministry in 1848, and the Rev. Robert Mitchell was ordained as his colleague and successor on 30th January, 1849. He died on 6th January, 1869. The following April of that year the two congregations were united. The succession of ministers in the New Licht Church is as follows :—

Rev. Hugh Crichton, ordained 16th January, 1826; translated to Liverpool, 18th April, 1838.

Rev. Andrew Rintoul Johnson, ordained 2nd May, 1839; resigned, 10th April, 1849.

Rev. James Henderson, ordained 26th March, 1851; left for Australia, 14th December, 1858.

Rev. John Stark, ordained 17th April, 1860, under whom the two congregations united as Craigs and Duntocher; died, October, 1889.

DUNTOCHER *QUOAD SACRA* PARISH CHURCH.

The parish of Duntocher was disjoined, *quoad sacra*, from West Kilpatrick in 1836, in which year the church was erected. It was opened on Sunday, 25th September, 1836, and the Rev. John Pollock, who had worked as missionary in the village, was ordained the first minister on the 6th October. Being translated to Baldernock parish, 29th November, 1838, the Rev. William Alexander was ordained October, 1838, and joined the Free Church on the occasion of the Disruption in 1843. The Rev. John Templeton then succeeded to the charge, and died in 1877; the Rev. John Ellis Rae was inducted the following year.

DUNTOCHER FREE CHURCH.

As already mentioned, the Rev. William Alexander left the Establishment at the Disruption, a large number of the congregation leaving with him. He acted as minister with great acceptance until 1885, when the Rev. James Harvey was ordained as colleague. Mr. Harvey was called to Lady Glenorchy's Free Church, Edinburgh, and was succeeded by the Rev. John E. Falconer.

W. Snell Anderson.

SCENE ON THE CLYDE AT BOWLING.

ROMAN CATHOLIC CHURCH.

The chapel of St. Mary, with dwelling-house and school attached, provides for the religious and educational requirements of the adherents to the Roman Catholic persuasion. Among its Fathers during the past half-century were the Rev. Messrs. Maloney, Munro, Danaker, Brown, Dowd, M'Conville, and Bird; the present incumbent being the Rev. James M'Cluskey.

COLQUHOUN HOUSE, DUMBUCK HILL.
(From a Sketch by W. A. Donnelly.)

CHAPTER XVII.

LANDS OF COCHNO AND BARNS, KILBOWIE, EDENBARNET, CRAIGBANZEOCH, AND LAW.

THE LANDS OF COCHNO AND BARNS.

THE estate of Cochno or Cochna, passing into the possession of Lord Claud Hamilton, commendator of Paisley Abbey, was held in feu by Andrew Hamilton, who is supposed to have been the eldest son of Andrew Hamilton of Ardoch, a younger son of James Hamilton of Torrance. On the 25th August, 1550, James Boyle and James Thomson, as the Abbey Rental Roll informs us, resigned their portions of Western Cochnay in favour of Andrew Hamilton, captain of Dumbarton Castle, and his son John, and in the following year Easter Cochnay was feued to him and his heirs.* For many · years governor of Dumbarton Castle, he was besides Provost of Glasgow in 1541, 1553, and 1558, and sat in Parliament for that burgh in 1546. In 1552 John Palmer

---

* See pages 87 and 89.

resigned the customs of Dumbarton in favour of Andrew Hamilton of Cochno ; Agnes Crawford of Kilbirnie, his wife ; and of their son Duncan, in fee. Andrew and his three sons sided with Queen Mary at the battle of Langside in 1568, and no doubt was the leader of the Hamilton contingent from Kilpatrick which took part in that fateful conflict.* In the "Diurnal of Occurrents," p. 136, the following entry appears:—" 19th August, 1568. Andrew Hamilton of Cochnocht, Johne, his sone and air, forfalfit after the battle of Langside" ; and the same year Robert, Lord Sempill, was ordained by the council "to pass be himself or his servandis in his name, and tak and intromit with the same tour and fortalice Cochnocht, and keep and use the samyn in our Soveranis name." On 7th March, 1570, the Diurnal again notes—"Andrew Hamilton, sonnes of Cochnach quha wes put in ward" for being in the Place of Paisley after it was rendered. " 14th June, 1571. Johnne Hamiltone, sone to Andrew Hamilton of Cochnoch, wes beheaded for the inter-prysing of the taking of Glasgow castell." In 1572 Andrew Hamilton is returned as "among the traitors and rebels of Cliddesdale." Married twice, first to Margaret, youngest daughter of James Noble of Ferme, he had a numerous family, and was succeeded ultimately

See page 87.

by Claud, who, with his two sons, were forfeited by Act of Parliament, 11th November, 1579. It is interesting to note that John Layng, parson of Luss, who died December, 1571, bequeathed to "Agnes Hammiltoun, dochter to Andro Hammiltoun of Cothnocht, ten pundis, to by her ane goun." Possibly the lady required such a thoughtful gift during these exciting times, her father was a rebel and the tower of Cochno in possession of the party of the Regent. The late David Wingate, the author of many pleasing songs and poems, made the Laird of Cochno's exile the subject of a short poem entitled "Cochno Braes," beginning—

> "Amang the braes whaur Cochno rins,
> Owre boulders brown and ferny linns."

In 1581 Claud Hamilton had a charter of vendition of Wester Cochnoch from Robert, brother of James Foulis of Colmtoun, to him and his wife, Margaret Beaton of Creich in Fifeshire, in liferent, and to their eldest son, Claud, in fee.

In 1585 the Hamiltons were restored to the Royal favour, and the Abbey estates held by David Erskine, Commendator of Dryburgh, were retransferred to Lord Claud Hamilton, the former Commendator, who two years later was made Lord Paisley, and whose eldest son was created Earl of Abercorn in 1606. The charter restoring the Abbey lands in the parish to Lord Paisley, which is dated 29th July, 1587, and confirmed 22nd March, 1592, at Linlithgow Palace, reads as follows :— "terras de Eister et Westir Kilpatrikis, Moreisland Kirktoun de Kilpatrick, Auchintoshane, Dunterclunane, Belwarthill, Eister et Westir Cochnoxhis cum carbonibus, etc., Drumtocher cum Molendinis granorum et fullonum ; terris Molendinariis et Multuris ; terras de Mylncroft, Edinbarnane, Craigbarneoch, Auchinleck, Faiclay, Braidfield, Maquhanrane, Auchingrie, Chapelland, Eister et Wester Kilbowies, Barnes ac prata earundem, cum piscariis de Cruikitschot et Linbrane, ac moris de Kilpatrik, Cochnoch, Auchingrie et Enbarnet, cum castris Manerais, pratis wardis parcis Molendinis, silvis, piscariis tenentibus, etc., omnium dictarum terrarum in regalitie de Paisley vic de Dumbartane."

In 1594 James Hamilton of Cochno had to find caution not to harm the tenants of West and East Cochno, Faifley, and Hutcheson.* A Crown charter dated 18th June, 1618, confirms to the Provost of Dumbarton the weigh-houses and petty customs of the burgh, with consent of Claud Hamilton of Cochno and James Hamilton, his son. Claud Hamilton of Cochno was a commissioner for the shire in 1610, and in 1615

---

* See page 90.

he is styled the Goodman of Cochno. Sir Claud
Hamilton, subsequently designed of Craigleith, who
married Marjory, second daughter of Sir James Edmon-
stone of Duntreath, sold in 1617 to James, Earl of
Abercorn, the lands of Easter and Wester Cochnoch,
Blawarthill, Hutcheson, Coilheugh, and Hoill. After 1622
no further notice is found of Sir Claud. He went to
Ireland and was heard of no more.

Matthew Hamilton of Auchentoshan, a younger son of
Andrew, now represented the Cochno family.

In 1633 the Earl of Abercorn sold Cochno, along with
his other lands in Kilpatrick parish, to Sir James Hamilton
of Orbiston, by whose family it was feued out, and afterwards, in 1647, acquired by Robert Hamilton or Barns.

The family of Barns is descended from Claud Hamilton, second son of Gavin, the seventh of Raploch, lineally
descended from Sir David Hamilton of that ilk. He
had a charter of Barns, in 1575, and also of Wester and
Easter Kilbowie. In 1610 Claud Hamilton of Barns was
one of the commissioners for Lanarkshire, and in 1611
he became surety for Hew Somerville of Drums in 300
merks. He died September, 1632.

From 1643 to 1666 Robert Hamilton of Barns was
one of the commissioners for Dumbartonshire.* He

---

* John Knox of Barns, a descendant of the Abbey tenants of that name, was
also one of the commissioners in 1643.

married, first, 1644, Mary, daughter of Walter Macaulay
of Ardencaple ; second, 1663, Anne, daughter of John
Brisbane of Bishopton. He died July, 1677, and was
succeeded by his son, Claud.

ARMS OF HAMILTON OF BARNS.

*Gules, a man's heart or betwixt three cinquefoils ermine, within
a bordure indented of the second.*

On 26th June, 1729, Robert Hamilton of Barns bought
the parsonage teinds of the lands of Barns, Easter and
Wester Kilbowie, Easter and Wester Cochno and Bel-
warthill, and the lands of Meikle Faifley, the lands of
Hutcheson, Coillheugh land, and Hoile, from Lord
William Cochrane, into whose possession they had come

from Thomas, Earl of Dundonald, having had a charter of the Lordship of Paisley, 13th February, 1727, who had inherited them from James, Earl of Abercorn.

Claud Hamilton of Barnes, who was Sheriff-Depute of the County, and sat in Parliament as its representative, 1689-1702, married, in 1670, Anne, daughter of Sir Walter Stewart of Allanton, Lanarkshire. He was succeeded by his son James, who married, 1714, Grizel, sister of Sir John Maxwell, Bart. of Pollock, and was succeeded by his eldest son, Claud Hamilton of Barnes, major of marines, who served at the siege of Carthagena, etc., and died unmarried, 1770; and was succeeded by his brother, John Hamilton of Barnes, who married Marion, daughter of John Bryson of Craigallian, Stirlingshire, by a sister of Sir John Maxwell of Pollock, and had (with a daughter Grizel, wife of John Hamilton Dundas of Duddingston and Westburn) James, his heir; Claud, captain in the 54th Regiment, and major of the Lanark and Dumbarton Fencible Cavalry, married Elizabeth, daughter of John Bardin, of the Colony of Rhode Island, and left issue—(1) John, died unmarried; (2) Claud, merchant, at Mirzapore, Bengal, died unmarried, October, 1863, having settled his property on his nephew Claud Brown, with a request that he would assume the surname of Hamilton. Grace, married Archibald Brown, merchant in Glasgow, son of John Brown, merchant in

Glasgow, of the family of Brown of Crofthead, county Ayr, by Jean Mayne, his wife, sister of William, Viscount Newhaven, and died in January, 1844, leaving issue— (1) John George Brown, died unmarried, 6th April, 1844; (2) Claud Hamilton Brown, now Claud Hamilton Hamilton of Barnes. The elder son, James Hamilton of Barnes, major commandant of the Dumbartonshire Yeomanry Cavalry, married Eleanor, daughter and co-heir of John Dun, Tannochside, county Lanark, and died 1833, having had issue—(1) John, major 11th Regiment, mortally wounded at Salamanca, 1813; (2) James of Barnes, married Margaret, daughter of Hugh Maclean of Coll, county Argyll, and died 26th August, 1852. His daughter, Grace Hamilton of Barnes and Cochna, died April, 1887, and was succeeded by her cousin, Claud Hamilton Hamilton, Esq., born 10th April, 1823; married, first, 26th November, 1862, Eleanor Margaret, daughter of Henry Walters, Esq., of Bath Easton, and had issue—Grace Hamilton, married, 8th December, 1886, George James Fergusson Buchanan, Esq. of Auchentorlie. He married, secondly, 26th November, 1874, Hon. Henrietta Anne Bruce, sister of Lord Balfour of Burleigh, and had issue—Robert Bruce Hamilton, born 1878; Claud Archibald Mackenzie Bruce; Nora Ann Bruce Hamilton; Anne Henrietta, who died in infancy, and Katherine Claudia Bruce.

On acquiring Cochno the Hamiltons of Barns resided upon it. The present house was built in 1757 and added to in 1842. It is tenanted by W. A. Donaldson, Esq., of the well-known firm of Messrs. James Watson & Co., Glasgow, and chairman of Messrs. J. & G. Thomson, Limited, Clydebank.

CLYDEBANK.

Our story of the rise of Clydebank will be brief. In 1870 Messrs. J. & G. Thomson, having been compelled to remove from Glasgow on account of the extension of the harbour, feued from Miss Hamilton several acres of the lands of Barns, and erected thereon their shipbuilding yard, which they called Clydebank. A busy town immediately sprang up, and fields which had been tilled for centuries were covered with houses and made noisy with the clang of hammers and other sounds of a big industry. A burgh was formed in 1886, and Mr. James R. Thomson, senior partner of the firm, was fittingly chosen the first chief magistrate.

THE LANDS OF KILBOWIE.

This name—meaning "the yellow ridge"—appears in many forms, the earliest being Cultbuthe. The lands were held by Dungallus, son of Christinus, Judge of the

Lennox, and Fergus Cunningham, both of whom resigned possession between the years 1235 and 1270 in favour of the Abbey of Paisley, by whom they were retained until about the Reformation. In the year 1553 Kilbowie was held by Barbara Hamilton who had a part of the lands from James, Lord Fleming.

Among the "traitors and rebels of Cliddisdale," proclaimed in 1572, John Hamilton * of Kilbowie is mentioned, and in the year previous David Hamilton of Kilbowie was summoned for treason.

In 1581 the Privy Council recalled the confirmation of a tack for 19 years of the tiends of Culbowie and Barnis, granted by Claud Hamilton to Robert Dalziell of that ilk.

Passing into the hands of Hamilton of Orbiston, Kilbowie was acquired by Barns, and later, in 1643, William Brock had a grant from Robert Hamilton of Barns of that piece of ground described as "that 25s. land of the lands of Easter Kilbowie, the crofting lands thereof, with the houses, biggins, and yards thereupon, as presently possessed by . . . Macindoe and Neil Forsyth ; and the lands of the same being as yet undivided frae the other 25s. land of the half town and lands of Easter Kilbowie. The equal half of the haill outfield of the

---

* See page 87.

said two 25s. lands is by lot and cabbil to be caster for that effect to belong to the said William Brock." In 1704 Brock's portion was sold by John and James Brock to Robert Morrison, and was known afterwards as Morrison's Easter Kilbowie.

In 1667 the other portions of Easter Kilbowie were owned by Andrew Morrison and his son, and the representatives of the umquhile John Buchanan. After passing through several hands, William Dunn in 1826 acquired Easter Kilbowie, along with White Crook and other lands from Sir Archibald Edmonstone, by judicial sale, along with the superiority of parts of Wester Kilbowie, previously held by the Edmonstone family.

Wester Kilbowie £6 10s. land. Prior to 1675 Robert M'Nair held part if not the whole of Wester Kilbowie,* and in 1754 John Hart was heritable proprietor of ⅝ths of the lands, and Mrs. Turner of ⅜ths. Hart's ⅝ths were acquired from parties of the name of Hunter, Morrison, and Lang.

---

* This tomb is still to be seen in the Churchyard, Kilpatrick. It is much defaced through weather. The inscription reads—

MEMENTO MORI.

This is the burying place of Robert M'Nair, Portioner in Wester Kilbowie and Dalmure, who died July 18th, 1675, aged 64 years.

Thomas M'Nair, late Tenant in Barns of Clyde, who died June   , 17 , aged 74.

This is the burying place appointed Robert M'Nair, Tenant in the Mains of Scotstoun, his wife and children, A.D. MDC . . .

In 1766 Sir A. Edmonstone acquired Hart's portion of Kilbowie, and in 1768 acquired from Major Claud Hamilton the superiority of all the lands in West and East Kilbowie that had belonged to Mr. Hart. In 1826 Mr. William Dunn acquired from Sir A. Edmonstone at this judicial sale the lands that belonged to Mr. Hart, and in 1852 Mr. Alexander Dunn acquired by purchase, also from Sir A. Edmonstone, the superiority of Hart's lands in East and West Kilbowie.

The disposition by Sir Archibald Edmonstone to Alexander Dunn of the superiority of the lands of West and East Kilbowie describes the second of those portions thus:—Half of the £1 12s. 6d. land of old extent of West Kilbowie as the half of the fourth part of the whole town and land of Wester Kilbowie lying by the ancient rights on the east side thereof, with houses, &c.; with the pro part of the Isle in Clyde; with the portion of the sandbeds in Clyde between the Horse Isle and Newshot Isle, as the said half of the £1 12s. 6d. land. Horse Isle sandbeds, pertments, pro rata, were of old possessed by the deceased Robert Morrison and James Cunningham, and afterwards by Robert Morrison, and thereafter by John Hunter, acquired by the said John Hart from Anna Hunter, his daughter, &c.

In 1754, at Hart's request, a boundary line of the lands of West Kilbowie was fixed between his possessions and that of Mrs. Turner, who held the other portion of the Kilbowie lands.

In the Kilbowie lands there are places named as the Muir Park and Butts, on which it is supposed in the time of James IV. and V. the people were in the practice of shooting with bows and arrows. The lands of Kilbowie were burdened with the annual charge of £1 1s. 7¾d., conform to use and wont, payable to the minister of New Kilpatrick.

On the death of Mr. Alexander Dunn, who succeeded his brother William, Kilbowie became the property of the heirs-at-law, William Park, John Macindoe and his twin brother George Park Macindoe, and James Black.

In 1881 the Singer Manufacturing Company purchased 46 acres of the Kilbowie lands, upon which their factory now stands. In May, 1882, ground was broken for the same in the presence of a large gathering, and in 1885 the immense works were in full operation.*

EDENBARNET AND CRAIGBANZEOCH, ALSO LAW.

Forming part of the Abbey possessions, and thus included in the lordship of Kilpatrick, these lands were

---

* Kilbowie, by E. W. M'Cormick: Helensburgh, 1893.

acquired by Andrew Stirling from Stephen Spreull of Edenbarnet, the charter being dated 12th July, 1569.

The adjoining lands of Law formed part of the lordship of Drumry and were acquired by William Stirling, first of Glorat, in 1528, from Sir James Hamilton of Finnart with consent of his spouse,

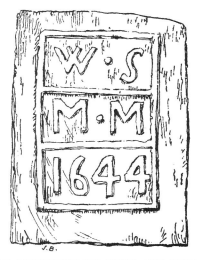

STONE FROM EDENBARNET OLD HOUSE, NOW BUILT INTO THE
KENNEL WALL.

Margaret Livingston, heiress of the Drumry and neighbouring lands, on 28th November, 1530. Cunningham of Drumquhassel, who had acquired the superiority of Law, granted a precept for infefting Andrew Stirling, son of the late William Stirling and Margaret Houston, in these lands, and Andrew was infeft the following day. Andrew Stirling married the second daughter of Gabriel Cunningham of Craigends, and was succeeded by his eldest son William, who was infeft the last day of March, 1582, by Crawford of Kilbirnie, who had acquired the lordship of Drumry. He also received from William, commendator of Paisley, a charter dated 16th April, 1581, of Edenbarnet and Craigbanzeoch on the resignation of John Spreull, heir male of the deceased Stephen Spreull. He married Margaret, daughter of Hugh Crawford of Cloberhill. He was succeeded by his son Andrew, who died December, 1646, and was in turn succeeded by his son William, fifth of Law, one of the commissioners of the county, who married Margaret Maxwell of Dargavel, the contract being dated 2nd December, 1641.* She died between 1694 and September, 1703, and in him the direct male descent ended.

William Stirling left three daughters—Margaret, Mary, and Agnes. Agnes married John Campbell of Succoth, W.S. They had two sons, John, the second, succeeding to Law. The seventh laird of Law was John Campbell, and he had a charter from Walter, Lord Blantyre, who had become superior, dated 17th August, 1708, of the lands of Edenbarnet and Craigbargeoch as heir to William Stirling of Law.

---

* See page 104.

EDENBARNET HOUSE.

Archd. Holmes.

He was succeeded by his only son James Stirling of Law, who "set tacks of the great part of the estate of Law and Edenbarnet to various parties," and these tacks were challenged by his successor in the estate. James Stirling died 15th January, 1809, and was succeeded by

MURAL TABLET.
Stirling of Law's Tomb. Kilpatrick Churchyard.

his cousin-uterine, Agnes Hamilton Stirling of Law and Edenbarnet, who died 2nd February, 1816, and was succeeded by her sister Anne Hamilton Stirling of Law and Edenbarnet. She died unmarried 11th July, 1817, and was descended from Mary Stirling, second daughter of William Stirling and wife of William Colquhoun,

Craigton ; they had a daughter, Margaret Colquhoun, who married Alan Colquhoun of Kenmuir. They had two sons, Alan, who died without issue, and William Colquhoun of Kenmuir. He married Judith Dunn Thibou, by whom he had one son, William, who succeeded to Law, and two daughters.

ARMS OF STIRLING OF LAW.

Shield, quarterly: 1st and 4th for Stirling, argent, on a bend engrailed azure three buckles or, in chief on an oak branch slipped vert a raven proper; 2nd and 3rd for Colquhoun, on a field argent a saltire engrailed sable and in chief a rose gules.

William Colquhoun Stirling of Law married Helen, youngest daughter of the late Archibald Calder, banker in Glasgow. They had a son, William Colquhoun Stirling, who succeeded, and was a lieutenant in the

14th Regiment of Madras Infantry. He died in 1866 and the estate passed to his cousin Alexander Murray Dunlop, of Corsock, advocate, and at his death to his son, Alexander Colquhoun Stirling Murray Dunlop, of Law, Edenbarnet, and Corsock, from whom Edenbarnet was purchased by Walter MacKenzie, Esq., son of Robert MacKenzie of Caldarvan. Mr. MacKenzie married Elizabeth, fifth daughter of the late Alexander Campbell, Esq., of Barnhill, and has, with other issue, Robert Campbell, born 1856. The family residence, originally at Law, was removed to Edenbarnet, where the first house was built by William Stirling about 1644. On acquiring the property, Mr. MacKenzie built a new mansion house in 1882, which was destroyed by fire a few years later, and immediately rebuilt.*

The ruins of the tower of Law were carted away some years ago by the tenant of Law farm, Mr. D. Ramsay, some of the stones from which were utilised by Mr. MacKenzie for repairs at the offices beside old Edenbarnet house.

---

* The rooftree at Edenbarnet is said to have been the identical oaken beam that held the same place of honour at Mugdock castle, the beam having been carried off after that edifice had been "herried" by the Buchanans.

CHAPTER XVIII.

EAST KILPATRICK.

THIS parish was disjoined from Old or West
Kilpatrick, 16th February, 1649.* Steps toward
the disjunction were first taken in 1643, when the Marquis
of Montrose, superior of much of the eastern lands, proposed that they should be transferred to the parishes of
Baldernock and Strathblane, while Crawford of Kilbirnie,
who held the Lordship of Drumry, and other heritors,
desired that their lands might be erected into a separate
parish. The matter occupied the Presbytery of Dumbarton
for several years. A church was immediately built and
opened for worship the following year. During its construction Sir Humphrey Colquhoun had to be inhibited
by an Act of Parliament, 28th July, 1649, from interfering
with the masons, quarriers, and other tradesmen employed
thereat. The Act reads as follows :—

"*Act in favor of the Parochiners of Eister Kilpatrick.*
28th July, 1649. Vol. 6, fol. 486.

" The Estaits of Parliament having hard and con-
siderit the supplicatioun givin into them be the parochiners

* See Appendix A.

of eister Kilpatrick shewing that the parochine of Kilpatrick being devydit in severall distinct paroches vpon the parochiners suplicatioun and the presbitries recommendatioun to the Commissioun for plantatioun of Kirks, ane new Kirk was appointit to be buildit in the eist pairt of the said parochin Quhairupon sex of the parochiners in name and at the Desyr of the haill parochine vndertook the building of the said Kirk and having agreet with meassouns quarriors and sledders hes now compleit moir nor the halff of the said building notwithstanding whairof Sir Umphra Colquhoun of Balvie ane of the heritors of the said new parochine and who wes one of these that agriet with the quarriors for winning of stains to big the said Kirk hes now upon what grounds they know not but malice as wold appeir to hinder Godes work sent and taking fra the quarriors thair haill Instruments at the quarrey hes stopit the carryers from leiding and the meassouns from hewing and building and hes chairgit all with Lawborrowis and so hes stopped the work unless the saides estaits of parliament provyd some speidie remeid to promove the samyne Thairfoir humblie supplicating the saids Estaits of Parliament to tak the premiss into thair serious consideratioun and give warrand heirby to ane messenger to wairne the said Sir Umphra to compeir befoir the parliament or Comittie that sall be sitting for the tyme at Eb^r upon thrie dayis

wairning with continuatioun of dayis to an[sr] to this
complaint and to heir and sie him decernit to pay the
haill chairgis of the quarriours carriers and meassouns
during the tyme of the stoping of the said work as the
saidis estaits of parliament shal be pleasit to modifie
with all costis skaithis and damnage that the undirtaikirs
of the said work sall sustein thairthrow and to heir and
sie such farder punishment imposed vpon him as the
saidis estaits of Parliament sall think fitt and that he
doe not imped the said work heireftir as at mair lenth
is conteinit in the said supplicatioun Quhilk being taken
into consideratioun be the saidis estaits of Parliament
They have ordainit and ordains ane messenger to chairge
the said Sir Umphra Colquhoun of Balvie to compeir
befoir the parliament or Com[n] of estaits the   day
of   with continuatioun of dayis To answer to
the complaint givin in against him be the parochiners
of eister Kilpatrick for taking away fra the quarriours
the haill Instruments at the quarrell and stoping the
caryers from leiding and the meassouns fra hewing and
building of the Kirk of Kilpatrick and chairging all the
workmen with lawburrowis and that vnder the paine of
rebellioun and to vnduly any vther censur the parliament
shall think fit."

The church which had such a troublous beginning was

pulled down towards the end of last century. The edifice which took its place has been so altered from time to time and enlarged that there is little left of the original building.

The stipend in 1792 amounted to 70 bolls of meal, 100 of bear, and £45 16s. 8d. sterling.

COMMUNION TOKEN—NEW KILPATRICK CHURCH.

In the "New Statistical Account," published 1845, we learn there was a small chapel at Lurg, on the Mains estate, of which few remains were extant. The place where it stood was then pointed out by the name of Chapel Couch, and in the tradition of the neighbourhood the auld kirk was then spoken about. There had been a cemetery attached to it and in the early part of the century several tombstones remained. These had, in 1843, all disappeared save one—an unpolished, unlettered, and rude stone.

In a grant to John Logan of Balvie, the chapel and yard in the neighbourhood of Gartconal, dedicated to St. Kessog, the patron saint of Luss, is mentioned.

SUCCESSION OF MINISTERS.

1650.   Walter Rollock had a call on completion of the church, and died the same year.

1651.   Robert Law, son of Thomas Law, minister at Inchinnan, was rejected on his trials, but latterly ordained. Expelled in 1662 for Non-conformity, he afterwards came under the Indulgence and preached in and around Glasgow, and is supposed to have died about the period of the Revolution.   His Journal of " The Memorable Things that fell out within the Island of Britain from 1638 to 1684 " is an extraordinary production.

1664.   Richard Laurie.

1666.   William Duncan " rabbled " by the people at the Revolution, and died 1692.

In 1667 Agnes Symmervel was accused of having used unlawful means for restoring sick folks to health.

1690.   John Dougall ; died 1712.

1715.   John Logan ; died 1730.

1731.   Andrew Gray was presented by the Duke of Montrose, and John Alexander M'Culloch was called by the people, Mr. Gray was preferred by the Presbytery and pending an appeal to the Higher Courts he was appointed to fill the vacancy, but was prevented by a mob which filled the church and filled the pulpit with stones and otherwise desecrated the building.

1776.　James Carrick ; died 1787.

1787.　George Sym ; died 1835.

1835.　Andrew Sym, D.D., ordained assistant and successor to his father in 1821 ; died 1870.

1870.　James Waters King, D.D., translated from Killearn, was presented to the living by the Duke of Montrose, this being the last presentation under the Patronage Act in Dumbartonshire prior to its abolition.

On the erection of the church in 1649 a few houses were soon grouped in its neighbourhood, the village being designated New Kirk.　About the year 1856 Mr. Colquhoun of Killermont decided to feu part of that and the Garscadden property, and some six or seven villas were soon built.　Of late years the natural advantages of this district have been fully recognised, and some 200 to 300 villas and cottages, not to speak of terraces and blocks of buildings, have been erected. No place near Glasgow has had such a rapid rise as New Kilpatrick.

DRUMRY AND DRUMCHAPEL.

In 1329 the lady of Drumry paid to the Chamberlain of Scotland one chalder of flour, " farine pro libertate suae terre."　She may probably have been of the Livingstons, who held this estate in later times, a branch of the Callander family of that name. Robert Livingston, Lord of Drumry, was, on 10th October, 1381, witness to a charter by William of Galbraith. Lord of Katconvall (Gartconnel), of the lands of Estir and Wester Bothernick and Kyncade, on payment of

ARMS OF LIVINGSTON OF DRUMRY.

Argent, three cinquefoils gules, with double tressurefleury and counterfleury azure.

40 pennies yearly at the fair of Glasgow, and also giving to him and his heirs a silver penny in the name of blench ferme, at Katconvall if asked. In 1385 Sir Robert and his lady took infeftment of the lands of Wemyss in Fife. Sir Robert Livingstone of Drumry, Lord Treasurer of Scotland, is recorded by

Pitscottie as having been executed at Edinburgh in 1447 in consequence of his being implicated in the charges against Sir Alexander Livingston of Callander, chief of the family, governor of James II. during his minority. Sir Robert Livingstone of Easter Wemyss and Drumry was killed at the battle of Flodden, 1513. His daughter married Sir James Hamilton of Fynnart, who received from James V. a grant of the lands of Drumry, which had probably escheated to the Crown in default of heirs male. Sir James exchanged them — 27th January, 1529 — with Laurence Crawford, for the lands of Crawfordjohn in Lanarkshire, by which means they came into possession of the Kilbirnie family, who took from them the title of Barons of Drumry.

From ancient times there had been a church at Drumry, the first notice of which is found in connection with the Paisley Abbey in 1476, when the abbot in that year disputed a tack of the chapel lands granted in favour of Thomas de Montgomery. Laurence Crawford of Kilbirnie founded a chaplaincy in the church of Drumry of his own patronage. The endowments of the church were considerable, among which were the lands of Jordanhill and those of Drumchapel. The former were gifted to the Drumry church about the year 1546 by Laurence Crawford — " pro salute animae suae and Helenae Campbel, spousae suae, etc."

On the dissolution of the religious houses Captain Thomas Crawford, who was a younger son of Laurence Crawford of Kilbirnie, and a valiant soldier, acquired the lands of Jordanhill in 1562 from Sir Bartholomew Montgomery, chaplain of the chapel of Drumry. In 1553 Robert, Lord Semple, had a deed of gift under the Privy Seal of the 20 pound land of auld extent of Drumry, with the fortalice, kirks, and chaplainries, etc. The Hamiltons some time later appear as connected with Drumry, as John Hamilton of Drumry became in 1575 one of the cautioners for William Hamilton of Sanquhar, and in 1579 Robert Bruce of Kennet became in turn surety for John Hamilton to the extent of £1000 Scots.

In the beginning of last century the adjoining estate of Cloberhill, which from a very remote time had been in the possession of the Crawfords, was conveyed by Hugh Crawford to John Spreul of Cowden, in Renfrewshire, who had married his only child, Isabel. John Spreul, in 1716, made a new deed of entail by which he destined the lands of Cloberhill and Drumchapel to the heirs male, and failing them, the heirs whatsomever of this marriage, binding them to assume the name and designation of Spreul Crawford of Cowdenhill.

George, Viscount Garnock, sold Drumry in 1747 to

William Colquhoun of Garscadden. Knightswood remained with the family and passed to the Earl of Glasgow with the other Lindsay-Crawford estates. In 1671 the Presbytery of Dumbarton reported that, "Mr. Thomas Melvin in Drumry, Hugh Smith at Garscadden, Patrick Sympsoun in Boquhanran are all proved to have held conventicles in their several dwellings during divine service whereby many elders are drawn away from the neighbouring churches, so that kirk services could not be held."

In the courtyard of the farm of Drumry stands the tower, evidently of a keep or peel, overlooking a steep bank. Formerly in a ruinous condition, it was repaired prior to 1836, and a year or two ago the upper portion was fitted up by the proprietor of the estate—Rev. J. Campbell Colquhoun, as a bothy for the male servants employed on the farm, the ground floor being used as a stable. It probably dates from the acquisition of the estate by the Crawfords. The corbelling on the tower is identical with that on the Crawford tomb at Kilburnie, which was erected 1594.

The farm buildings seem to have been built largely of stone taken from the old peel and chapel. On a stone built into one of the barns the name "Laurence Crawford," in Old English lettering, can still be deciphered with difficulty. The smithy adjoining has also been built, as is shown by the tooling of the stones, from material taken from the old castle—a species of vandalism only too common.

The chapel of Drumry is said to have stood on the roadside close to the South Drumry farm, the spot being marked by an ancient thorn tree which was removed in the year 1891. Human remains have been found at this spot from time to time.

Part of the lands of Drumry and Drumchapel belong to the Rev. J. Campbell Colquhoun, and part to John Black, Esq.

During the past few years building sites have been feued off, and some fine villas erected.

The Barony of Drumry included also the lands of Law, Cloberhill, and Jordanhill.

LANDS OF GARSCADDEN.

Sir Robert Erskine of Erskine granted Garscadden to Patrick Galbraith, his armour-bearer, 8th June, 1444. In 1489 John Galbraith of Garscadden, in common with his neighbours, took an active part in the capture of Dumbarton Castle.

On 19th May, 1563, Robert Galbraith of Garscadden was one of a party of 47 who, along with John Hamilton, Archbishop of St. Andrews, was called upon to underlie

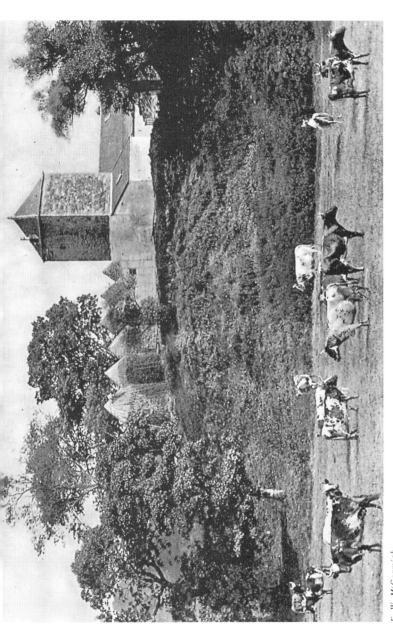

E. W. M'Cormick.

DRUMRY TOWER.

the law for assisting at the celebration of Mass in the chapel of his own house. Garscadden's punishment is not mentioned, but three of those indicted along with him — viz., Malcolm, prior of Whithorn, Sir Thomas Montgomery, and Sir William Failyofen—were adjudged to be put in ward within the Castle of Dumbarton.

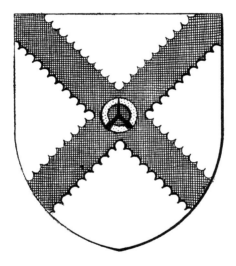

ARMS OF COLQUHOUN OF GARSCADDEN.
Argent, on a saltire engrailed sable a buckle or.

The Garscadden lands were sold by Walter Galbraith in 1611 to Matthew Wallace of Dundonald, who in turn disposed of them in 1620 to Hugh Thomson of Derry. In 1655 the Colquhouns became possessors, and later on in the century they acquired Killermont, which in 1628 had been sold by John Cunninghame of Drumquhassil.

Both estates are now held by the Rev. J. Campbell Colquhoun, who is descended from John Colquhoun, second son of Robert, sixth laird of Camstradden, who was a true soldier-patriot. The present house of Garscadden has been added to at various times, the oldest date, 1723, is on a back window lintel.

The entrance gates, now much shorn of their early fantastic adornment, were erected in 1789 from design by Charles Ross, architect, of Greenlaw, near Paisley.

Hutcheson House, erected by a cadet of Hamilton of Barns, is now occupied by the farmer of the lands, and belongs to Messrs. Tait & Crighton, W.S., Edinburgh.

GARTCONNEL.

In the north and east of New Kilpatrick lay at one time the spacious domains of the Galbraiths, whose family residence was at Gartconnel or Katconvall. The chief of this name in the 14th century, during the reign of Robert III., had three daughters who carried in marriage his estates to the families of Douglas of Mains, Logan of Balvie, and Hamilton of Baldernock. The Galbraiths appear early in the records of the

Lennox, there being several charters in the chartulary showing the extent of their possessions. From one of these we learn that in 1238 William Galbraith had a charter of the lands of Brothernockis and Kyncaith. Some time before this, the year not being mentioned, Maurice Galbraith had a charter of the carucate (104 acres) of the lands of Cartonvenach or Gartconnel. Tombothy and Letyrmolyn are also mentioned in the chartulary in connection with this family, likewise Auchencloich, near Strickelmakessog. In the Exchequer Rolls for 1377 Robert de Galbraith appears as the recipient of a present from the King.

In 1381 William of Galbraith gave a charter of the lands of Bothernock and Kyncade, which in a few years after fell into the possession of John Hamilton, and were confirmed in 1394 to his wife Margaret.

On 23rd April 1411 Alexander de Logan, Lord of Catconwell, Knight, was witness to an agreement, signed at the church of Kilpatrick, between Duncan, Earl of Lennox, and Sir John Colquhoun of Lus. Sir John de Hamilton, Lord of Bardowie, was also a witness to same document.

Robert Livingston on 20th November, 151?, was infeft "by John Logan of Carconell of the east half of the lands of Bannachtan, extending to a 25s. land of old extent in the lordship of Carconell."

On 17th June, 1531, Hamilton of Bardowie and John Logan of Balvie chose arbiters to decide regarding all slaughters, hurts, and debate between the contracting parties, their kin, and friends.

In 1594 the Galbraiths are named in the Acts of Parliament for that year amongst the lawless men to be suppressed on account of " dalie herrschippis of the wicked thevis and lymaris."

Kilmardinny. These lands were, in 1440, partly owned by Donald Lennox of Balcorrach, and in 1465 Sir John Colquhoun had a reignation of part of the lands from Alexander de Auchencross.

John MacHutcheson, heir of Eugene Mackessog, was, in 1505, vested in the whole £5 land of Kilmardinny. In 1563 John Colquhoun of Kilmardinny appears as factor of John Layng, parson of Luss. Thereafter the estate was feued out in small portions.

The Colquhouns of Kilmardinny were descended from Walter, third son of Sir James Colquhoun who died some time before 22nd August, 1536. Walter died before 26th October, 1541, and John Colquhoun of Luss was infeft in the lands.

John Graham of Kilmardinny and Clober was an active supporter of Prince Charlie in the rebellion of 1745. He had been an ensign in a Scots regiment in the Dutch service,

Garscube. These lands were included in the Barony of Luss in 1457, and were acquired in the middle of the 17th century by John Colquhoun of Succoth.

Mains. The Douglases of Mains are descended from Nicholas Douglas, fourth son of James, Lord Dalkeith, who, in September 1373, married Janet Galbraith, heiress of Mains. Space will not permit us to deal at length

THE ARMS OF DOUGLAS OF MAINS.

with the history of this ancient and illustrious family further than to say that the present proprietor of Mains, Archibald Campbell Douglas, is the twenty-first in descent from Nicolas first referred to.

Baljaffray. These lands were acquired in 1449 by Robert Noble of Ferme, Bailie of Dumbarton, by charter from the Crown on the resignation of two sisters, Molinara and Mariotta, or Marion, Newlands. In 1557 they passed to the family of Douglas of Mains who still remain the proprietors.*

* History of Parish of Strathblane, J. Guthrie Smith, fol. 76.

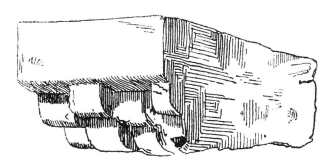

CORBELLED STONE.   See Page 263.

APPENDIX A.

SCOTS ACTS OF PARLIAMENT.

Decimo sexto Februarij, 1649. Vigesima Septima
Dies Parliamenti. Prayers said—Rolls called.

Act in favors of the Ministers of Drumery and Kirkpatrick.

The Estates of Par. ratifies and approves of the Act
of Diuisioun of ye presbitrie of Dumbartane underwritten is the haill heids articles and clauses whereof
the tenor followes—At D'biton Presbitrie the 23rd of
Januar 1649. The q^{lk} day Forsameikle as it is agreed
betuix the heritors and others of the two paroches of
easter K. and wester K. on the ane part And us the
moderator and remanent bretherene of the presbitry of
Dumbartane In maner following That is to say Quhair
the minister of the old Paroche of K. before the
Diuision thairof into Two paroches had belonging unto
him yeirlie of stipend six chalders meall two chalders
bear with ye vicarage of ye said old paroche undivyded
Together with six bolls beir yearly for the Comunion
elements The said stipend and victuall for the Comunion
elements shall be divided betuix ye ministers of these
two paroches in maner underwritten viz. Thrie chalders

and Tuelff bolls meal and Tuentie bolls bear extending in wholl to fyve chalders victuall shall with the vicarage of ye wester diuision or paroche appertayne in stipend to ye first entrant minister and his successors of ye said wester paroche serving ye cure theirof at ye old Kirk of Kirkpatrick in all tyme comeing, together with three bolls beir for ye comunion elements begining the first yeirs paiment theirof for the cropt and year of God 1648 yeirs and that tuo chalders four bolls meal and tuelff bolls beir extending in wholl to three chalders victuall shall with ye viccarage of ye easter diuisioun and paroche appertayne in stipend to ye minister of ye said eastern divisioun together with three bolls beir for the comunion elements and that for the cropt ye year of God 1648 and so furth in all tymes coming lykeas for helping ye forsaid stipends to the said ministers.   Q'as thair are restand auchland in ye Earl of Abercorn's hand tuo vaiking yeirs stipend of ye cropt and year of God 1646 and 1647 extending in wholl to tuelff chalders meall and four chalders beir and tuelff bolls beir for the comunion elements, together with ye vicarage duties of ye said old undivyded paroche resting awing in the hands of ye said parochine the said years.   The said vaiking stipends of meall bear viccarages and bear for the comunion elements is be agriement forsaid mortified and to be uplifted and employed, the one half thairoff for yeirlie arent for buying of potatoes to help ye stipend of ye minister at ye old kirk and the other halff thereof in lykmaner for the minister of the eastern diuisioun the helping of his stipend and seing for ye establishing ye said diuision of ye old diuisioun and of ye mortification and diuisioun of ye said tuo yeirs vaiking (vacant?) stipend victuall viccarages and half bolls bear for the comunion eliments. It is necessarie that the ratification of the hono[ll] estates of parlement be had thereto, thairfor it is ordained to be recommended lykas the forsaid diuisioun of ye old stipend mortification and diuisioun of ye vacant stipends vict[ll] viccarage and bolls bear for the communion elements is earnestlie and humblie recomended by this parties. To the hon[ll] estates of this present parlement. To be ratified and established in maner above spelt, and this part to be extracted and sub[t] be o[r] moderato[r] and clerk in o[r] names. Sic sub[r] M. J. Elphinston, moderato[r] Mr. J. Stewart, clerk. Siclyk the said estates declares that the ratifica[oun] above written shall nowise prejudge ye ministers of ye said parochines in yair seeking for augmentation of y[r] stipends according to former Acts of Parlement in cais they have not competencie after the divisioun of the said parochin.

Decimo Nono Junij. Prayers said—Rollis callit.

Act anent the [Presbitrie] of Dumbartan anent the devyding of the parochin of Kirkpatrick.

The estaits of Parliament now portlie conveined in this third sessioun of the second Trienniall parliament. Taking to their consideratioun the desyn of ane supplicatioune givine in to them be the Presbitrie of Dumbartaine humblie shewing that q[r]as it pleasit the estaits of Paisley to ratifie ane Act of the said Presbitrie of the dait the day of   Ratified in Parliament the 16th

day of February, 1649 yeirs, anent devyding of the old
paroch of Kilpatrik and the erecting of ane new kirk in
respect of the largnes of that paroch and for the better
helping of the ministers stipeinds of the said two
paroches, to approve of the divisoune of two years'
stipeinds auchtand be the Erle of Abercorn, viz., the
years 1646 and 1647, to be equallie devydit betwixt the
ministers of the saidis two paroches : And whairas thair
is a necessarie clause omitted in the close of the ratification granted be the said estaits of Paisley, to witt, ane
ordor for directing letters of horning to pass heir upon
against the Erle of Abercorn for payment of the fousadis
two years' vacand stipend to the collector appointed for
receiving thairof, upon ten dayis allenarlie. Thairfor,
humblie supplicating the saidis estaits of Paisley to cause
add the said clause to the ratification therewith producit,
or that the said estaitis of Paisley would allow letters
to be direct be verteu of thair act to follow upon the
said suplica^{oun}, as at mair lenth is conteinit in the said
suplica^{oun} quhilk being [tare] in consideratioun be the
saidis estaitis. They have ordanit and ordains letters
of horning to be direct upon the fousaid Act of the
Presbitrie, ratified in Parliament in maner above written,
and chairge the Erle of Abercorne to mak payment of
the fousaid two years' vacand stipend to the collector
appointed or to be appointed for receaving thereof, upon
the simple chairge of ten dayis allenarlie nixt eftir he
be chargit to that effect, under paine of rebellioun and
of putting him to the horn.

Sexto July, 1649.

ACT IN FAVOR OF THE ERLE OF ABERCORNE.

The estaits of parliament taking into thair consideratioun the supplicatioun givine in to them be James, Erle
of Abercorne, Lord Paisley and Kilpatrick, schewing that
quhair the saidis [estaitis] be thair act, the 16th February
last, ordainit the s^{d.} suplicant to pay tua yeirs' byrune
stipends for the parochin of Kilpatrick, which the saidis
estaits of parliament hes modified for the helping of ane
provisioun to the ane ither minister of the said parocheand;
lykwayis be ane other act, daited the 19th of Junij instant,
the saidis [estaitis] hawe ordainit lettres of horning to be
direit againis the suplicant for payment of the saidis tua
yeirs' stipends whairupon he is presentlie chargit and
distrest, both the which acts are past without the suplicant
evir being aither cited or hard befoir the saidis estaits.
Thairfoir humblie suplicating the saidis estaits of parliament that the saidis act is in sua far as concerns his
present payment of the stipend may be recallit, and the
samyne remittit to the judgis ordinarie in the lyk cases,
or at leist all farder executioun of the chargis following
vpon the saidis act is dischargit and suspendit till the
said suplicant be hard befoir the saidis estaits of parliament, or ady others whom they shall appoint for that
effect. Seeing the prycis of the victuall chargit for are
not liquidat, and so the chairge in that respect cannot
receave any implement or obedience; and farder, the
chairge is not agrieable to the foirsaid decreit. The said
suplicant hes still offerit and yit is willing to give that

satisfaction for ye saidis tua yeirs' stipend which, if the
commission for surrenders and teinds were sitting, could
not in equitie be refusit. And if the said estait will not
be pleasit vpon the foirsaidis consideratioun to grant the
suplicant continuation till he be hard befoir them, or
others to be appointit be them for that effect, he doeth
humblie crave the lyk favor and expeditioun of justice
againis the heritors of the saidis parochins at his awine
instance for thair valued teinds, out of which the ministers'
stipends are justlie appointit to be payit, as the saidis
estaits grantis to the presbitrie of Dumbartan and thair
collectors against him, so that he may not presentlie put
to the payment of the saidis stipends, and postponed in
his relief thairof be the ordinarie delayis of the judicatories
as at mair lehth is contenit in the said suplicatioun.
Quhilk being takine in consideratioun be the saidis estaits
of parliament, they have ordainit and ordains and be their
presents grant warrant to ane messenger of arms to cite
the persons eftersteit to compeir personallie before the
estaits of parliament or comittie of estaits the   day
of July instant, with continuation of days, to answer at
the instance of the said Erle of Abercorne, and to what
he can lay to any of thair chairgis anent the premiss ;
and the said estaits of parliament dischargis and suspends
all execution to follow upon the said lettres direit againis
the said Erle for the saidis tua yeir's stipend vntil the
first day of August nowtocome inclusive.

Vigesimo Septimo July, 1649.

ACT AND RATIFICATIOUN OF THE LOCALLITIE OF THE
MINISTER AT THE KIRK OF KIRKPATRICK.

The estaits of parliament taking into thair consideratioun the desyr and supplicatioun of James, Erle of Abercorne, titular of the teinds of the parochine of Kilpatrick, and Mr. Harie Sempell, Mr. Alleine Ferguson, and Hew Crawford of Cloberhill, commiouners of the presbitrie of Dumbartan within the quhilk presbitrie the said parochine doeth lye and having warrand from Mr. Matthew Ramsay, present minister of the said kirk, schewing that quhairas by decreit of the commiouners for plantaoun of kirks the saidis kirks is provydit to sex chalders of meíll and tua chalders of bear and fourtie pundis yeirlie for the comunione elements as the said decreit of the dait the day of the yeir of God and in the selff at mair length proportis. And quhairas thair is not any localitie givin to the minister of the said stipend which hes bred severall contests betuixt the former ministers and the titular for payment of the said stipend as thair is presentlie betuixt the presbitrie and him for tua yeirs byrune stipends of the said kirk he offering to give valid [   ] heritors for payment thairof, and they refusing to accept the same till it be legallie and judiciallie givine them as a locallitie, and that the said supplicants for taking away the first contraversie and to prevent the lyk in tymecoming are all vnanimouslie willing the one to give and the other to accept a localitie which cannot now be done. In regaird thair is no comissioun for plantatioun of kirks now sitting thairfor, the saidis supplicants does humblie desyr the said estaits of parliament to interpose thair authoritie for approving the localitie heirwith givin in and subseryint be both the pairties that it may stand for a locality in all tyme heirefter according to the ordinaince of the foirsaid decreit which will be ane readie means for the present payment of all byruns and securitie to the ministers in tyme herefter as at mair length is conteinit in the said supplicatioun. Thairfoir the saids estatis of parliament have ratified and approvin and doe heirby ratifie and approve the localitie of the minister his sttpend of the kirk of Kilpatrik whairof the tenno^r followis:—

Imprimis out of the—

	Chalders.	Bolls.	Firlots.	Pecks.
Laird of Luss for the Barony of Gar- scube, Colquhoun, Dunnerbock, ⎰m. and Auchentorlie, with thair per- ⎱b. tinents, - - - - -	3 1	6 3	2 —	1⅖ ½, ⅓, ⅙
Sir William Hamiltoun of Erlistoun, ⎰m. his landis of Wester Kilpatrick, -⎱b.	1 —	— 4	— —	— —
John Colquhoun, his halff landis of⎰m. Myltonn, - - - - -⎱b.	— —	3 2	— —	— —
Walter Colquhoun, his tua-third pairts⎰m. of the landis of Barnhill, - -⎱b.	— —	2 1	— 1	— 1⅓
William Johnston, his twenty-five⎰m. shilling land of Auchinleck, - -⎱b.	— —	— —	3 2	— —
Patrick Brysoune, his 12s. 6d. land⎰m. thair, - - - - - -⎱b.	— —	— —	1 1	2 —
Walter Logan, his landis of Spittel⎱m. of Tambowie, - - - ⎰	—	1	2	1⅗
John Stark of Killermont, his lands⎱b. of Killermount, - - - -⎰	—	3	—	—
John Balloch, his landis of Temple⎰m. of Holiedayre, - - - -⎱b.	— —	1 —	2 1	— 2

Laird of Lauchope, his £10 land of Craigton, Tombowie, and Careddin, - - - -	m.	—	2	—	—
	b.	—	4	—	—
Kilmahew, his landis of Laid Cameloche (Ledcameroch), - -	m.	—	—	—	—
	b.	—	2	—	—
And out of his landis of Mayns and Littil Balvie, - - - -	m.	—	14	—	—
	b.	—	1	2	$\{$ $1\frac{1}{2}$, $\frac{1}{3}$, $\frac{1}{2}$ of $\frac{1}{3}$, $\frac{2}{5}$ $\}$
Which extend in haill to - - -	m.	5	15	3	$1\frac{2}{5}$
	b.	2	6	2	$\frac{4}{5}$

the which tua pecks 4-5th pairts bear is in place of so much intaiking of the maill, which localitie abovewritten whairinto the ministers entrie is to be and begin this instant yeir of God 1649. The said James, Erle of Abircorne and the Com[nrs.] aboune namit, in testimonie of their mutuall agriement to give and accept the same, they have subscryvit the same with thair handis. Written be Mr. Johne Algoe, writer, E'bro, att the Cannogat, the 23rd July, the yeir of God 1649, befoir this witnesses, viz., to the subscription of the said James, Erle of Abircorne, Sir Alexander Hamiltoun, his brother-german, Robert Fork, sheriff clerk of Renfrew, and the said Mr. Johne Algoe ; and to the commissioners thair subscriptions the said Robert Fork and Mr. Johne Algoe. And the saidis estaits of Parliament ordains the foirsaid locallite to stand for the croft and yeir of God 1649, and in heireftir and to be ane rule for payment of byrunes conform to the foirsaid ordinance and decreit of the commissiouners of plantatioun of kirks, and if neid be is ordanis lettres of horning and uthers neidfull to be direcit against the foirsaidis persouns in form as offeirs.

APPENDIX B.

See page 25.)

PRE-HISTORIC REMAINS.

A strict search on Carleithhill, instituted after the finding of the portion stone axe referred to in p. 25, has not led to further discoveries. Subjoined is a drawing of the axe in question. It was found by Master Herbert Shields, Dunclutha, Dalmuir.

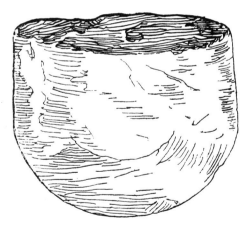

PORTION STONE AXE FOUND ON CARLEITHHILL (ACTUAL SIZE).

On pages 18 and 212 we ventured the remark that the pre-historic remains in the parish were few in number. Since these words were penned, the estate of Auchentorlie has been found to contain not only the remains of a vitrified fort, but a most important group of the rock sculpturings known as cup and ring marks; these, with the interesting finds made at Dunbowie, make a group of archæological discoveries probably the most important hitherto found in the valley of the Clyde.

The remains of the vitrified fort on the summit of Ardconnell or Sheephill were discovered by the proprietor of the estate, G. J. Ferguson Buchanan, Esquire, in company with the writer, last autumn, and recent excavations, conducted at the instance of the Helensburgh Naturalist and Antiquarian Society at the request of the Society of Antiquaries of Scotland, have fully proved the interesting nature of the discovery. It is the only fort of the kind hitherto discovered in the Clyde valley; it has been of large extent, and has been protected by earthworks on the southern slope of the hill, the precipitous face of the hill to the west, north, and east dispensing with the necessity of any artificial defences. The vitrification is very marked, and in some places the stones adhere to the living rock, in others the vitrification appears on the top of loose stones, the lower portions of which have been untouched by fire.

The group of cup and ring markings which Mr. W. A. Donnelly, the well-known artist, with the writer, were instrumental in discovering, lies in the hollow behind Ardconnel towards the north-west, on the natural surface of a sandstone rock which slopes gently towards the south. These markings have been considered of great importance by leading authorities on such matters, Mr. Romilly Allen, F. S. A. Scot., considering the group of seven holes, which will be seen in the plate attached, as being specially interesting. The markings consist of 45 sets of concentric rings with cups, and over 200 cups without rings. The concentric rings range from a single circle with a cup in the centre to a series of as many as 9 concentric circles with central cup. A duct or radial grove from the cup to outermost circle, and even extending beyond, is a conspicuous

Sketch No. 1.

feature, although it is absent from some of the smaller sets of circles. The cups vary in size, and some measure about 3 inches diameter and have a depth of about 2½ inches. The largest rings on this rock are only 12 inches diameter, while those at Cochno are more than double this size. The theory which finds most acceptance regarding the use of these cups and rings is that they have been used for pouring libations on, notwithstanding that in some instances these sculpturings are found occasionally on vertical surfaces. An instance of this can be seen on

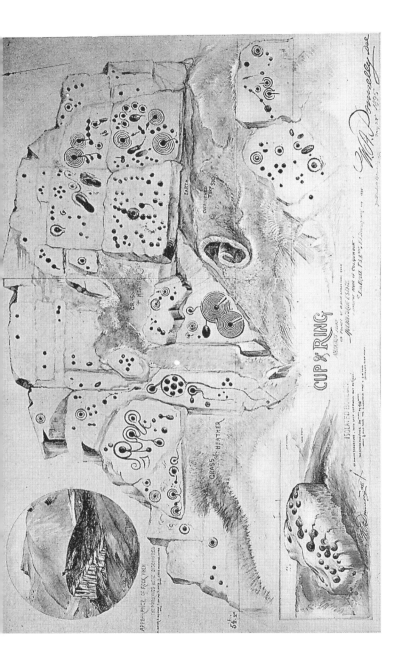

AUCHENTORLIE GROUP ARCHAIC MARKINGS.

a much smaller rock about 30 yards to the north east of the group (sketches Nos. 1 and 2). The markings have been made with a sharp-pointed instrument, the picking with same being clearly discernible. The study of this branch of archæology is not yet 50 years old, but in that

Sketch No. 2.

time cup and ring marks have been found not only in Britain but in Ireland, Scandinavia, France, and North America. In this country they occur in association with Bronze Age burials, and the opinion is held that the districts where they are found were considered specially sacred. The cup and ring stones found at Auchentorlie,

Sketch No. 3.

referred to on page 24, may have been taken from the group behind Ardconnel, which shows signs of some portions having been quarried. A boulder of sandstone with three cup marks (sketch No. 3) lies on the slope of the Hill of Dun, about 100 yards north of Dunerbuck farmhouse, while a boulder with a large basin and a duct leading therefrom was found by Mr. Donnelly at the foot of Dumbuck hill.   To the north of Greenland farm, which lies about a quarter of a mile up the hill from Ard-

Sketch No. 4.

connel hill, three boulders with cup and ring marks were found on the removal of one of the dykes. (sketch No. 4.)   The carvings are well executed, and are different in design from those previously referred

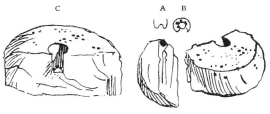

Sketch No. 5.

to.   At same time a most peculiar stone was found 2 feet 3 inches in diameter and 1 foot 8 inches deep (sketch No. 5), covered over with pittings too small to be called cups. In the centre is a hole 3 inches in diameter and 7 inches deep (c). At the foot of this hole there is a cone rising from the inside 2½ inches high (see section A), and at the base of same a cluster of cups are cut into the side of the hole (B). These peculiarities are all the better seen through the stone being broken into two unequal portions. Efforts are being made to secure this stone for the museum of the Society of Antiquaries, Edinburgh.

Close by Dalmuir station traces of Palaeolithic man have been found during the excavation of the new railway

Sketch No. 6.

cutting. A full account of the find is given in the January number of *The Scottish Antiquary*, 1895, by the Rev. Frederick Smith.

Referring to the Cochno cup and ring marks (see page 22), Mr. Donnelly, while engaged making a careful drawing of these for the illustration of this volume, discovered an incised cross within an oval frame, and also a sculpturing resembling two footprints, which, curiously enough, shows only four toes. (See plate attached.) The cross has been rarely found in this country in juxtaposition with cup and ring markings. At Aspatria in

Cumberland a stone taken from a cist shows some rings with crosses cut in relief (sketch No. 6), while at Newgrange in Ireland a stone showing a similar cross in combination with a cup and ring and a star-like design, has been found (sketch No. 7).* In connection with the footprints, examples of which are found on rock surfaces at Dunad and other places in Scotland, there are two sculpturings on the Auchentorlie group having a general

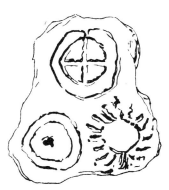

Sketch No. 7.

resemblance to footprints, but closer examination leads us to the supposition that they are rather oval-shaped cavities or basins.

On the report of Mr. Donnelly, whose antiquarian zeal is beyond all praise, excavations have been carried on by the Helensburgh Naturalist and Antiquarian Society at the fort or watch tower on the summit of Dunbowie hill, Barnhill estate. The fort is fully 30 feet in

* Sir James Y. Simpson's *British Archaic Sculpturings*, pages 76 and 137.

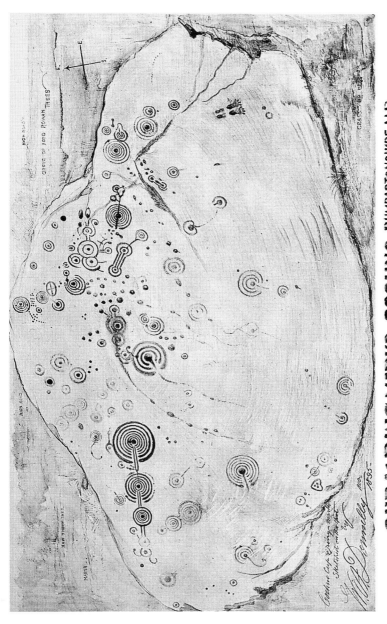

CUP & RING MARKS COCHNO DUMBARTONSHIRE N.B.

diameter inside, and the walls, which are from 13 to 14 feet thick, constructed of metamorphic sandstone from the neighbourhood. The entrance, which is clearly defined, is from the north-east. The floor originally had been formed of flat stones loosely jointed together. Several hearths, or large flat stones showing action of fire, were found *in situ ;* also quantities of black earth with pieces of charcoal and a small quantity of animal bones. A portion of deer's horn was found. The interior has been entirely cleared of all the debris, and the finds

Sketch No. 8.

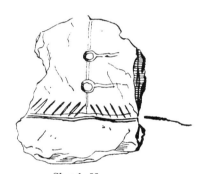

Sketch No. 9.

consist of the upper portion of a quern ; stone pounders ; cooking stones and pebbles with artificially polished surfaces ; whetstones ; an oyster shell (sketch No. 8) perforated in the centre and with a rude ornament scratched or cut on it ; a piece of slate (sketch No. 9) with two perforations and ornamented with a simple design, which, when cleared out, showed signs of a pigment of a red colour ; a small piece of sandstone (sketch No. 10) with similar ornamentation ; and also a limpet shell (sketch No. 11) perforated at the sides for the purpose of putting a cord through, having in the

Sketch No. 10.

Sketch No. 11.

interior the likeness of the human face, with two small perforations for the eyes, the nose and mouth being cut with a sharp instrument.

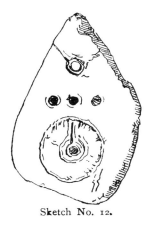

Sketch No. 12.

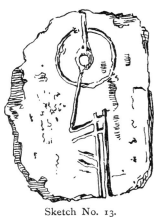

Sketch No. 13.

Most interesting of all is perhaps the ornament of soft

clay slate (sketch No. 12), showing a cup and ring marking in conjunction with an upper row of three cups. Sketch No. 13 shows an entirely novel combination of cup and ring, with zig-zag ornament, a feature present on many of the pre-historic stones and also metal ornaments

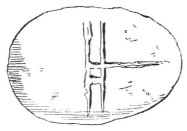

Sketch No. 14.

found in the east of Scotland. The stone is a flake of the red sandstone of which the fort is constructed. Sketch No. 14 is that of a small sandstone pebble showing some artificially-formed lines. A flint pebble was found showing signs of colouring taking the form of

Sketch No. 15.   Sketch No. 16.

a dot with a surrounding ring. Many of the stones show the action of fire, some of them being reduced by this agency to fragments. White quartz pebbles are numerous. No. 15 is sketch of a spear-head of slate found outside the fort, and No. 16 that of a bone arrow-head unearthed from same place. Operations are not yet finished, and when the exterior of the fort is cleared of the accumulated debris other finds of importance may be made.

These discoveries have caused a great deal of talk in the neighbourhood, and there are those who are sceptical as to the origin of the cup and ring marks. The following humorous sketch by Mr. Donnelly well illustrates the opinions of these folks.

AUCHENTORLIE.

The coat of arms shown on page 203 is far from being what it should, a rejected block having been inserted in error. The illustration herewith is correct in every detail.

During recent alterations of the walls on Middleton farm, a great number of stones, evidently forming part of the old castle of Colquhoun (see page 231), were turned out of the foundations. A portion also of the grouting which formed the interior of the castle walls was also found.

OLD KILPATRICK PARISH COUNCIL.

EXTRACT FROM MINUTES OF PROCEEDINGS.

Dalmuir, 17*th May,* 1895. *Inter alia.*—In reference to the remit as to official seal, the clerk was instructed to inquire of Mr. John Bruce, F. S. A. Scot., late of Bowling, as to a suitable seal connected with the district, and to obtain specimens from Mr. D. Cunninghame, engraver, Glasgow, and to report.

SAM. LECKIE, *Convener.*

Dalmuir, 13*th June,* 1895. *Inter alia.*—The clerk submitted specimens of official seals obtained from Mr. John Bruce, F.S.A.Scot., and Mr. Cunninghame, engraver, Glasgow. After inspecting, in considering the same, the committee recommend that the coat of arms containing St. Patrick's Cross, as submitted by Mr. Bruce, be adopted as the common seal of the parish council.

SAM. LECKIE, *Convener.*

W. FRASER MACKENZIE, *Clerk.*

APPENDIX C.

(See page 68).

SCOTS ACTS OF PARLIAMENT, Vol. i. fol. 85.

PROCESSUS PRO TERRA DE MONACHKENNARAN RE-
CUPERANDA CORAM JUDICIBUS A PAPA DELEGATIS,
A.D. 1233.

Intentio Abbatis et Conventus de Passelet est probare
quod tota illa terra de Monachkennaran super amnem
de Clud injuste in Gilbertum filium Samuelis alienata
est quid de jure ad ecclesiam eorum de Kylpatrik debet
pertinere unde petunt ipsum Gilbertum adicta terra
amoveri et sandem terram ad jus et proprietatem dicte
ecclesie legittime revocari. *Prima* productio testium per
Abbatem et Conventum contra dictum Gibertum die
lune proxima ante festum Sancti Mattei in parrochiali
ecclesia de Yrewin (Irvine) anno gratie millesimo
ducentesimo tricesimo tertio. Alexandre filius Hugonis
juratus dicit quod sexaginta annis et co amplius elapsis
vidit quendam nomine Bede Ferdan habitantem in
quadam domo magna fabricata de virgis juxta ecclesiam
de Kylpatrick versus orientam et tenuit illam terram de
Monachkennaran quam Gilbertus filius Samuelis nunc
tenet. Interrogatus cujus nomine dictam terram possedit
dicit quod tantum nomine ecclesie nullum aluid
servitium faciendo pro dicta terra nisi tantummodo

recipiendo et pascendo hospites illic venientes. Dicit etiam quod cum puer effet aliquando receptus est ibi cum patre suo ficut hospes et quod dictus Beda eodem jure et servitio tenuit terram de Cultbuthe et de Dumtechglunan Thomas Gaskel juratus dicit quod vidit dictum Bedam Ferdan maventem in eadem domo in terra ecclesie Sancti Patricii sita tenentem easdem terras eodem modo eodem jure et idem servitium faciendo sicut Alexander testatus est Addidit etiam quod vidit postmodum Cristinum filium dicti Bede possidentem easdem terras eodem jure quo pater ejus possidebat et quod totalis terra ecclesie divisi erat in quatuor partes quorum unam partem dictus Beda Ferdan possedit et tres alii tres alias partes quorum quilibet nomine ecclesie respondebut hospitibus inter se divisis. Requisitus de tempore dicit quod plus quam quadragenta anni elapsi sunt quia ibidem nutritus est ab infantia. Interrogatus que alie terre pertinent ad eccleziam dicit quod Cochmanach Fimbelach Edmbernan et Cragnentalach et que dam alie terre quas Dufgallus filius Comitis nunc tenet Dufgallus filius Comitis juratus dicit idem per omnia quod Thomas Gaskel et adjecit quod dicta terra de Monachkennaran et jeures alie terre per defectum et negligentiam ipsius a dicta ecclesia suerunt alienate quia noluit patrem vel fratrem suum vel parentes suos offendere. Secunda productio testium per Abbatem et Conventum de Passelet contra dictum Gilbertum filium Samuelis die Sabbati proxima post festum Sancti Martini in parrochiali ecclesia de Are (Ayr) anno supradicto Malcomus Beg juratus dicit quod vidit Bedam Ferdan

habentem domum suam sitam juxta cimiterium ecclesie
de Kylpatrick ex orientali parte et tenuit nomine ecclesie
illam terram de Monachkennaran quam Gilbertus filius
Samuelis modo tenet et prodicta terra et aliis quas
tenebat de ecclesia recipiebat hospites ad ecclesiam
veinates nullum aluid servitium faciendo pro eis Requisitus in tempore cujus Comitis hoc vidit dicit quod in
tempore Alwini Comitis et quod idem Comes dedit
Sanct Patricio et ecclesie illam terram de Kachconnen
quam ipse Malcomus postea tenuit et vendidit pre timore
et dicit quod omnes terre ecclesia quas dictus Beda
tenuit et quas Dufgallus etalii modo tenent libere et
quiete erant ab omni temporali servitio et quod homines
in illis terris manentes et habitantes defendi erant
semper per ecclesiam et in curia ecclesie contra omnes
Anekol juratus idem dicit per omnia quod Malcomus
Beg et odjeut quod Comes Dauid frater regis Wilelmi
eo tempore quo habuit comitatum de Levenax et
possedit voluit de dictis terris ecclesie de Kylpatrick
habere auxilium ficut de ceteris terris comitatus et non
potuit quia defense erant per ecclesiam Gilon juratus
idem dicit per omnia quod Malcolmus Beg Gilbethoc
juratus concordat in omnibus cum Malcolmo et Anecol
et adjecit quod dictus Beda interfectus erat pro jure et
libertate ecclesie Fergus filius Cunigham juratus concordat cum Gilbethoc in omnibus Hilarius juratus dicit
idem per omnia quod Fergus and Gilbethoc Nemias
juratus idem dicit per omnia quod Anecol et adjecit
de tempore quod quinquiginta anni et eo amplius
elapsi sunt post quam hoc vidit et pro certo habet

quic quid dicit quia natus fuit in illa parróchia Ressin juratus idem dicit per omnia quod Nemias Gillemor juratus idem dicit per omnia quod Ressin et Nemias Rotheric Beg de Carric juratus concordat in omnibus cum Malcolmo Beg fratre ipsius Requisitus qualiter hoc scivit dixit quod hoc vidit ab adolescentia oua quia natus et nutritus erat in Parrochia de Kylpatrick Rathel juratus concordat in omnibus cum predicto Rotheric Gillekonel Manthac frater comitis de Carric juratus dicit idem per omnia quod Malcomus Beg.

OLD OVERTOUN FARM-HOUSE (page 244).

(From a Sketch by W. A. Donnelly).

E. W. M'Cormick.

ST. PATRICK'S OR TREES' WELL, OLD KILPATRICK.

(See page 137).

APPENDIX D.

At Ebro, 28th July, 1681, reign of Charles II., 3rd Parliament. Members for D'shire— Sir Pat. Houston of Houston and W$^{m.}$ Noble of Dalnottar? for the burgh—W$^{m.}$ M'Farlane.

No. 146—RATIFICATION in favor of W$^{m.}$ Hamilton of Orbitoun of the Lordship and Barony of Erskine, Dunnotar, Kilpatrick.

Our soveraigne Lord with the speciall advice and consent of his Estates of P'ment ratifies approves and confirmes to and in favour of his Maties lovit W$^{m.}$ Hamilton of Orbitoun And the airs male lawfullie procreat or to be procreat of his own bodie whilks failing to James Hamiltoun his brother germane and the airs male lawfullie to be procreat of his bodie whilks failing to the said W$^{m.}$ Hamilton his nearest lawfull heirs male whilks all failing to his nearest lawfull airs and assigneyes whatsomever Are chartor made and granted be his Matie under the Great Seal of this his ancient Kingdom of the date at Whitehall the last day of April 1672 whereby his Matie for himself as King and as Prince and Stewart of Scotland with advice and consent of the Lords and uthers comissioners of his Maties Exchequer Gave granted and disponed And for him and his Royall successors perpetually confirmed to the said Wm. Hamilton and his airs male and of Tailzie above specified heretablie and irredeemablie All and sundrie the lands of Easter Kilpatrick Wester Kilpatrick Moriesland Kirktoun of Kilpatrick Auchintoshan Govanburne Dunteglenan Bowwarthill Easter and Westir Cochnochs Duntocher with the Corn milnes and walk milnes thereof milnelands multures and milne dewties and pertinents of the samen The lands of Milnetoun Milnecroft Edinbarnet Craigbanzoch Auchinleck Ffairclay Braidfield Balquharien Auchingae Chappelland Easter and Wester Culbowies The lands of Barnes and meadows thairof with the fishigs of Cruikedshott and Linbranie and with the muirs of Kilpatrick Cochnoch Auchingrie and Edenbarnet with all and sundrie Castles Towers fortalices mannor places houses biggins yairds Orchyairds Dowes Dowcots Coalls Coallheughis parks meadows wards annexis comonis tennents tennendries and services of free tennents etc. All unit and incorporat in ane haill and free Baronie and Regalitie called the Baronie and Regalitie of Kilpatrick Whilk haill Lands Lordship Baronies Milnes teinds Right of Patronage fishings and privilidge of Regalitie pairts pendules and pertinents thereof particularlie and generallie above written are erected in Ane haill and free Lordship and Baronie called the Lordship and baronie of Erskine And the mannor place of Erskine Ordained to be the Principall messauge of the said Lordship and Baronie And als the Towne

of Kilpatrick with the tenements cottages houses and
yairds thereof Is erected in ane burgh of Baronie of
Kilpatrick with the privilidge of haveing a weekly
mercat on Thursday weeklie and als Two free ffaires
in the year to be holden within the said burgh the
first upon the tuentie seventh day of June called
              and the uther upon the tuentie eight day of
October called   and each of them to continue
for the space of eight days yearlie and to collect the
tolls customes and casualties thereof and apply the
samen to their owne proper use and with all other
privilidges liberties freedomes and jurisdictions granted
to any other Baronie or Burgh of Baronie within this
his Maties ancient Kingdom At length mentioned in
the said chartor Moreover be the said chartor the
foresaids lands of Easter and Wester Kilpatrick Moreis-
lands and others formerly erected in ane haill and free
Baronie and Regalitie called the Baronie and Regalitie
of Kilpatrick are of new united and Erected in ane
haill and free Regalitie and Justiciarie To be in all
time coming called the Regality of Kilpatrick with the
priviledge and jurisdiction of ane free Regalitie Chappell
and Chancellarie and with all other privilidges Immunities Casualties Comodities profites and dewties thereto
belonging siclike and als freely and fully in all respects
as any other regality within this Kingdom And siclike
The saids haill Lands Lordship Baronies Milnes teinds
Right of Patronage fishings Burgh of Baronie and
Regalitie with the liberties priviledges and Jurisdictions
thereof above mentioned pairts pendules and pertinents

of the samen particularlie and generallie above exprest
Are of new united erected created and Incorporated
In ane haill and free lordship and Baronie called the
Lordship and Baronie of Erskine ordaining the Tower
fortalice and mannor place of Erskine to be the prin-
cipall messuage thereof.

PARISH CHURCH COMMUNION TOKEN, 1787.

TWO CUPS OF THE COMMUNION SERVICE WERE DATED 1704.

APPENDIX E.

COUNTY VALUATION, 1657.

JUST copy of the Old Valuation Roll, which was subscribed by the Commissioners in the year 1657, with the sub-divisions, and the valuation of the freeholders of the shire of Dumbarton.*

WESTER KILPATRICK.

Luss, with Barnhill, ...	£930	0	0
Laird of Luss, his sub-divisions in W. Kilpatrick—			
Mains of Colquhoun, ...	164	0	0
Barnhill, Overtoun, and Middleton, . . .	156	0	0
Chappletoun, ...	200	0	0
Miltoun, ...	84	0	0
Overtoun and Dunglass, ...	125	0	0
Dunerbuck and Auchintorlie, ...	237	0	0
Andmore, ...	42	0	0
Dargavell, ...	90	0	0
Spittle of Dunerbuck, ...	56	0	0
Gavinburn, ...	220	0	0
Dunnotre Castle, Dalnotter, ...	40	0	0
Arch. Colquhoun of Blackmailing, ...	42	0	0
J. Burnside of Closs, ...	38	5	0
Jas. Cunningham, ...	36	0	0
Dalmuir, ...	187	10	0
W. Hamilton of Auchentoshan, ...	80	0	0

---

* Irving's History of Dumbartonshire, fol. 498.

Wᵐ· Johnstone, portioner, there,	£30	0 0
Boquhanarn,	460	0 0
Edenbarnet,	95	0 0
John & Wᵐ· Johnstone in Auchinleck,	90	0 0
Wᵐ· Johnstone there,	28	10 0
Margaret Grey there, now John Bryson,	13	5 0
John Douglas, Milton Douglas,	85	0 0
Barns,	800	0 0
Robt. & Jno. M'Nair in Kilbowie,	116	13 4
Robt. Morrison,	95	0 0
John Sprewl, Milton Sprewl,	97	10 0
Faifley, Wester,	24	0 0
Orbistoun's Lands (Hamilton), a feu duty,	741	0 0

EASTER KILPATRICK.

Drumry lands,		£774	0 0
Cloberhill,		115	0 0
Drumchapel,		120	0 0
Hutcheson,		150	0 0
Law,		125	0 0
Garscadden,		240	0 0
Kilmahew?	Ledcameroch,	240	0 0
John Stark,	Killermont,	148	9 0
	Lochbrae,	23	13 0
	Chappletoun,	65	0 0
Laird of Luss,	Garscube,	488	6 8
	Kilmardiny,	135	0 0
Kilmahew,	Mains & Keystoun Lands,	390	0 0
Wltr. Logan,	Spittle of Tombuy,	25	0 0
Kilmahew,	Balvie Lands,	557	13 4
Laird of Lauchope,	Craigton,	315	0 0
	Auchincloich,	385	0 0

Transcribed by John Colquhoun of Garshake, at Milton, the 20th day of June, 1690.

POPULATION.

OLD KILPATRICK—

In 1755 the parish was said to have contained	1281	souls.
according to the Old Statistical Account,	2452	,,
1801, - - - - - - - -	2844	,,
1811, - - - - - - - -	3428	,,
1821, - - - - - - - -	3692	,,
1831, - - - - - - - -	5879	,,
1836, - - - - - - - -	6123	,,
1841, - - - - - - - -	7020	,,
1861, - - - - - - - -	5577	,,
1871, - - . - - - - -	5346	,,
1881, - - - - - - - -	8862	,,
1891, - - - - - - - -	17,715	,,

NEW KILPATRICK—

In 1653 (the Records of the Dumbarton Presbytery) the population is estimated at about - - - - -	1000	souls.
1755, - - - - - - - -	1390	,,
1791, - - - - - - - -	1700	,,
1801, - - - - - - - -	2312	,,
1811, - - - - - - - -	2608	,,
1821, - - - - - - - -	2530	,,
1831, - - - - - - - -	3090	,,
1839, - - - - - - - -	3250	,,
1861, - - - - - - - -	4910	,,
1871, - - - - - - - -	6038	,,
1881, - - - - - - - -	7414	,,
1891, - - - - . - - -		

Many thanks are due to Mr. Robert Balderston, Cathcart, and Messrs. E. W. M'Cormick and W. Snell Anderson, Helensburgh, for the excellent negatives from which some of our illustrations have been printed ; also to Mr. W. A. Donnelly, artist, for several sketches, and to the many friends, some indeed entire strangers, who have assisted in every way possible in the compilation of this volume.